BORN TO
RULE

BORN TO RULE

BRITISH POLITICAL ELITES

ELLIS WASSON

SUTTON PUBLISHING

First published in the United Kingdom in 2000 by
Sutton Publishing Limited · Phoenix Mill
Thrupp · Stroud · Gloucestershire · GL5 2BU

British Library Cataloguing in Publication Data
A catalogue record for this book is available from the British Library.

ISBN 0-7509-2313-X

Typeset in 10/14pt Times.
Typesetting and origination by
Sutton Publishing Limited.
Printed in Great Britain by
Biddles, Guildford, Surrey.

To Diana

Contents

List of Figures

List of Tables

Acknowledgements

I am grateful for the support given to my research by a travel fellowship from the English-Speaking Union and a Bernadotte E. Schmitt Grant from the American Historical Association.

Ever since my first visit to the offices of the History of Parliament Trust over two decades ago, I have learned to respect the scholarship and generosity extended to other researchers to be found in that institution. My first contact, while working on another project, was with E.L.C. Mullins and Roland Thorne. Later David Hayton and his staff were extraordinarily generous with their time and data. I am also indebted to Valerie Cromwell, Linda Clarke and Andrew Thrush. I gratefully acknowledge that the copyright of any unpublished material (which may appear differently when published) included in this study lies with the History of Parliament Trust and is used by their permission.

An equally great debt is owed to Edith Johnston-Liik, editor of the *History of the Irish Parliament 1690–1800*. My visits to her office at The Queen's University, Belfast, and her home in County Down were characterized by helpful discussions and warm hospitality. It was reassuring to me that my most 'difficult cases' in tracking down social origins turned out to be at the top of her trouble list as well. I would never have been able to disentangle the Hamiltons without her help.

Computers made this study possible. My colleagues Bill Chase and Joe Smolko helped me out in emergencies. My student Kaizar Campwala designed the graphs and charts. The omniscient Christopher Smick listened patiently and dispensed invaluable advice. Michael Chupa, whose ability to appreciate the problems I encountered in a historical as well as a statistical context, was a wise and creative guide to the mysteries of number crunching.

I owe a great deal to my cousins Elizabeth Black and Robin Black for their kind hospitality during my visits to Northern Ireland. Rachel McMullen, Virginia Forbes and Joanna Hawthorne provided not only indispensable base camps in London and Cambridge but also constant friendship and encouragement.

Innumerable people along the way have answered questions and given me good service or advice. Special acknowledgement is owed to David Brown, Nigel Davis, James D. Galbraith, Aaron Gillette, Stuart Halliday and Bruce Lenman. Richard W. Davis, Abraham D. Kriegel, Michael McCahill and Wilfrid Prest offered encouragement and advice. They have shown me their unpublished work and taken the time to read what I have written. They are not, however, in any way responsible for the blemishes and errors that may be found in this book.

David Spring has remained a constant sounding-board, critic, and friend as I have pursued my work.

Finally, I owe gratitude to my friends and family. Their support has been both practical and emotional. Joey's belief in me has been indispensable. My debts to Diana and to my mother are beyond recompense.

Abbreviations

AHR	*American Historical Review*
BNE	Christie, *British 'non-elite' MPs*
BSM	*British Studies Monitor*
CB	*The Complete Baronetage*
CL	*Country Life*
CP	*The Complete Peerage*
DFBA	Cannadine, *Decline and Fall of the British Aristocracy*
DNB	*Dictionary of National Biography*
DWB	*Dictionary of Welsh Biography*
EcHR	*Economic History Review*
EE	Clay, *Economic Expansion and Social Change*
EHR	*English Historical Review*
ELS	Thompson, *English Landed Society in the Nineteenth Century*
HJ	*Historical Journal*
HP	*History of Parliament*
HR	*Historical Research*
IHR	Institute of Historical Research
IHS	*Irish Historical Studies*
JBS	*Journal of British Studies*
JMH	*Journal of Modern History*
MDE	Habakkuk, *Marriage, Debt and the Estates System*
NH	*Northern History*
OE	Stone and Stone, *An Open Elite?*
PA	*Parliamentary Affairs*
Parl. Deb.	*Parliamentary Debates*
PER	*Parliaments, Estates & Representation*
PH	*Parliamentary History*
PP	*Past and Present*
SC	Whiteley, *Social Composition of the House of Commons*
SH	*Social History*
SHR	*Scottish Historical Review*
TLS	*Times Literary Supplement*

TRHS	*Transactions of the Royal Historical Society*
UHC	Porritt, *Unreformed House of Commons*
VCH	*Victoria County History*
WHR	*Welsh History Review*

Introduction

Elusive as Proteus, the British elite has long escaped precise definition. Although the 'upper classes' have been exhaustively catalogued, terms such as aristocracy and gentry, nobility and country gentlemen, governing class and social elite have never achieved standard definition.[1] Wales, Scotland and Ireland were unique in their social and political development. Not all hereditary titles conferred political position; not all government offices brought membership in the social elite. Comparisons with the continental experience are difficult to make because in England titular aristocrats were rare. The line of demarcation between members of the social elite and those rising towards acceptance was fluid and ill-defined.

Each list of the elite offers a means to draw lines and to count. In England ownership of land was until the twentieth century the essential foundation for high economic, social and political status, but no accurate and comprehensive data exists on land ownership between the two Domesday surveys of 1087 and 1876. To conduct a longitudinal survey of even a handful of landowners over four or five centuries requires prodigies of research, and what evidence survives is rarely intact. Registers and directories of the nobility and gentry are a relatively recent development; they contain much erroneous information, and inclusion often rested on the whims of editors. The value of baronetcies and knighthoods rose and fell in the market of social discriminators. Tax records and lists of pedigrees compiled by heralds were flawed, erratic or only available for certain periods. Monographs on county communities have yielded rich pictures of elite society, but they are confined to brief periods or single shires, and employ diverse approaches that render comparisons difficult or impossible.[2] Tracing the ownership of country houses offers interesting possibilities. Recently, Lawrence Stone and Jeanne Fawtier Stone strove to gain a three-century perspective by conducting an ingenious analysis of houses in three counties.[3] They escaped the teleological bias of studies focused on a single event such as the Civil War, the narrow vision afforded by looking only at the titled, and the incompleteness of tax records, wills and private lists. It is unlikely, however, that their sample is typical of the national experience. No method of measurement seems to provide a systematic, long-term set of data covering all of England, let alone Wales, Scotland and Ireland. Hence estimates of the size of the landed elite vary widely. Our image of the governing class is fractured and evanescent.

Absence of a usable morphology of the British patriciate poses serious problems for historians because the elite was extraordinarily influential in the social, economic, cultural and political history of the nation from the Middle Ages to the twentieth century. The two most recent comparative histories of European nobilities both emphasize the unique grandeur and importance of the aristocracy and gentry in England. Jonathan Dewald's survey of the years 1400 to 1800 calls them 'the richest and most powerful landed elite in Europe'. Dominic Lieven, who concentrated on the nineteenth century, believes that they 'came closer to being an hereditary ruling class in the fullest sense of the word than any other European nobility'.[4]

Many of the central issues which interest historians are inevitably intertwined with the size and structure of the governing class. For instance the rate at which new entrants were ingested into the elite has been a perennial source of debate. 'Aristocratic it has been from the first,' the great constitutional authority Frederic Maitland wrote of the English elite, 'but never oligarchic; always ready to receive into itself new members who would have the time, the means, the will to do the work, without inquiring into the purity of their pedigrees or their right to coat armour.'[5] This analysis made in the morning of modern scholarship became a prevailing orthodoxy. A flexible, mobile, entrepreneurial society has been traced as far back as the thirteenth century. Scholars poise important interpretations of English history on the hinges of a door open to advancement. The unique stability of constitutional government, the elastic social fabric that survived the challenges of war and revolution, capitalistic agriculture and innovation in industry which made England the first modern society, imperial expansion that led to the most far-flung empire in history, and the descent from glory in the twentieth century have all been attributed to the fluid interpenetration of ranks and classes. Because of the elite's ability to absorb newcomers some historians argue that in the nineteenth century no separate bourgeois culture arose to challenge aristocratic hegemony. Uniquely among European countries at the dawn of the twenty-first century, land in England and Scotland is still widely held in large blocks by noble families, and the high aristocracy long retained hereditary seats in the legislature.

Of course, not all scholars embraced the open door argument, either as a historical reality or as an explanation of stability, expansion and decline.[6] As a result, much effort has been expended on measuring social mobility in English society, although this is not the only controversy which directs attention to the character of the governing class. Architectural historians study the proliferation of country houses and the conventions of aristocratic life which changed the elite's self-image and way of meeting the world rendered in brick and stone. Economic historians are interested in the proportion of national wealth held by the elite and their agency in overseas expansion and the Industrial Revolution. Political analysts investigate the consequences of electoral reform in the nineteenth century. Studies of county elites illuminate the role of the gentry and nobility in the shaping of medieval society and in the outbreak of the Civil War. The interaction of the English, Welsh, Scottish and Irish elites within the context of the Atlantic archipelago has recently become a lively area of scholarly debate.

This book offers a new route to understanding the character of the governing class in Great Britain and Ireland. Although it is focused most sharply on the years between the Restoration and the First World War, the data assembled here also have implications for the study of England ranging between the reigns of both Elizabeths. Not all of the questions raised above can be definitively answered. The lesser gentry, by far the most numerous and porous element within the landed elite, is perforce ignored. Nevertheless an analysis of the parliamentary elite is set on the most solid and reliable foundation of any long-term survey of the governing class. It is made possible for the first time by the development of computerized database programs.

Although Britain leads the world in the comprehensiveness of the information available about its governing class, here as elsewhere those interested in the role of the elite in society and the state have under-utilized parliamentary data and relied on fragmentary studies of particular periods based on incompatible systems. This study corrects that deficiency. I have collected data about 18,025 individuals who were members of 2,800 Welsh, Scottish, Irish and English families. These men and women provided most hereditary members of the House of Lords and up to four out of five members of the House of Commons (and considerable portions of the Irish and Scottish Parliaments) between the Middle Ages and the Second World War. No anatomy of the elite heretofore has been based on such a large and comprehensive set of individuals.

Members of parliament have borne names such as Wildblood, Spriggy, Ryebread, Overdo, Groggy, Steppingstones, Baa, Spitling, Bastard, and Silly as well as Smith and Jones. Thieves, saints, traitors, fishmongers, pirates, murderers, bakers, nabobs, carpenters, admirals, brewers, headmasters, duchesses, cardsharps, bell-founders and virtually every other human type and occupation have been represented there. Edward Grimston (MP 1563–93), while imprisoned in the Bastille, cut open the bars of his cell with a file, let himself down the walls with sheets knotted together, and made his way on foot to Caen disguised as a Scotsman. Young Winston Churchill (MP 1900–64) did much the same thing in South Africa three hundred years later. Both were men of enterprise; both were from patrician families; neither was typical, but both epitomized a type continuously to be found among the English elite. The range of employment and social backgrounds of men called to become medieval *viri parliamentarius*, seventeenth-century parliament men, and nineteenth-century MPs may seem so vast and varied that no useful conclusions about their lives and social origins can be drawn.

To call an assembly of mercers, ironmongers, tallow chandlers, lawyers, country gentlemen and aristocratic buccaneers collectively a national elite is perhaps to exaggerate institutional continuity. Moreover, the meeting place, rules and constitutional position of parliament changed over time, as did the balance of social categories represented there.

However, one theme runs consistently through parliamentary history from the fifteenth to the nineteenth century: a desire by members to perpetuate their descendants in high rank. The House of Lords gradually came to guarantee that outcome. Increasingly the Commons became a means of confirming status in a society where few legal privileges were automatically available to the merely wealthy. As an authority on the Hanoverian political system writes: 'The retention or enhancement of social prestige – those most powerful of all social pursuits – seem sooner or later to have involved membership of the House of Commons. . . . The country gentry class regarded a seat in Parliament as the pinnacle of its ambitions, the sure seal of local approval for family merit and achievement.'[7] A great historian of the English elite used membership in the House of Lords as *the* criterion for inclusion in his most famous book and concluded another study at 1880 because the landed elite had by then lost their predominance in the House of Commons.[8]

Power held by families is the essence of aristocracy.[9] The ability of a family to gain election to the Commons over a number of generations displayed a dynasty's capacity repeatedly to *reassert* high rank. The status of MP was not the outcome of an inexorable law of inheritance, like a peerage. Nor were MPs elected in fits of absence of mind, and the office was not a product of self-description. A conscious choice had to be made by a candidate to stand, and non-family members participated in the electoral process. Deference or preference had to be elicited to win a seat, frequently at great expense to the candidate's family in time, care and money. The process had to be repeated regularly in a sequence of electoral re-endorsements. Moreover, only men who could meet the property qualifications for membership and maintain a style of life suitable to the position from private means could usually get elected. Being an MP or peer did not necessarily mean a man sought or exercised power, though few outside parliament possessed significant political influence at the national level. The office of MP and/or noble birth conferred status and marked individuals as 'governors' even if their dominance was residual and authority held in reserve. Considerable evidence suggests that the office of MP was the key divider between the national governing class and gentry of middling and lower status. Most families whose economic resources allowed them to aspire to the socio-political elite elected MPs in quantity.

Social and political history are often treated as if they were separated into hermetically sealed boxes. In England, however, the political system was the framework for social structure as well. In no other European country was the process of gauging social status by political influence more institutionalized than in Britain.[10] The centrality of parliament, the nation in council, to English history stretches over more than half a dozen centuries. The people perceived it as a key element in governance, defining the development of the state and distinctive to English nationhood.[11] This was true when the institution existed merely as an advisory body and later when it began to take the initiative, whether it was regarded as a mechanism for legislation or as a place to make policy, both in the years when it was itinerant and intermittent and when it settled down to more regular meetings. The membership of the English parliament was never uniform. Only in the seventeenth, eighteenth and nineteenth centuries did the political strength of the landed class become fully organized there, but the institution was elastic enough to meet the elite's changing needs, including absorption of the Edinburgh and Dublin MPs, over a longer period than 1660 to 1832.

The English parliament has few rivals for continuous survival as an institution, and a number of the families associated with it have lasted nearly as long. The roof of Westminster Hall, damaged by Nazi bombs in 1941 and 1944, was repaired with timber taken from an estate held by the same family believed to have supplied the original oak in the reign of Richard II.[12] A recent comparative study of European elites found that 'England represents an extreme instance of the continuity of aristocratic power in European history.'[13] Outward appearances, of course, mask profound interior changes. Fossilized procedures such as the Speaker's reluctance to make her way to the chair after election, the pink ribbons attached to cloakroom hooks for the suspension of swords, and the monarch's exclusion from the Commons chamber mark little more than fondness for quaint traditions. On the other hand, for three-quarters of a millennium dozens of aristocratic families have repeatedly sent representatives to the Commons and the Lords. An historian's discussion of a sixteenth-century election will often include names of candidates who stood for the same seats three centuries later. The Virgin Queen's first Privy Council of nine men included a Cecil, Herbert, Russell, Stanley and Talbot, families still active politically in the twentieth century. In 1997 a Cecil sat in the current Elizabeth's cabinet just as his ancestor did in her namesake's council four hundred years ago.

Because status, land ownership and political authority were closely linked in England, 'new men' purchased estates as a prelude to entering parliament. They consolidated their social position by gaining political recognition.[14] Absence from the electoral lists or loss of access to office could reduce the status of even great families and for lesser ones might mean social obliteration.[15] David Cannadine, though writing about the Victorian era, has summarized the position that prevailed from the later sixteenth until the later nineteenth century: 'the status elite and the wealth elite were essentially the same people. In the main, the power elite was recruited from the wealth elite.'[16] As late as 1881 the 15th Earl of Derby believed 'political influence' was the first object of owning a landed estate.[17] The price of land reflected not merely its economic value, but also the unique combination of social and political power that it brought its owner.

We cannot write the social history of England in terms of the membership of the Commons. Westminster was not what Namier called a 'marvelous microcosmos' of social life. We do not have to agree, however, with Sir Lewis's flawed notions about eighteenth-century politics any more than we need to accept his exaggerated belief in the paramount place of parliament in social history in order to appreciate two of his important insights into the role of prosopographical research. First, he understood that studying the origins of MPs offered a unique opportunity to trace social mobility within the elite over long periods of time. Second, he saw that membership in parliament was the single most verifiable indicator of social status available to historians, largely free of the problems which bedevilled previous research.[18] Analysis of parliamentary families also has the immense advantage of providing a national picture, not a mere sample based on what were often unique regional experiences.

The History of Parliament Trust

The reason we can have such confidence in the abundance and accuracy of detail about parliamentary families is due to the compendium of noble lives in *The Complete Peerage*, the vision of Josiah Wedgwood and Lewis Namier, and the exacting labour of dozens of editors and research assistants of the History of Parliament Trust. Wedgwood proposed a biographical dictionary of English and Welsh Members of Parliament in 1928 and edited the first instalment. Namier revived the project after the Second World War and his last work was the editorial supervision of the volumes covering 1754 to 1790. The Trust, established in 1940, continues to publish and will complete the Commons up to 1832 some time in the twenty-first century. Nearly all the relevant volumes for the central years of this study are complete except for 1820–32. Stimulated by the English example, a committee on the history of the Scottish parliament was created in 1937, and their biographies were issued in the early 1990s. A similar though less comprehensive undertaking for the Irish House of Commons is being completed in Belfast by Dr Edith Johnston-Liik.[19]

The critics of the *History of Parliament* have attacked the project with more asperity than one might assume would be generated by mere professional jealousy or desire to see money spent on their own pet projects.[20] Some of the vitriol may be due to guilt by association with Namier's now excessively blackened reputation. The introductory surveys have many weaknesses. There is too little about procedures and institutional development, and the growth of political ideology and parties were largely ignored.[21]

None the less, much of the criticism has been unfair. Scholars ask the project to answer questions the Trust never intended to investigate. At the heart of the problem, however, is a fundamental divide between different visions of the past. To some the essence of history lies in the details of innumerable biographies, while others keep their eyes fixed on the horizon searching for big themes: foxes and hedgehogs. It is true that the majority of MPs never held high office and their life stories tell us only in the most general way about how parliament affected the national destiny. None the less, as Sir Herbert Butterfield (no supporter of Namier) understood, the biographies of these often obscure men represent 'a new way of finding contact with a historical world'.[22] The long line of blue volumes offers us a panoramic view of the cavalcade of families who formed the directing force of British and Irish history for centuries.

Imperfections in the Study

One cannot understand complicated problems in history by imposing a single template any more than one can close an over-stuffed suitcase by clipping around the edges with scissors. It is impossible to eliminate the ragged margins in a study such as this. Therefore at the outset I need to post some warnings and issue a few disclaimers.

Historians rightly fear to tread too far outside 'their' chronological period. Obvious and good reasons exist to account for this. Hence the focus of my analysis is confined principally to the years between the Restoration and the First World War, although data for the pre-1660 and post-1914 periods have been included. Some readers may be looking for answers to questions which the data on the parliamentary elite cannot provide or that I have not had the time or resources to address. It is not that I believe that topics such as party or ideology are unimportant. However, the purpose of this study is to reconstruct the shape and structure of the governing class, not the policies individual statesmen pursued.

Although the criticism of Namier and his followers is sometimes unfair, I agree with Plumb's judgement that they mistook 'genealogy for political history'.[23] The importance of kinship relations between MPs can be exaggerated.[24] Family groups linked by marriage, even in the Middle Ages when kinship was strongest, did not act monolithically. There can be hatred as well as love within families. Examples exist of brothers and fathers with influence over parliamentary seats denying access to them or being challenged for control by siblings and sons. Nevertheless, kinship connections among the elite were carefully charted. Even well established peerage families were highly sensitive to distant connections. Trivial family associations could benefit those related to grandees. In pre-twentieth-century Britain and Ireland a broad web of kinship helped to sustain membership in the governing class. As early as 1422 Sir William Sturmy of Wolfhall, Wiltshire, a shire knight, brought into the House of Commons with him his illegitimate son, his nephew and his grandson.[25] Groups of related families can be seen to have pursued coherent political policies over periods of a century or more.[26] Though Namier, Walcot and others exaggerated the dominance of family alliances in eighteenth-century parliaments, some clan-based parties, such as the Grenville connection, were of real political significance and persisted into the nineteenth century. Aristocratic marriages in the 1700s were still contracted to achieve political goals. Lord Grey included seven members of his family in the Whig reform administration of 1830–34. As a young man, the 3rd Marquess of Salisbury was helped by his Cecil kinsman the Marquess of Exeter in his election for Stamford in 1853 even though their last common ancestor lived in the sixteenth century. Salisbury was succeeded as Prime Minister in 1902 by his nephew. The 9th Duke of Marlborough helped to pay his cousin Winston Churchill's election expenses, and the latter's uncle aided him in finding a constituency. One in ten cabinet ministers in the years 1868–1955 were the sons of ministers.[27]

There is considerable debate about the extent to which kinship played a role in economic and social interaction. Undoubtedly such influences varied in effect over time and between regions. But there is little disagreement that kinship was more important and elaborate among the elite than at other levels of society, especially at the top.[28] Most peers inherited their seats in the Lords and most MPs in this study gained a place in the Commons because they inherited land or were blood relatives of wealthy men or women. They formed, and were conscious of forming, a governing class born to rule.

Influence and status within English society rested on many complex factors other than membership in parliament, including personality, education, luck, wealth, birth order, marriage and a host of other phenomena. This mixture of forces operated on many axes in multi-dimensional planes. The picture of the ruling class that emerges in this study offers only one perspective on the structure of power in Britain and cannot answer all of the questions that arise about social mobility, regional interaction and institutional reform. But the evidence adduced below brings us nearer to a full understanding of the political elite than any previous method has been able to do.

A challenge to the conclusions of this book may come from those who argue that computer studies can impose a false sense of unity and simplicity on a subject which has neither. I do not accept Namier's contention that studying the interconnectedness of commerce and landed families is impossible because the subject is 'too vast and complex for an exhaustive statistical examination'.[29] It seems to me this is just the sort of topic to be assisted by analysis of aggregated data. Habakkuk's magnum opus on landed society contains some important insights, but his decision not to systematize his findings leaves at best an outline so densely overlaid with individual cases that it is often impossible to decide what Sir John finally concluded. Statistical studies sometimes resemble Victorian phrenology in that the bumps and humps may only accidentally coincide with reality. Change over time renders a line drawn in one period suspect in another. My assumption is that readers will understand the distortion to individual, class, regional and institutional reality that numbers laid out in tables and graphs can impose. I have tried to compensate for these dangers in a variety of ways. For example, I have usually separated data by country and by the number of MPs a family accumulated. Individual cases are introduced to flesh out the statistics while not overwhelming the text with endless examples. It is, however, the small size and unique continuity of the English elite, less disturbed by change over time than lower levels of landed society and other social categories, which affords the opportunity to analyse large amounts of data over long periods. The prosopographical skeleton can achieve enough shapeliness to reveal the outline of its limbs.

A possible flaw in this study is failure to incorporate analysis of the losing candidates in parliamentary elections.[30] This does not mean, however, that half or more of the families that might have been included had they won elections fail to appear in the data pool. Until the mid-nineteenth century the majority of elections went uncontested. In many cases when open fights did take place the defeated contenders came from families already included in the study, and many of the men trounced in one election found a place in parliament for another seat. For example, over two-thirds (70% in 1727 and 73% in 1774) of the losing candidates in eighteenth-century contests were either MPs earlier or later, or were members of parliamentary families. In most cases losers who were not included in this study ranked lower than their opponents in both wealth and status, and the mechanism of parliamentary election did its work of winnowing out the most potent members of the elite.

Other absentees from this study include women, bishops, Roman Catholics, Jews, dissenters and unacknowledged illegitimate sons. In-law relationships, which were sometimes quite important, at least in the short term, could not be included. In the latter case the research involved to trace the social, economic and political importance of every marriage connection would be impossibly vast.

With regard to women involved in parliamentary history, cultural and legal factors limited their participation as MPs or peeresses until the twentieth century. It should be noted, however, that aside from their roles as wives and mothers of members of parliament, women played a direct part in the operation of the electoral system. As widows, guardians and heiresses, aristocratic women managed pocket boroughs and county campaigns over the centuries.[31]

Bishops inhabited a grey area. They became members of the House of Lords and some exercised electoral patronage and commanded incomes and estates comparable to those of peers, but they could only pass on to their progeny savings made during tenures that were usually brief. For that reason bishops are not counted as the equivalent of peers for the purposes of this study. A few other oddities such as the Brooke family, with only one MP but several Rajas of Sarawak, are also not included.

Some Jewish and dissenting families may have failed to enter the data pool or, as in the case of the Rothschilds, would have elected more MPs had they not suffered from denominational discrimination. Catholic families were prevented from holding office, but they were not excluded from high status. Some enjoyed great social prestige, especially in areas where there were a large number of co-religionists among the gentry such as in Lancashire. More families survived the crippling fines for recusancy than is sometimes assumed, but inability to conform also led to removal from political influence and often to heavy debts or even ruin.[32] Perhaps fifty Catholic families of parliamentary status disappeared from the landed elite prematurely, or had the total number of MPs they might have elected significantly reduced. No more than a dozen families, however, were permanently excluded from the national elite because of their religion after 1660. All the families with peers after 1829 are counted and a number of families such as the Cliftons, Petres, Stonors, Stricklands and Towneleys managed to elect at least one MP after emancipation.

Some families are included in the study who should not be, such as medieval and Tudor burgess families. At the other end of the time continuum, there are non-landed modern families which sprang from careers in the press, politics or unions such as the Aitkens, Foots or Hardies. A number of poor peers unavoidably creep into the study. During the Middle Ages, if a lord's family sank in wealth or prestige, they ceased to be summoned to parliament, but once titles became hereditary, succession (with a few exceptions) became automatic. Most peerage families in financial difficulties were artificially supported by government intervention intended to preserve the dignity of the order. The 3rd Baron de la Warr, who succeeded in 1602, lamented that he was 'the poorest baron in the kingdom' and was shunted off to Virginia as governor. The Earl of Monmouth alleviated his poverty in 1589 by winning a £2,000 wager that he could not walk to Berwick from London in twelve days. Pensions were also granted to the peers in greatest distress. Most poor nobles ended their lines without issue unless saved by marriage to an heiress.

Overview

Chapter 1 describes the methodology employed in this study, and demonstrates that examining the membership of parliament is the best means comprehensively to analyse the governing class. Chapter 2 examines the rate of entry and exit in and out of the English elite, and the size and composition of the governing class from the late Middle Ages until the First World War. Grandee families of immense wealth and influence surviving over long periods and forming a largely indestructible nucleus of aristocratic power between 1660 and 1914 are identified and analysed. The proportion of new families entering the elite from various backgrounds is examined in Chapter 3. Particular attention is paid to men made rich in business, whose rate of penetration into the governing class has aroused controversy. Chapter 4 looks at the Welsh, Scottish and Irish elites, and analyses the similarities, differences and interactions between them and the English governing class. To what extent was there a merged elite in the nineteenth century? The last chapter measures the effect of parliamentary reform and the forces hostile to hereditary privilege on the aristocracy.

A central theme of the book is the remarkable continuity and small size of the core elite. The data show that previous estimates of the number of families in the governing class have been too high. This was an elite largely closed to newcomers in its upper reaches, but outside the grandee circle it was open to penetration by commercial wealth. Social mobility was lively, rapid and continuous from the Middle Ages to the twentieth century. The currently fashionable notion of an emergent 'supra-national' elite in the British Isles too readily neglects important distinctive characteristics of the Welsh, Scottish and Irish aristocracies. The increasingly popular view of a persistent old regime which survived intact until the 1880s and beyond is not supported by the data uncovered by this study.

At the heart of this story is parliament. It gave the elite a means to combine status and power. It was used to secure property and prestige. It emulsified the new and the old. It invited consensus and supported, by the standards of the time, efficient and effective government. Its relationship with the executive has changed from grovelling compliance to irreconcilable conflict, and now in the late twentieth century to what some see as helpless obedience. Yet it was the place to be if you were rich and wanted to be powerful.

The direct connection between the landed elite's control of the legislature and the maintenance of its wealth and status is obvious, but in England the phased withdrawal of the aristocracy from the Commons tends to obscure how vital retention of political authority was to continued social and economic leadership. The dramatic electoral obliteration of the Welsh and Irish elites during a few years in the second half of the nineteenth century left them impotent in their attempt to sustain their values and save their estates. An historian of the Protestant Ascendancy has pointed to the change that took place when members of the Anglo-Irish elite failed to gain election as MPs. Competition for local honours such as High Sheriff and Deputy Lieutenant assumed much greater significance. Henceforward they could only set their sights on empty pomp, 'the small change of the old order'.[33] Soon even those offices were no longer available, and they had no visible means either to establish a pecking order within their own ranks or to exert leadership in shaping the national destiny.

The long-term stability and continuity of the English social structure at its highest levels allows us to measure degrees of both equilibrium and change by applying criteria that retained validity during many centuries. The eminence of the governing class was due to a desire for wealth and status channelled by the institution of parliament into a narrow frame, which identified and organized its power.

Chapter 1
The English Governing Class

No ruins remain to mark the site of Otes, a manor house in Essex situated not far from Harlow. A medieval moat surrounded the Tudor dwelling when William Masham purchased the estate late in the reign of Elizabeth I. He was the son of a London merchant and alderman who died in 1575. The family was never really rich, but the next William managed to purchase a baronetcy in 1621 and gained election as MP for Maldon in 1624. His acceptance in county society was marked by selection as a knight of the shire in 1640. He took a leading part against Charles I and served in the Council of State from 1649 to 1652. The 3rd Baronet also managed to sit for Essex (1690–98 and 1701–10). His wife was a friend of John Locke, who became their paying guest at Otes from 1691 to 1704. The house was frequented by Shaftesbury, Newton and other friends of the great philosopher. Locke left his library to the Mashams.

Samuel Masham married a plain and penniless servant at court who rose by royal favour to become Queen Anne's closest friend. Abigail Masham displaced the Duchess of Marlborough from her perch of privilege and arranged for Samuel, MP for Ilchester and then Windsor, to be raised to the barony of Masham in 1712. The 2nd Baron was a wastrel and spendthrift. Before inheriting the title, he could not even manage to retain his place in the Commons, being unseated on petition. He ran through his inheritance, disposed of Locke's books and papers, and consumed the dowries of two wives. In 1766 he sold Otes, and the peerage became extinct on his death ten years later. Nothing remained of the fortunes carefully accumulated by the Tudor merchant. Even the house was pulled down.[1]

Between 1621 and 1766 the Mashams stood at the centre of English cultural, social and political life, supported by an estate founded in commerce and enlarged by marriage, literature and royal favour. Four members of the family were elected to the House of Commons between 1624 and 1712, and two peers sat in the Lords. However, the family lacked luck and the biological fortitude to sustain itself. The Mashams joined the company of a thousand or so families which became parliamentary dynasties, sometimes ascending even to the highest reaches of the social pyramid, but which did not last. A century or so of importance and influence was followed by decline or disappearance. About half the English families in this study fall into this category.

By no means all such happy beginnings petered out so quickly. For instance, the Holtes of Aston, Warwickshire, enjoyed a long tenure as members of the ruling elite.

Simon del Holte purchased his first manor in 1331 with money made in the wool trade. His grandson acquired Aston in 1367. The first Holte elected to parliament took his seat in 1378, and they continued to send representatives to Westminster in each of the following four centuries until 1782. Eight Holtes became MPs, half of them sitting for the county. The family prospered. They acquired one of the first baronetcies in 1611 and in the 1620s built a new mansion that was not only beautiful but also prodigious in scale. The title became extinct in 1782 and the house was sold by the heirs in 1817. Today Aston is a museum marooned among the terraced houses, motorway flyovers and the eponymous football ground in what has become metropolitan Birmingham. Like the Mashams, no Holtes now inhabit the ancestral seat, but the latter lasted much longer and sustained a continuous line of parliament men.[2] Their service as knights of the shire reflected the important place they held in Warwickshire society for five centuries.

The Mashams and Holtes were typical of important gentry families, some of whom even gained a peerage. However, within the ruling class a small group of grandees formed an inner circle among whom wealth and power were luxuriantly distributed. For example, the Stanhopes prospered and proliferated to a degree that made members of even the greater gentry seem modestly endowed. The founder of the dynasty was a wool merchant. He became mayor and MP for Newcastle-upon-Tyne in the 1360s and 1370s. His son married an heiress and became a member of the Nottinghamshire gentry. The grandson of the Newcastle burgess was knighted in 1399 and sat for his county in parliament between 1402 and 1433. His son continued the tradition for much of the rest of the century. Rapid advancement led to important marriages and the world of high politics. Sir Edward Stanhope was one of Henry VII's commanders at the Battle of Stoke in 1487. That knight's daughter married the Protector Somerset. While this led her brother to an appointment with the headsman on Tower Hill – an occupational hazard for sixteenth-century government officials – the momentum of the family's rise seems hardly to have been dented. The first peerage came to a younger son in 1605, followed quickly by a proliferation of titles and MPs of almost manic proportions. The senior line seated at Shelford in Nottinghamshire and Bretby in Derbyshire became barons in 1616 and Earls of Chesterfield in 1628. The eldest son of a younger son of the 1st Earl of Chesterfield achieved a peerage in his own right in 1718 as Earl Stanhope of Chevening in Kent. A third earldom came to a grandson of another younger son who was created Lord Harrington in 1742. This line was seated at Elvaston Castle in Derbyshire. A younger son of the 3rd Earl Stanhope succeeded to estates in Lincolnshire and the Midlands, establishing a rich cadet branch. Another junior line became the Spencer Stanhopes of Yorkshire. Both of these families inherited incomes that in the nineteenth century stood at well over £10,000. Finally another cadet succeeded to the Collingwood estates in Northumberland worth £5,000. By the eve of the twentieth century the various elements of the Stanhope family had accumulated a grand total of 76,000 acres. The Chesterfield stem family elected twenty-three MPs (including an Irish one) over six centuries. Added to this were the Harrington ten and the (Earl) Stanhope seven and four from the other cadets totalling forty-four parliament men plus over a dozen peers sitting in the House of Lords. Several of the earls served as lords lieutenant of their counties, four were made Knights of the Garter, and they held cabinet level office following the Restoration in 1714–21, 1730–51, 1745–48, 1885–92, and 1936–40. Members of the family achieved fame as diplomats, patrons, sportsmen and men of letters. Not every Stanhope was distinguished. One served as the model for Disraeli's Lord Fitzbooby in *Coningsby*, another earl blew himself up in his private laboratory at Elvaston, and the family was notorious for adultery. However, from the time of Bosworth to Dunkirk virtually every generation produced an ambassador, a general or a privy councillor. Chesterfield House, one of the most handsome aristocratic palaces in London, has been demolished. Chevening was donated to the nation and still serves as the official residence of the Foreign Secretary. But the Earl of Harrington, who succeeded to titles from the other lines as they became extinct, is still prosperous and his daughter recently married into the royal family. Unlike the Mashams and Holtes neither biology nor insufficient funds have managed to halt the Stanhopes. For over five hundred years they accumulated riches, honours and power in an unrelenting progress that fed on itself, bolstering the family's fame.[3]

Who is Included in This Study?

Families are at the centre of this book, so we begin with their histories. For the purposes of this study all families which elected at least three male or female MPs to the Commons, enjoyed three tenures[4] in the House of Lords, or held three memberships of either House in combination are counted as part of the parliamentary elite (an MP who became a peer is only counted once).[5] I have followed the practice of other surveys of the English elite, such as those made by Lawrence Stone, Barbara English and Lewis Namier, in counting families as continuous so long as their principal properties were passed intact to designated heirs, even if this occurred through the female line or via illegitimate or remote kin. In the vast majority of cases, the individuals included in this study were brothers, sons or grandsons of the head of the family, almost always the direct beneficiaries of the wealth and influence connected with their name (see Table 1.1). Englishmen holding seats in the Irish or Scottish parliaments and representative peers from those countries serving in the British House of Lords are included in the count. MPs/commissioners/peers from Welsh, Irish and Scottish families in the Dublin, Edinburgh and London parliaments are analysed separately in Chapter 4.

Table 1.1 Examples of members of the English parliamentary elite and family relationships

PECCHE

John Pecche MP London 1361, 1369, 1371, 1372	**Head**
Sir William Pecche MP Kent 1394, 1397	**Head**
Sir William Pecche MP Kent 1450	**Head**

The first MP was a successful fishmonger and Mayor of London who purchased estates in Kent. The line died out in the sixteenth century.

CORBET

John Corbet MP Norwich 1536, 1554	**Head**
Thomas Corbet MP Dunwich 1593	**Head**
Francis Corbet MP Aldeburgh 1601	**Younger Son**
Sir John Corbet, 1st Baronet MP Norfolk 1624	**Head**
Miles Corbet MP Great Yarmouth 1640–53	**Younger Son**

The father of the first MP was a brazier in Norwich. The last baronet was a royalist who suffered financial setbacks during the turbulent years of the mid-seventeenth century, sold his estates and died unmarried in 1661.

CARTWRIGHT

Thomas Cartwright MP Northamptonshire 1695–98, 1701–15, 1748	**Head**
William Cartwright MP Northamptonshire 1754–68	**Head**
William Cartwright MP Northamptonshire 1797–1831; S. Northamptonshire 1832–46	**Head**
Henry Cartwright MP S. Northamptonshire 1858–68	**Younger Son**
Fairfax Cartwright MP S. Northamptonshire 1868–81	**Grandson**
William Cartwright MP Oxfordshire 1868–85	**Head**

The family was founded by a successful lawyer, the son of a yeoman sheep farmer, who purchased Aynhoe, Northamptonshire, in 1615. The last head of the family and his heir were killed in a car crash in 1954 and the house was sold.

GUEST

Sir Josiah Guest, 1st Baronet MP Honiton 1826–31; Merthyr Tydvil 1832–52	**Head**

<u>Arthur Guest</u> MP Poole 1868–74	**Younger Son**
<u>Montagu Guest</u> MP Youghal 1869–74; Wareham 1880–85	**Younger Son**
<u>Ivor Guest 1st Baron Wimborne</u> HLds 1880–1914	**Head**
<u>Ivor Guest, 1st Viscount Wimborne</u> MP Plymouth 1900–06; Cardiff 1906–10; HLds 1914–39	**Head**
<u>Christian Guest</u> MP E. Dorset 1910; Pembroke Boroughs 1910–18; N. Bristol 1922–23; Drake Div. Plymouth 1937–45	**Younger Son**
<u>Frederick Guest</u> MP E. Dorset 1910–22; Stroud Div. Gloucestershire 1923–24; N. Div. Bristol 1924–29	**Younger Son**
<u>Oscar Guest</u> MP Loughborough Div. Leicestershire 1918–22; Camberwell N.W. 1935–45	**Younger Son**
<u>Ivor Guest, 2nd Viscount Wimborne</u> MP Brecon and Radnor 1935–39; HLds 1939–45	**Head**

The Guests began as Welsh industrialists but later set up as landed gentleman in England.

FOLEY

<u>Thomas Foley</u> MP Worcestershire 1659; Bewdley 1660, 1673–77	**Head, Witley**
<u>Philip Foley</u> MP Bewdley 1679–81; Stafford 1689–90; Droitwich 1690–95; Stafford 1695–1700; Droitwich 1701	**Younger Son, Witley**
<u>Paul Foley</u> MP Hereford 1679–81, 1689–99	**Head, Stoke**
<u>Thomas Foley</u> MP Worcestershire 1679–81, 1689–98; Droitwich 1699–1701	**Head, Witley**
<u>Robert Foley</u> MP Grampound 1685–87	**Nephew, Witley**
<u>Thomas Foley</u> MP Weobley 1691–1700; Hereford 1701–22; Stafford 1722–27, 1734–37	**Head, Stoke**
<u>Thomas Foley, 1st Baron Foley</u> MP Stafford 1694–1712; HLds 1712–33	**Head, Witley**
<u>Edward Foley</u> MP Droitwich 1701–11, 1732–41	**Younger Son, Witley**
<u>Richard Foley</u> MP Droitwich 1711–32	**Younger Son, Witley**
<u>Paul Foley</u> MP Aldborough 1713–15; Weobley 1715	**Younger Son, Stoke**
<u>Thomas Foley, 2nd Baron Foley</u> HLds 1733–66	**Head, Witley**
<u>Thomas Foley</u> MP Hereford 1734–41; Herefordshire 1742–47	**Head, Stoke**
<u>Thomas Foley, 1st Baron Foley</u> (2nd creation) MP Droitwich 1741–47, 1754–68; HLds 1776–77	**Head**

<u>Thomas Foley, 2nd Baron Foley</u> MP Herefordshire 1767–74; Droitwich 1774–77; HLds 1777–93	**Head**
<u>Edward Foley</u> MP Droitwich 1768–74; Worcestershire 1774–1803	**Younger Son**
<u>Andrew Foley</u> MP Droitwich 1774–1818	**Younger Son**
<u>Thomas Foley, 3rd Baron Foley</u> HLds 1801–33	**Head**
<u>Thomas Foley</u> MP Droitwich 1805–07 Herefordshire 1807–18; Droitwich 1819–22	**Grandson**
<u>John Hodgetts-Foley</u> MP Droitwich 1822–34; E. Worcestershire 1847–61	**Head, Prestwood**
<u>Edward Foley</u> MP Ludgershall 1826–32; Herefordshire 1832–41	**Head, Stoke**
<u>Thomas Foley, 4th Baron Foley</u> MP Worcestershire 1830–32; W. Worcestershire 1832–33; HLds 1833–69	**Head**
<u>Henry Hodgetts-Foley</u> MP S. Staffordshire 1857–68	**Head, Stoke**
<u>Henry Foley, 5th Baron Foley</u> HLds 1880–1905	**Head**
<u>Fitzalan Foley, 6th Baron Foley</u> HLds 1905–18	**Head**
<u>Gerald Foley, 7th Baron Foley</u> HLds 1918–27	**Head**
<u>Adrian Foley, 8th Baron Foley</u> HLds 1944–45	**Head**

The Foley line(s) of MPs look more complicated than they really are. The first MP's father founded a great nail-making concern in the mid-seventeenth century. He purchased two estates: Witley Court, Worcestershire, for his heir and Stoke Edith, Herefordshire, for a younger son, who was active in the business and had a large income in his own right. Had the senior line continued uninterrupted, the Stoke Edith cadets would have been treated as a separate family in this study. However, on the death of the 2nd Lord Foley of the first creation in 1766, the Witley and Stoke Edith estates were merged and the family title was recreated for the new head a few years later. A grandson succeeded to the Hodgetts estates at Prestwood. His son inherited Prestwood and was also allocated Stoke Edith, but no further MPs followed. So, despite determined efforts to break up the family into branches, the Foleys remained a single unit. The 3rd, 5th, 7th and 8th Barons inherited their titles while minors and could not have served as MPs.

EDGCUMBE

<u>William Edgcumbe</u> MP Plymouth 1447	**Younger Son (?)**
<u>Sir Richard Edgcumbe</u> MP Tavistock 1467–68 (? 1485, 1487)	**Head**
<u>Sir Peter Edgecombe</u> MP Cornwall 1515, 1529	**Head**
<u>Sir Richard Edgecombe</u> MP (Cornwall?) 1542; Cornwall 1547	**Head**

Peter Edgecombe MP Totnes 1555; Cornwall 1563; Devon 1571; Cornwall 1572; Liskeard 1584; Cornwall 1586, 1589, 1593	**Head**
Richard Edgecombe MP Totnes 1563	**Younger Son**
Sir Richard Edgecombe MP Liskeard 1586; Totnes 1589; Grampound 1593; Bodmin 1614; Grampound 1624; Bossiney 1628	**Head**
Piers Edgcumbe MP Newport 1628; Camelford 1640–44; Newport 1662–67	**Head**
Richard Edgcombe MP Newport 1640–44	**Younger Son**
Sir Richard Edgcumbe MP Launceston 1661; Cornwall 1679–81	**Head**
Richard Edgcumbe, 1st Baron Edgcumbe MP Cornwall 1701; St Germans 1701–02; Plympton Erle 1702–34; Lostwithiel 1734–41; Plympton Erle 1741–42; HLds 1742–58	**Head**
Richard Edgcumbe, 2nd Baron Edgcumbe MP Plympton Erle 1742–47; Lostwithiel 1747–54; Penryn 1754–58; HLds 1758–61	**Head**
George Edgcumbe, 1st Earl of Mount Edgcumbe MP Fowey 1746–61; HLds 1761–95	**Head**
Richard Edgcumbe, 2nd Earl of Mount Edgcumbe MP Fowey 1786–90; Lostwithiel 1790–91; Fowey 1791–95; HLds 1795–1839	**Head**
William Edgcumbe, Viscount Valletort MP Lostwithiel 1816–19	**Eldest Son**
Ernest Edgcumbe, 3rd Earl of Mount Edgcumbe MP Fowey 1819–26; Lostwithiel 1826–30; Plympton Erle 1830; Lostwithiel 1830–32; HLds 1839–61	**Head**
George Edgcumbe MP Plympton Erle 1826	**Younger Son**
William Edgcumbe, 4th Earl of Mount Edgcumbe MP Plymouth 1859–61; HLds 1861–1917	**Head**
Piers Edgcumbe, 5th Earl of Mount Edgcumbe HLds 1917–44	**Head**
Kenelm Edgcumbe, 6th Earl of Mount Edgcumbe HLds 1944–45	**Head**

The Edgcumbes (spelt here as the volumes of the *History of Parliament* present them) acquired Cotehele in Cornwall in the mid-fourteenth century. An unbroken chain of thirteen generations of the head of the family sat in the Commons.

The three MP/peers demarcation line guarantees that at least two generations of a family were in parliament, and in most cases three or more generations.[6] As a measure of membership in the social elite, this method has some flaws. For example, caution must be exercised in ascribing congruence between social and economic prominence and political office in England before the reign of Elizabeth I. However, for England and Wales after the mid-sixteenth century and Scotland and Ireland after the Restoration selection as an MP was the highest accolade commonly available to the landed elite other than a title. Knights of the shire came to outrank knights by appointment. Lord lieutenancies were the reserve of a tiny handful of magnates, and sheriffdoms were held only for a year and for a time came to be regarded as an onerous duty. This chapter will demonstrate that tenure by three or more participants at Westminster proves to be the most accurate measure of a family's membership in the English governing class at the national level, at least until the mid-nineteenth century.

The Governing Class and Parliament

'Mad', 'Merciless', 'Diabolical', 'Drunken' and 'Unlearned' are among the not entirely respectful sobriquets applied to medieval parliaments. In early centuries neither the king nor the nobles necessarily centred their political struggles within the institution, and its full panoply of powers was not achieved until the seventeenth century. This is not the place to enter into the controversies surrounding the gestation of the embryonic institution. For our purposes it is enough to know that at some time in the thirteenth century, nobles, clergy, knights of the shires and borough representatives began to gather on a regular basis.[7] The formation of a permanent, hereditary parliamentary peerage developed during the 1300s. Peter Coss believes that it was not coincidental that the emergence of a territorial conception of status in the mid-fourteenth century was concurrent with the emergence of the Commons as a significant political force. Both the nobles and gentry thus began to define themselves in part by their relationship with the central government and their capacity for collective self-expression through parliament.[8] Although among commoners office-holding was not the sole criterion by which an individual could be identified as of greater gentry status, in terms of *families* this was increasingly the case. Parliament was where landed society and the crown converged. Two developments occurred, which were of great importance to this study.

First, from about 1400, with occasional exceptions, knights of the shires, who previously had been often recruited from the ranks of the lesser landed families and self-made men, became more exclusively drawn from the higher gentry usually connected by blood or association with magnates. Geoffrey Chaucer's franklin 'ful ofte tyme . . . was knight of the shire', but neither the poet nor the pilgrim probably would have qualified in a county election a century later.[9] As prowess on the battlefield, jousting at tournaments and the massing of liveried henchmen became less useful and important, membership in parliament became a new means to assert status. The number of baronies declined substantially between the early fourteenth and the early fifteenth century, which left the Commons as the place for most influential landowners to make their mark. A shire seat became largely out of the reach of ordinary country gentlemen.[10]

From the fourteenth century onwards great lords were meeting to discuss who should be returned for shire seats.[11] County elections were increasingly contested. Rivalry for status within the hierarchy of an elite obsessed with finely graded social distinctions now came to govern competition for knighthoods of the shire, and this remained true until the late nineteenth century. County elections, often decided before the official nomination process took place but sometimes in an open contest, emerged as gauges of standing, the new battlefields for honour and arenas of acclaim.[12] By the Tudor period most knights were drawn from the richest and socially pre-eminent county families.[13] Election became, in S.T. Bindoff's words, the 'most coveted prize'.[14]

By Elizabeth's reign contentious elections could produce county meetings of 7,000 to 10,000 voters and were accompanied by skulduggery, violence and in contemporary parlance 'great ado'.[15] Contests were usually not fatal, unless they provoked a duel, but they had the attraction of both producing a clear winner and offering a satisfying opportunity publicly to humiliate rivals.[16] Nursing even a quiet county constituency began to cost money.[17] By the reign of Elizabeth, exclusion from a shire seat for two consecutive elections could be seen as a serious demotion in the county hierarchy.[18] The number of contests and the expense of electioneering during the seventeenth and eighteenth centuries continued to grow, owing to inflation and to an elite expanding in size, while the number of county places in the Commons remained inelastic. One nineteenth-century nobleman described being a county MP as 'the most honourable situation an Englishman can enjoy'. 'Kings might make peers,' another remarked, 'but they could not make a county member.'[19] Only after the First Reform Act did county seats become regularly available to men with commercial backgrounds. As late as 1868 Sir Watkin Williams Wynn, 3rd Baronet, a Welsh landowner of princely fortune and lineage, declared: 'It is a position which for more than a century and a half has been the most prized distinction of my family; it was preferred by my great-grandfather to an earldom, by my father to an earldom, and by myself to a peerage.'[20] Nowhere in the British political system, save the monarchy and a few medieval baronies, does one find greater continuity than in the high social standing of the families who were first elected shire knights in the late thirteenth or early fourteenth centuries and continued repeatedly to hold the office into the late Victorian period. Heirs to such traditions were born predestined senators.[21]

The second important shift in medieval parliamentary practice began as early as 1320 when country gentlemen started to gain election for borough seats, which unlike the county constituencies were neither socially prestigious nor usually open to non-residents. Borough representatives were drawn either from commercial oligarchies or from the company of modest tradesmen of the towns. Although some candidates considered election as an MP to be an undesirable duty, others regarded it as confirmation of their high status in the municipal hierarchy.[22] By the 1420s, however, resident burgesses were more frequently giving way to local gentry and later to men from further afield. Practice varied from borough to borough, but the statutes enacted with increasing frequency during the fifteenth century requiring MPs to reside in their constituency showed in which direction the wind was blowing.[23] The Reformation Parliament included a significant number of great names among the burgesses. From the 1530s the numbers of leading gentlemen sitting for boroughs expanded explosively (see Table 1.2 below). Even a borough seat in parliament now could be considered the summit of a country gentleman's ambition.[24] Men of great wealth and rank began to fill the benches of the Commons from the mid-sixteenth century onwards.[25]

A number of developments were occurring simultaneously which caused the change in borough representation. It was expensive to maintain burgesses at Westminster. The Reformation Parliament, commencing in 1529, had seven sessions lasting 407 days (up to 600 for those travelling from distant places), which produced prodigious bills for wages and expenses. Corporations found the money to support two MPs hard to come by. This gave impetus to finding candidates who would pay for themselves, and perhaps contribute to local charities or public works as well. The boroughs gained socially prestigious representatives, often with connections at the bar or in the royal court, who could look after the legislative interests of the town more effectively than most burgesses, and for free. During Elizabeth's reign it was rare for small boroughs to pay wages. By 1601 only a few large cities such as York were still doing so.[26]

Other factors contributing to the 'invasion' of the boroughs included interference by great lords who sought to enhance their power by finding more rewards to confer on their followers, and subsequently places of honour and influence for their sons. There were not enough county seats to satisfy the demand, and some shires were not amenable to the wishes of magnates. Borough seats were answers to noble prayers. The Crown also competed for places in the Commons to elect men capable of arranging its affairs. Leading lawyers found membership in the House useful for 'networking' and generating business, and this remained true in subsequent centuries. Great financiers and merchants eager to consolidate their social prestige began to sit for borough seats distant from the towns which produced their fortunes, because a seat in parliament had ceased to be seen as a burdensome duty and had become an object of ambition. Finally, the tiny size of the House of Lords and the restricted number of shire seats meant that country gentlemen were left no alternative but to seek a borough seat if they wanted to raise themselves to social eminence above their neighbours.

The 'invasion' of the boroughs did not begin as a gadarene rush. In 1422 only one out of ten burgesses was a carpetbagger. But a medievalist can speak of a 'parliamentary class' of families having emerged by the mid-fifteenth century. Soon afterwards at least half of the borough representatives were not resident townsmen. At the accession of Elizabeth I less than one-quarter of such MPs fulfilled the original qualifications of the office.[27] Native sons were 'virtually extinct' in Wiltshire boroughs by the end of the century. Of the thirty-nine MPs for Reading between 1604 and 1754 only one was a townsman.[28] Only a few great cities such as Bristol, Norwich and London continued to return their own.[29]

A number of factors enhanced the prestige of a seat in the Commons. Liberty of speech was granted explicitly in 1523 and confirmed at all subsequent parliaments.[30] Some of the changes mentioned above grew out of the increased stature of parliament earned during the Reformation. The unprecedented number and intensity of sessions in the 1530s gave the members a new sense of corporate identity and importance. MPs began to meet on a regular basis outside the chamber to discuss parliamentary matters, assert the Commons' parity with the Lords, and proclaim independence from royal interference. The move to St Stephen's Chapel and the regularization of division procedures took place in the 1540s. Determined attacks on government policy could produce minorities of up to a hundred MPs, and leading figures such as Sir Christopher Hatton delivered polished oratorical performances of two hours in length.[31] The drought of peerage creations under Elizabeth became acute, and the size of the House of Lords actually began to shrink.[32] This made membership in the House of Commons even more desirable. The tone and timbre of the lower chamber changed as more self-confident, established and influential gentlemen and sons of nobles asserted themselves.[33] In the 1570s an MP explicitly compared the lower house to the Roman Senate. Attendance at important debates packed the benches.[34] The Commons came progressively to be the senior partner in the legislative process. This led to even more strenuous efforts by the peers to control the nomination of MPs, and the interest of a lord in elections to the Commons became as potent a symbol of his status as the size of his estate.[35] The Stuarts confronted the socio-political elite in more concentrated form and in greater numbers than any of their predecessors.

The role played by parliament in the Civil War conferred additional authority on the institution. Sequestration, confiscation, fines and punishments issued forth from the chamber in Westminster, and parliament became more obviously the direct shaper of the national destiny. As Mark Kishlansky has observed: 'When the lessons of the power of parliament over men's lives and estates had been fully digested,' the landed elite 'came to believe that it was more important to secure a seat than to avoid defeat.'[36] During the Georgian and Victorian eras parliament reached a kind of apotheosis as a model for self-government both in Europe and around the globe. The disfranchised and oppressed at home sought redress within the system, not revolution. Barry and Pugin's neo-Gothic Palace of Westminster commemorates the era of pre-eminence.

The close identification of social status with political standing in the electoral process and the minuscule size of the titular nobility raised the English House of Commons to a unique place among early modern national assemblies. Hence from the mid-fifteenth century pressure mounted to add more seats, as the size of the gentry increased. The number of borough places rose from 296 in 1510 to 462 in 1586, an expansion in which the addition in the 1540s of Welsh seats was only a minor part. Parliament became the largest representative body in Europe both in proportion to population and absolutely.[37] In the seventeenth century fewer new constituencies were established and the number of English MPs remained stationary from 1677 to 1832. Thus, as the size and prosperity of the elite grew, the possession of a seat became all the more prized. Indeed, the shire knight membership became as exclusive as the peerage. The development of continuous sessions and frequent elections made it possible for the elite to gain communal sanction for its leadership and to assert their rank on a regular basis in a public and dramatic way.[38]

Soon after the death of Henry VII Sir Thomas Seymour noted that 'the most part of Parliament' was now composed of gentlemen.[39] Hitherto, for many MPs, standing for election once or twice was enough, much as they might demonstrate courage or preserve honour by exposing themselves a few times on a battlefield or in a duel. Now regular attendance became more common and service in seven, eight or even more sessions became normal practice for dozens of noble scions and greater gentry.

The interconnectedness of the parliamentary elite thickened through intermarriage among politically prominent families.[40] In the Middle Ages family representation in the Commons was usually restricted to one member at a time, and it was by no means automatic that son would succeed father as an MP. Again, the mid-Tudor period marked a shift. Under Elizabeth I twenty-four families elected five or more MPs, including seventeen Herberts. Six Knollys and seven Throckmorton brothers sat as MPs, and a dozen other families elected three or more siblings.[41] Another new phenomenon was the number of family members sitting simultaneously in the same session of parliament. This began to occur on a regular basis from the 1590s. For example, five Wingfields sat in 1593 and the same number of Townshends in 1601.

Such electoral exhibitionism was made possible by magnates choosing family members as candidates, not their retainers or servants.[42] This was the era of the rise of the 'family' seat.[43] Bindoff judged that by Elizabeth's reign families with three or more MPs became 'the governing class *par excellence*'.[44]

The elite of the realm was now fully gathered in parliament. Geoffrey Elton, who criticized fellow historians for according parliament unwarranted importance before the Civil War, none the less admitted that by 1600 the Commons had achieved a social homogeneity that made it representative of the richest and most powerful men in the country.[45] The hiatus in the meeting of parliament during the 1630s caused a crisis for political and for *social* reasons. Between the Restoration and the Great Reform Act, economic, social and political power were most fully integrated and represented in parliament. W.D. Rubinstein believes that even as late as 1895 it is likely that a state opening of parliament 'saw a greater concentration of Britain's economic wealth at one time in one place than ever in British history, and possibly among any legislature anywhere'.[46] It was this process that makes parliamentary families as defined in this study uniquely useful in mapping the English social and economic as well as political elite.

The Privileges of Rank

Social status was not the only incentive to stand for parliament. Many practical advantages accrued from holding a seat in either house. Some of these 'perks' were useful to men of widely different backgrounds, while others more exclusively reflected patrician interests. Taken together, they enhanced the value of membership in the legislature and were a further inducement to wealthy men with aspirations to power and status to covet a seat there.

Class privilege and property were maintained by the power of parliament. The elite could pass legislation protecting game and the price of corn. Individual families also benefited. Personal participation gave gentlemen access to local patronage and private legislation to arrange for divorce, enclosure, jointures, succession to property, settlements, drainage projects, road diversions, legitimizing children, protecting fisheries, reversal of attainders, canal or harbour schemes and other profitable endeavours. MPs could protect their own interests and those of their clients; they could spike the guns of opponents and rivals. Private legislation occupied much of the Commons' time from the sixteenth century to the early nineteenth century. Battles to promote local interests became frequent, and thus a voice in the process of apportionment and mediation of interests became more vital than ever. Membership also provided opportunities to benefit from lucrative sinecures, wardships, grants of lands and appointments to or promotions in the services, church, court and government jobs. Admission to Westminster gave access to officials, business contacts, marriage partners and the notice of the monarch. Nabobs could block inquiries into their sources of wealth; ex-Jacobites could fight to regain lost estates. Welshmen sought recognition from their English peers.[47] Other practical advantages included freedom from arrest in civil suits and for debt during parliamentary sessions. In the eighteenth century Edward Wortley found it cheaper to keep his son out of gaol by bringing him into parliament than by paying his creditors.[48] Franking privileges were a boon when mailing letters was expensive. The frank became an inexhaustible gift of minor patronage and social power.[49]

Fathers sent sons to Westminster to rub shoulders with the nation's elite, to breed them to the nation's business and to add to their experience of life. In 1585 Sir Henry Bagnall requested a seat in the Commons 'for my learning's sake'. Sir George Trenchard wished in 1601 'to train up and make serviceable to her Majesty' his eldest son as a knight of the shire for Dorset. Lord Ashburnham wrote in 1701 that by becoming an MP his son's abilities 'will be improved, I hope daily, by the good company of the gentlemen of the House of Commons'.[50] Nor should one rule out as an attraction of membership the desire to sample the delights of the capital, which the permanent settlement of parliament at Westminster made possible. Thomas Bulkeley declared in 1584: 'I am one that loves to see fashions and desires to know wonders,' and therefore he wanted a seat.[51] The times and seasons of meetings were arranged so as not to disturb shooting, hunting, gambling and other aristocratic pastimes. When it developed, the 'Season' coincided with a convenient period to be in town. From the early eighteenth century, if not before, the dates of the English elite's annual calendar were literally set by the meeting of parliament: the political schedule dictated the social one. Holding elective office was also closely linked with the admission of wives of 'new men' to their first presentation at Court.[52] Renewing old friendships and social gossip were as much a part of the Commons as politics. After the parliament buildings burned down in 1834 a new facility was built with all the amenities of a luxurious social club.

We should not entirely exclude nobler motives for membership. Only a cynic could dismiss the sense of responsibility that some men brought to their duties in parliament. Francis Alford (MP 1563–89) felt proud of his years of public service 'for that I know I have done my country some good, where unto we are all born'. Sir Edward Dering stated in 1641 that the electors 'sent us hither as their trustees'.[53] Religion, honour, philosophical ideals and regional loyalties all played a role in impelling wealthy men to bestir themselves to their duty. The self-image of a senator was attractive, and service in parliament satisfied the psychological needs of paternalistic and idealistic aristocrats, giving members of the elite a means 'to display their virtue to the nation', in what one MP called 'the Great Theatre of the World'.[54]

The Price of Admission

Nothing better illustrates the value placed by the social elite on membership in the Commons than the financial price they were willing to pay to gain admission. Indeed, election became so expensive that only the top layer of English society could afford to contend for a seat, and even great landowners beggared themselves to ensure victory on the hustings. As early as 1534 the son of one MP complained that he had been unable to acquire a university education because his father had spent so much on service in parliament. Sir Richard Grenville calculated that five years in the Commons in the 1530s cost him £333, at a time when a country gentleman could maintain his whole establishment for less than £100 a year.[55] Sir Matthew Morgan, MP for Brecon Boroughs in 1593, had to borrow £300 to finance his election and service in London.[56] Once wages and expenses ceased to be provided, only wealthy men could serve unless subsidized by a patron, which was uncommon. The cost of travel to and from London, which was expensive until the nineteenth century if large distances had to be covered, lodgings in the capital and maintenance of a style of life suitable to the rank of an MP placed the position out of the reach of all but a few thousand individuals by the reign of Elizabeth I. Three-quarters of the MPs in the Long Parliament were estimated to have had incomes of at least £500 a year.[57] Legislation enacted in 1711 and in force until 1858 required MPs to own landed property (personal property was allowed after 1838) worth at least £300 for a burgess and £600 for a shire knight. Collusive transfers made it possible to evade this provision, but a substantial income was necessary to support living expenses as an MP, and as the sessions grew more frequent and lasted longer this became ever more the case. Barristers could usually combine a career with being an MP, as could some businessmen, but both categories provided a comparatively small proportion of the Commons until the later nineteenth century.

Evidence about election expenses is not always accurate. Outside observers liked to sound authoritative, but their estimates were often unfounded speculation. It was not unknown for those who had underwritten the expenses of an election to minimize or exaggerate the total for personal reasons. On the other hand, many costs were concealed. Estates were run in a manner to maximize political potential and ensure the return of family members to parliament. For example, holding down rents in order to keep the tenantry cooperative, paying excessive prices to tradesmen to win their loyalty, maintaining a herd of deer to provide gifts of venison or a pack of fox-hounds free of subscriptions to provide entertainment, philanthropies and dues all placed heavy financial burdens on the parliamentary elite, yet rarely showed up on the lists of election expenditures to be found in muniment rooms. Moreover stewards and agents spent much time 'tending the family interest' and electioneering, which could have been more profitably directed to increasing the productivity of the estate.[58] The hours spent by the elite themselves canvassing, serving on asylum boards, arranging concerts and races, and making themselves agreeable to prospective voters, while sometimes enjoyable or necessary for other reasons, also cost them time away from the pursuit of pleasure and often produced much boredom and discomfort. This is to say nothing of the lawyers' fees, the costs of food and drink, transportation, and the hiring of thugs to molest and kidnap opposing voters, and the massive distribution of bribes which could rise to staggering expenditure.

Bribery in elections can be traced back to the reign of Henry IV. The 'mad scramble' for a place in parliament drove up the market price. By the early Stuart period some borough seats cost £300 or £400. County contests reached the same level.[59] J.H. Plumb believed that many seats remained cheap before 1690. However, there is evidence to suggest that expenses began to rocket earlier. At least five MPs crippled their estates through election expenses between 1660 and 1690. Robert Coke of Holkham spent £10,000 in 1675 to win a contest in Kings Lynn.[60]

The passage of the Septennial Act in 1716 made elections less frequent and thus further increased the amount families were willing to spend on them. Borough elections could go to £30,000 or more while county costs occasionally rose to £100,000 per candidate. Welsh and Scottish seats, despite their small electorates, could swallow tens of thousands of pounds, and Irish contests also reached very high figures. Even magnates sometimes embarrassed their finances by electioneering on this scale. This was a period when the entire expense of maintaining an earl's eldest son and his family in considerable luxury stood at less than £3,000 per year.[61]

The Reform Acts of the nineteenth century were supposed to improve the efficiency and probity of the electoral system, but campaigning was still costly. Bribery continued. The Clives spent £40,000 between 1837 and 1841 struggling to preserve their ascendancy over a few thousand electors in Ludlow. The increasing number of contests after 1850 meant more expense, and landed gentlemen were still spending large sums to buy additional estates to increase their standing for electoral purposes. In 1866 the North Riding of Yorkshire cost the candidates £27,000.[62] After 1884 expenses declined and party war chests took up more of the burden, although Harold Macmillan told the story of a selection committee he attended in the 1920s where the chair asked each applicant to write his name on a piece of paper together with the amount he was prepared to donate to the local association – the highest bidder was adopted forthwith.[63]

For centuries most English magnates spent hugely merely to give their sons an opportunity to occupy a bit of free time in London during the Season in a more constructive way than gaming or whoring. While relatively few wasted their patrimony at £100,000 per election, many significantly diminished their capacity to provide for their younger children, to invest in more property or simply to enjoy themselves in order to assert mastery on the hustings. All the practical advantages of a seat in the Commons listed earlier could hardly justify spending like this. It is only when one recognizes that success in elections was seen as intimately connected with identity as a member of the governing class, that frittering away such vast sums no longer seems an irrational act.

For the established elite winning election to parliament was a matter of 'honour' and for new men it meant gaining the imprimatur of acceptance. The selection process for the Commons winnowed out the elite. It was the most effective means at the disposal of landed society not in the hands of the Crown to distinguish between those who mattered and those who did not. Whether a seat was won by intimidation or because the competition was not too intense, as was often the case in the fifteenth and sixteenth centuries, or gained by the expenditure of great sums of money and careful cultivation of the voters, as was more common in the eighteenth and early nineteenth centuries, it was a mark of arrival rather than a step along the way. Membership in the Commons moved from conferring gentility to confirming it. Huge investments were made to buy boroughs, yet not a single fortune is known to have been made by acquiring electoral influence. The letters 'MP' after one's name spelled out social primacy more clearly than 'Gent.' or even 'Bart.' and its potency did not become diluted over time.

Parliament and Social Status

Did parliament include *all* the leading families? Or were the Lords and Commons merely a cross-section of the elite ranging from minor squires to magnates? We know how attractive a seat in the legislature was, but what evidence is there to demonstrate that from the mid-sixteenth until the mid-nineteenth century the membership of parliament was largely congruent with the top layer of the social and economic elite?

The English obsession with rank made parliament the central pillar of social as well as political life because it provided the supporting framework for both a permanent titular aristocracy and the opportunities for the affirmation of honour by election to the Commons. The extraordinary table of precedence that used to be found in *Burke's Peerage*, listing by *number* every member of the British nobility down to remote kinsmen of junior baronets, is an artifact too little noticed by historians.[64] Precedence was of the gravest concern in medieval times, and competition for titles did not diminish as English society modernized and became a capitalist democracy. No other Western society has retained such an elaborate hierarchy of titles and honours still widely distributed both by Conservative and Labour governments. Compulsive attention to honorifics is found in the most unlikely corners even of contemporary life.[65] Peerages legitimized authority and leadership. Nobles were automatically members of both the political and social elite.

From the late fourteenth century onwards it became the ambition of new men to achieve a peerage. So potent was the claim of noble status that members of the Catholic clergy, including a monk and several bishops, renounced their vows and married in the hope of producing an heir after succeeding to Irish peerages.[66] Even in the late twentieth century, when peers were released from their legal obligation to bear a title, only a handful have abandoned their rank. The route to the summit of English society, other than by military exploits or personal friendship with a monarch, *lay almost exclusively through membership in the House of Commons*. Titles were the reward for long and loyal service as an MP.

Table 1.2 shows how close a connection developed after the Reformation Parliament between service in the Commons and the creation of peerages. In every decade except three from 1530 to 1900 more new peers were MPs than not. Under Elizabeth I only three men were created peers who had not been MPs and two of those were Howards, cousins of the queen, and the other was a younger son of the regent Northumberland. Under the early Stuarts some men were able to purchase titles without membership in the Commons, but most of the 'buyers' were also MPs. If one leaves out military heroes, husbands of heiresses to titled families, younger sons of dukes, judges and the like the number of new peers who had not been MPs never rises above 15% between 1559 and 1900.[67]

The close link over a long period between service in the Commons and gaining a peerage made the most crucial step in social advancement after acquiring a fortune and buying land the establishment of a hereditary presence in the elective chamber. The integration of new families into the governing class took place at Westminster. This was possible because the membership of parliament was largely composed of already well established families.

Men also built up electoral empires to put at the service of what they hoped would be a grateful king or prime minister. Once a title was gained there was further jostling and pushing to gain promotion in the ranks, which also encouraged assemblage of family members in the Commons. Prime ministers were pressed 'without mercy', Earl Grey once lamented, for advancement into and within the House of Lords.[68] Noble dynasties such as the Talbots, Earls of Shrewsbury, struggled to control parliamentary seats as early as the fourteenth century.[69] Gatton may have been a pocket borough from the day of its creation in 1450. All twenty-six seats in Sussex during the early sixteenth century were dominated by members of the nobility. By the early seventeenth century it is estimated that the peerage was involved in between one-third and one-half of all constituencies during elections.[70] Moreover, by the reign of Elizabeth I great landowners were involved in elections not to place followers in the Commons but because they wanted a seat for themselves or for members of their families.

Table 1.2 Number of newly created English, British and United Kingdom peers* who previously served in the House of Commons, 1450–1899

	MPs		Not MPs	
	Number	%	Number	%
1450–99	5	25.0	15	75.0
1500–49	14	41.2	20	58.8
1550–99	15	78.9	4	21.1
1600–49	66	72.5	25	27.5
1650–99	39	75.0	13	25.0
1700–49	55	98.2	1	1.8
1750–99	75	93.8	5	6.2
1800–49	83	85.6	14	14.4
1850–99	138	71.1	56	28.9

* The definition of newly created peer used here excludes foreigners, peeresses, royal bastards, heirs to peerages, promotions within the peerage, life peers and titles called out of abeyance or reversed attainders. It includes Scottish, Irish and Welsh families who gained English, British or United Kingdom peerages. The first title only is counted, even if it is an English family getting an Irish peerage.

The psychological investment in achieving victory was an indicator of how pervasive the compulsion to win elections had become among the elite. When Sir Edward Knyvet realized he would not gain his desire in a 1539 contest, 'he fell into a rage'. In 1572 a neighbour noticed that one of the greatest landowners in Norfolk and cousin of the queen, Sir Edward Clere of Blickling, 'leaveth no stone untouched that may further his part' to be a knight of the shire. The eldest son of a great landowner 'made very great labour' in 1586 to gain election for a borough. Francis Slingsby of Scriven, the son of a sister of the Earl of Northumberland, wrote in 1597 that being an MP 'is [a] thing I do exceedingly desire'. During the same year a peer got so carried away during a contest for Staffordshire that he voted for his own brother even though members of the House of Lords did not enjoy the franchise. The very rich father of nineteen-year-old Edward Noel (ancestor of the Earls of Gainsborough) of Rutland wrote that he would obtain his son's return in the election of 1601 or 'lie in the dust'. Sir John Wynn of Caernarvonshire called the defeat of his son, in 1620, 'the greatest publick disgrace that ever I had in my time'.[71] And it is evident from other correspondence that among the Tudor and Stuart peerage such losses were considered humiliating indignities. Lord Halifax wrote in 1695: 'A desire to serve the nation in

Parliament is an Englishman's ambition.' 'To be out of Parliament is to be out of the world,' observed a country gentleman in 1780.[72] The 2nd Earl of Radnor told his heir on the latter's election for Salisbury in 1812 that this success was intimately related to the family's honour and was a 'noble distinction'. 'I feel that a woman's life is only half a life,' said Trollope's Lady Laura Standish, 'as she cannot have a seat in Parliament.'[73] The Marchioness of Bute lamented the loss of her candidate at Cardiff in 1852, believing the defeat to cause 'the abasement of the family'. When the brother of the 13th Earl of Pembroke was defeated by a neighbouring landed gentleman in an election in 1885, it was reported that the grandee 'could hardly contain his rage and vexation. . . . His steward incited the mob by the Pembroke Arms to duck [the baronet who won] in the river.' For the son of Lord Addington in the early twentieth century, a seat in parliament was still 'the ambition of a lifetime'.[74]

From about 1570 men began to take such pride in their election to the Commons that they had etched on their tombstones and funerary monuments their service as MPs.[75] Aristocratic families hurried their sons into the Commons when they had hardly been breeched. The increasing number of young nobles and gentlemen becoming MPs at a tender age caused complaints from as early as 1571. One can understand why when one hears of Richard Edgcumbe's election as an MP at sixteen in 1586 or the Duke of Albemarle's son, elected at thirteen, making his first Commons speech a year later. This tradition would long continue. Forty-three MPs were elected as minors between 1660 and 1690, of whom twenty-four were peers' sons. The heirs of Whig grandees were still regularly entering the Commons in their twenties during the last years of Victoria's reign. As late as 1904 Viscount Turnour became an MP while still an undergraduate.[76]

Nothing better illustrates the increasing inclusion of all important and prestigious families in parliament than the rate of representation of *already established* peerage families there. In the thirteenth and fourteenth centuries shire knights of noble birth were infrequent. During the fifteenth century many of the great medieval noble houses were represented in the Commons. Well over one hundred MPs between 1386 and 1421 were related to members of the parliamentary peerage.[77] The first heir to a title who sat while his father was in the Lords was Sir Richard Poynings, MP for Sussex in 1423, the eldest son of the 4th Baron Poynings.[78]

Edward Porritt asserted that in medieval and early Tudor times it was the custom to exclude eldest sons of peers from the lower house. This was the practice in the Scottish parliament, but Porritt misunderstood the debate that occurred after the election in 1547 of Lord Russell, son of the Earl of Bedford, who was the first MP to bear a title while in the Commons. It was the entrance of a man holding 'courtesy' rank that provoked some members to question the propriety of Russell's participation.[79] The turning-point came in the sixteenth century. One can see from

Table 1.3 Number of peers by succession, newly created peers and close male relatives of peers* who sat in the House of Commons, 1386–1603

1386–1421	1439–1509	1509–1559	1559–1603
22	52	107	221

* Brothers, fathers, nephews, sons, uncles and grandsons.

Table 1.3 that a significant shift took place in the active participation of the peerage during these years, at a time when the number of title holders actually declined. In addition a further number of first cousins, illegitimate sons and claimants to abeyant peerages also sat.[80]

Heirs to peerages also began to sit for borough constituencies during this period, especially after 1553, including the heirs of ancient and high-ranking families such as the Percys, Radcliffes, Staffords and Stanleys.[81] About 8% of all MPs were direct male relatives of peers in Elizabeth's reign, the same proportion achieved after the Restoration.[82] Moreover, over a hundred MPs between 1509 and 1558 married the daughters of peers or had mothers who were the daughters of peers, and this number *doubled* during the reign of Elizabeth I. From the time of the 2nd Earl of Bedford's election, almost every heir to that title qualified by age to sit was returned to the House of Commons until the accession of the 11th Duke in 1893. From the late sixteenth century onwards it became normal for the heirs to peerages to serve an apprenticeship in the Commons, and the numbers of noble MPs grew both as the size of the Lords increased and as more peers survived to an age when their sons could enjoy a career in the lower house.[83] It is hard to think of many prominent Elizabethans or Jacobeans other than cultural and clerical luminaries who did not sit in parliament. The names of most great landowners were now represented in the Commons. *Every* peerage family with a member sitting in the Elizabethan House of Lords had at least one MP in the Commons.[84] Thenceforward until the twentieth century the upper and lower houses were thoroughly homogenized.

It could be argued, however, that because parliamentary families had such a firm grip on the electoral system many families who might otherwise have been fully qualified members of the elite did not appear in this study because longer established and luckier dynasties monopolized entry into the Commons. Was the system rigged to give an advantage to those who had gained control over pocket boroughs, which kept them pre-eminent at the expense of equally wealthy gentry who had failed to get in line for a borough in time? Did the paucity of open contests and deferential tenantry in county elections make even seats with larger electorates easy pickings for a small handful of magnates?

First, it should be noted that peerages were in the gift of the Crown and were thus not restricted to existing families who held a grip on the political system. In 1719 the only serious attempt to freeze the size of the peerage failed. The monarch was free to increase the number of peers as he or she saw fit, and except under Elizabeth I the nobility constantly expanded to include new entrants to the top tiers of wealth.

As regards a monopoly on seats in the Commons held by only a portion of the elite, recent research suggests that control of boroughs was rarely absolute, even at the high water mark of the 'rotten' era. Challengers could poach successfully in private preserves and patron turnover was frequent. The chief constants in parliamentary history from the Middle Ages until 1832 were the eccentric and irrational regulations governing the franchise and an electorate with many voters who were informed and independent. Counties could fall under the suzerainty of a great family for a time, but such imperiums evaporated with striking rapidity. Few constituencies failed to register a contest at some point, and even in the smallest boroughs, landlord influence had to be exercised with tact and willingness to serve local interests.[85] Room was always available for those with money and ambition. The political process ensured that the governing class consisted of the families most respected (or feared) by – and most effective in winning the loyalty and esteem of – the community.

Of course, families might not appear in the data pool collected for this study owing to a string of insane, imbecile or under-age heirs. Repeated service abroad in the military or diplomatic corps might also eliminate a family from the count. As we have seen, Commons seats were difficult and expensive to gain. Perhaps some individuals preferred to spend their time and money elsewhere – at the race-course, rebuilding country houses, foreign travel – or were simply homebodies who disliked the bustle and publicity attendant on a political life in London.

Undoubtedly, many *individuals* did fail to gain election to parliament for just these reasons. However, it was very unusual for generation after generation of a *family* to eschew service in parliament if it qualified by wealth for elite status. This fact can be illustrated in a number of ways. As we have already noted, virtually every peerage family is included in this study. Other useful checks on the comprehensiveness of the data on parliamentary families include country house ownership, records of estate sizes, county office holding, indicators of social leadership, employment of servants, and analysis of landed families who produced fewer than three MPs/peers.

Lawrence Stone chose country house ownership as the key indicator of elite membership. He and Jeanne Fawtier Stone found that about 10% of the owners in their survey (1540–1879) served in the Commons.[86] About one-third (129) of the houses they studied were owned at one time by members of the parliamentary elite.[87] I found only sixteen houses owned by parliamentary families that were not in the Stone list.[88] So while it is clear that their survey dipped a good deal deeper down the social range than the families included in this study, there is a substantial overlap.

The Stones used a three-county sample because the amount of research necessary to identify and establish records of ownership of all the houses in England of the right size would be extremely difficult and impossibly time-consuming. If we widen the field by turning to architectural surveys of country houses, we find that they usually do not yield accurate lists of the social elite. The acreage of the estates surrounding the buildings is rarely given, and inclusion is based on the antiquity of pedigrees, the quality of the architecture or for what sometimes appear to be entirely random reasons. None the less, a rough sense of the proportion of large houses owned by parliamentary families can be gleaned from the work of some recent county studies where the authors made an attempt to distinguish major from minor residences. In recently published surveys of country houses in Cheshire, Dorset, Gloucestershire, Northamptonshire and Warwickshire an average of four out of five big residences were owned by parliamentary families.[89] Using parliamentary participation as the test of elite status means that fewer of the greater gentry families are missed and fewer of the lesser landowners are included than with the Stone system.

We can also check the proportion of landed families with incomes large enough to sustain membership in parliament who were members of the elite in the 1870s in John Bateman's compilation taken from the raw data of the New Domesday survey of all landowners in the British Isles. Four out of five (79%) of the English landowners with 3,000 or more acres and an annual income of at least £3,000 listed in the 1883 edition of Bateman belonged to parliamentary elite families. More than nine out of ten of those with estates of 10,000 acres producing £10,000 per annum in income – in other words the great landowners – were similarly qualified. Families with big estates were almost always politically active. Most of those who were not 'parliamentary' were Roman Catholic, had only recently inherited additional acreage or were 'new men'.[90]

J.T. Cliffe's list of 141 seventeenth-century gentry compiled for his recent book on country house life is ranked by income. Four out of five (84%) of those worth over £500 p.a. were members of the parliamentary elite, while only 14% of those with less than £500 enjoyed that status. The proportion among those worth over £1,000 (94 out of the 141) was nine out of ten (92%).[91]

Another means of cross-checking membership in the social and political elites is looking at the holders of top county offices. The lords lieutenant were usually the most prestigious and powerful men in their shires. Since the first appointments made by Tudor monarchs until gradual 'democratization' began to set in after the Second World War, only landed magnates held the position. With a handful of exceptions, every English lord lieutenant was a member of a parliamentary family.[92]

The medieval office of High Sheriff gradually declined in power, but retained some influence over the political life of the county through its role in the management of the nomination process for knights of the shire and in calling county meetings. By the eighteenth century it was largely an honorary position and was usually held for a one-year term. The social status of sheriffs varied over time and differed from county to county. In modern times it often went to newcomers who had placed their feet successfully on the ladder to social advancement but were still parvenus. None the less, throughout the period covered by this study the office was regarded as an hereditary duty by many leading gentry families. Four or more generations might serve in sequence without a break. Even during the twentieth century the office has been held both by newly established men who can afford the expenses incurred by service and by the heads of old families who take their turn alongside the newcomers.

A detailed analysis of the sheriffs of Oxfordshire from the Middle Ages to the twentieth century shows fifty-eight families with three or more sheriffs. Thirty-two of these had three MPs as well. Most of the older families established a significant presence in Westminster. Those with four or more sheriffs (with three exceptions) were all members of the parliamentary elite.[93] A more cursory survey of other counties, based on lists of sheriffs from the Middle Ages to 1831, shows that some of the home counties such as Essex had only a handful of families with four or more sheriffs, while other regions with more stable social structures such as Staffordshire had dozens.[94] A study of thirteen randomly selected counties revealed variations from all regular shrieval families being members of the parliamentary elite to less than one-third. However, the average in the thirteen counties was 85%.[95]

Another prestigious position in many counties was the mastership of the local fox-hunt. This office had no direct political authority or legal standing but was usually associated with landed wealth. (Professional huntsmen were occasionally employed to chivvy up a slack pack of hounds or to fill a gap in aristocratic leadership.) It is impossible to survey all hunts. In many cases published records do not exist, especially for the seventeenth and eighteenth centuries when the sport was still evolving into its modern form. Some hunts were less important than others, and inclusion is a subjective decision. But it is worth noting that aside from the packs totally dominated by magnates, which were all in the hands of parliamentary families, such as the Beaufort, Berkeley and Belvoir Hunts, a group of other leading hunts were also controlled largely by the parliamentary elite. All the masters of the Bramham (1740–1945), Brocklesby (c. 1700–1921), Burton (c. 1672–1882) and Cottesmore (1660–1913, except for eight years) were from families with three or more MPs/peers. Among the grandest hunts, eleven of the fourteen MFHs of the Quorn 1698–1863, sixteen out of twenty of the Tarporley 1745–1911, and twenty-two of the twenty-seven of the Pytchley 1756–1919 were similarly placed.[96]

Additional examples of the connection between social leadership and membership in the parliamentary elite can be found among the landowners of Devon, Wiltshire and Carmarthenshire. Mary Wolffe's recent study of Devon during the early seventeenth century identified a list of nearly a hundred leading gentry of whom three-quarters were members of families included in this study.[97] A collection of diaries written between 1809 and 1925 by members of the Grove family, baronets of Ferne, Wiltshire, who had been greater gentry in the county since Tudor times, elected four MPs and had an income of £7,000 p.a. listed in Bateman, was recently published. The editor provided lists of *dramatis personae* to enable readers to follow the events described by various Groves. Two-thirds of the diarists' social world in 1809–58 and four-fifths in 1855–1925 were members of parliamentary elite families (excluding clergy).[98] A study of nineteenth-century Carmarthenshire landed society found that even after the Great Reform Act important families *without exception* produced parliamentary candidates.[99]

One of the most interesting lists with which the parliamentary elite can be cross-referenced is that of persons taxed for employing male servants in 1780. As with every other measure of social rank, this compendium is imperfect. None the less, the tax was socially selective. The manuscript lists for Yorkshire have been collated and published.[100] A clear dividing line between parliamentary families and those without much representation in the legislature is revealed by the data. Three-quarters of families with seven and 85% of those with eight or more male servants (about the minimum number of butlers, footmen and grooms needed to maintain a fully rigged household in the later eighteenth century) were members of the governing class as defined in this study.[101] Although some families with fewer than seven servants did elect three or more MPs, the number was quite small.[102] If families who had only recently acquired land, minors who succeeded to the family estates but were living at school or university, and Roman Catholics are not counted, nine out of ten employers of seven or more male servants in Yorkshire were members of the parliamentary elite.

Perhaps the most effective check on the accuracy of the system of selection used in this study is to look at families *not* included in the parliamentary elite. Of the one in five MPs between the Restoration and Reform who were not members of 'three-plus' or associated families, most fell into one of three categories: 'singletons' (obvious outsiders), rising stars who failed to sustain a parliamentary line, and a scattering of established middling and lesser gentry.

The first group included tradesmen and small town merchants who slipped into the Commons through inattention or on the crest of opposition aimed at the established electoral authorities. These were men of small fortune and little standing outside their immediate neighbourhood. Few of them managed to serve for more than one constituency or in more than one parliament. They quickly lapsed back into obscurity after more prominent and wealthy candidates resumed representing the borough. A sprinkling of adventurers added spice to the fellowship of the Commons. These men insinuated themselves into friendships with the great through charm or usefulness. One was a billiard marker at a coffee-house whom a lunatic earl brought into parliament as a prank. More respectable protégés of the elite were nominated to act as stopgaps to keep a seat warm until an heir came of age, to look after family legislation or to supplement numbers and debating talent in a dynastic political corps. A small body of military officers and civil servants were brought in by governments to advocate ministerial policies or to do its business. (Many such men were from elite families anyway.) The largest contingent in the 'one-off' category were the lawyers. One in five of all non-elite MPs from 1660 to 1832 were legal men who sought to establish their reputations and broaden their contacts at Westminster. Although some lawyers were members of or succeeded in founding landed families, many more never intended to enter the elite. Some substantial merchants without apparent dynastic ambitions also entered the Commons bent purely on lobbying for a particular policy or making contacts for business purposes. Many lacked a male heir, or as in the case of Christopher Potter (MP 1781–84) were 'too eccentric and speculative to hoard a fortune'.[103] Most of the individuals listed above maintained themselves on incomes that disappeared with their deaths, leaving little trace behind them.

The second category of non-elite MPs were less easily distinguishable from those who were successful in founding patrician families. Some non-elite MPs were unmarried and their wealth was divided among multiple heirs or left to charity.[104] Others were unable to build up a fortune large enough to guarantee long-term security for their heirs. A few eccentrically disposed of their patrimony by disinheriting sons or composing bizarre wills while deranged or intoxicated.[105] Those with children sometimes divided their estates equally among three or four, or even six or seven sons and/or daughters.[106] In other cases disaster struck. One MP father of three lost one son in a duel, while his second was hanged for murdering the other sibling. In another case the heir was murdered in prison and the estates sold.[107] Landed property was divided among illegitimate children to the exclusion of legitimate descendants. Spendthrift heirs sometimes finished off a family before it could get properly started.[108] In other cases it was the reckless spending of a father that forced a son to sell out.[109] Many initially successful businessmen died in straitened circumstances owing to bad luck or incompetence.[110] More often than one might suppose MPs died deeply in debt or even in prison.[111] Successful careers crashed after the discovery of corruption or fraud that led to expulsion from the Commons and the sale of estates. Few terms in office ended more spectacularly than John Ward's (MP 1710–26). An unscrupulous businessman ejected for forgery, he was placed in the pillory in Palace Yard and pelted into insensibility in the presence of his former colleagues.[112] The indebted fled abroad and even prosperous MPs emigrated to America.[113] As more bankers entered the Commons in the later eighteenth century, the peculiarly fragile nature of that business precipitated many financial failures, and nabobs were also likely to take tumbles.[114]

What is striking, however, is the paucity of important landed families among the fewer-than-three-MP category.[115] Among the third category of families not in the parliamentary elite only a handful of the greater gentry such as the Reresbys, Massingberds and Fenton/Fletcher-Bougheys, who at one time held significant acreage, failed to establish a significant presence in parliament.[116] Even fewer old and substantial landowners elected no representatives at all. The Greswoldes of Malvern Hall, Warwickshire, an ancient family credited with 9,000 acres in the 1870s, were an example from this very unusual category.

On the other hand, middling and lesser families rarely produced MPs. For example, the Thorntons of Brockhall, Northamptonshire, who entered the gentry in the sixteenth century and extended their estates in the seventeenth, never held much more than 3,000 acres, which was not enough to support electoral ambitions. The Kingscotes, seated at Kingscote, Gloucestershire, from about 1188 to 1956, never owned more than 4,000 acres and produced their first and only MP in 1852. They and their like were content to serve as JPs and occasionally to gain the limelight for a year as sheriff.[117] Typical examples of one-MP producers were the appropriately named Minors family, who held land in Staffordshire as early as the thirteenth century, produced an MP in the mid-seventeenth, and then faded to yeoman status, and the aptly named Clerk baronets (created 1660), old gentry who elected an MP 1710–15 and then declined into professional wage earners as clerics and civil servants.[118]

In the fifteenth and early sixteenth centuries at least five hundred families elected two MPs but failed to elect any more. Many were either burgesses or gentle families who did not yet see seats as vital to their social standing or were eliminated by the high mortality and turbulence of the times. As the importance of membership in parliament increased, the greater gentry and nobility engrossed more and more of the representation. Under Henry VIII and his children only 171 'two-MP' families can be identified, with 135 in the next century and 116 in the one following that, although this was a period when the number of seats was greatly expanded. A modestly increased rate of 'two-MP' families, reaching 117 between 1832 and 1885, was due in part to new dynasties such as the Sassoons or the Goschens entering the political arena being cut off by the extension of the franchise before they could reach the 'three-MP' level. Few families elected two MPs with intervals of a century or more between years of service, which might indicate a fortune sufficient to sustain electoral activity beyond a couple of generations. Only about sixty families fall into this category during the past six centuries.

The social and economic divide between those with two or fewer and three or more MPs/peers was often stark. The placement of more than two generations into parliament required substantial resources that only could be secured by families who did not divide inheritances equally among siblings and with enough income to weather the inevitable upsets human vagaries are likely to produce. The quantitative data relating to the participation of the peerage, country house ownership, landed estates, sheriffs, employment of servants and non-elite MPs all tell a similar story. So too does the more impressionistic evidence. In every county century by century individuals were elected who stood at the top of the social and economic hierarchies of shire society. They came from families who formed a small and closely connected elite, among whom becoming an MP was *de rigueur*.

Chapter 2

The Size and Composition of the English Parliamentary Elite

Two recent authorities on the gentry have despaired of getting the count of landed families right and declared the task to be 'well-nigh impossible'.[1] One can see what they mean if one looks, for example, at a list of estimates of the size of the Hampshire elite during the nineteenth century. Depending on who was counting there were 66, 168, 178, 300, 557 or 600 gentry families in the county.[2] Estimates of the size of landed society as a whole between the fourteenth and eighteenth centuries range from 5,000 to 25,000 families depending on the century and the social discriminators applied.[3] Of these, most were small gentry. In the nineteenth century fewer than 5,000 families were listed as substantial landowners in Burke's various registers of the elite.[4] Henry Fielding's definition of 'No Body' was 'all the people in Great Britain except about 1,200'.[5] The New Domesday count of great landowners of the 1870s showed 1,363 English peers and gentlemen with 3,000 acres or more.[6]

Just under 2,000 families in this study were predominantly English in wealth and political participation.[7] They produced a total of 12,788 MPs. Between 13 and 14% of this total served in each half century from 1603 to 1832. Some of these 'English' MPs sat either in the Irish or Scots parliaments or for Welsh, Scottish or Irish constituencies.[8] Three-quarters of the English families elected at least one MP in the years between the Restoration and the end of the Second World War.[9]

The graph (Figure 2.1) illustrates the proportion of the House of Commons composed of members of the parliamentary elite. As one can see, from the Long Parliament until the Great Reform Act over three-quarters of the Commons was composed of MPs from a small body of families. One can safely assume that their dominance in the House of Lords, at least until the late nineteenth century, was virtually complete.

The picture of the House of Commons presented in Figure 2.1 is open to the objection that the first couple of MPs in a family are indistinguishable statistically from MPs who came from families without further representation. The inclusion of the first and second MPs is contingent on what would happen in the future. Therefore, in Table 2.1 the data has been arranged in such a way as to show only MPs who were elected as the third or later member of their family to serve in parliament, removing

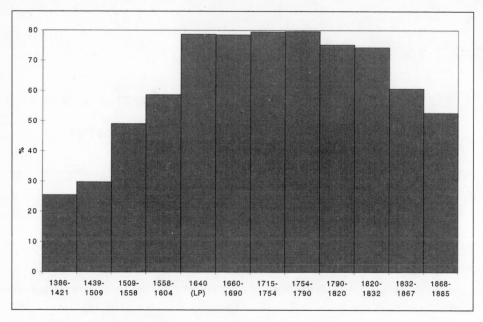

Figure 2.1 Proportion of members of the English, British and United Kingdom House of Commons from parliamentary families, 1386–1885

from the count (presented in Figure 2.1) the first two representatives. Even when the initial MPs in elite families are not counted, more than two-thirds of the Commons between the Restoration and the Great Reform Act were members of established governing families.[10]

Categories within the Parliamentary Elite

Within landed society many intricate distinctions were made. The largest category among the governing class was composed of families with comparatively modest resources unable to sustain parliamentary membership over more than about a century.

Table 2.1 Proportion of MPs for England and Wales from families who had previously elected at least two MPs, 1661–1875

1661	1700	1725	1750	1775	1800	1825	1850	1875
68.6	66.9	67.3	73.1	72.1	64.5	63.2	56.8	43.7

They rarely elected more than four or five MPs and infrequently entered the upper house. Only sixty-two English gentry families included in this study who produced fewer than six MPs/peers held estates worth over £10,000 p.a. in the New Domesday survey. A few were quite modest landowners, such as the Hutchinsons of Owthorpe, Nottinghamshire, who rose to gentry rank in the sixteenth century, elected three MPs between 1626 and 1695, and then, loaded with debts, disappeared in the late seventeenth century. Others like the Millers, clothiers and maltsters prominent in Chichester, Sussex, from the mid-sixteenth century, purchased a moderately sized estate and elected four MPs between 1689 and 1816.[11]

As Table 2.2 illustrates, by far the largest proportion of MPs in the House of Commons in the seventeenth and eighteenth centuries came from families who elected six or more members to the legislature. Not all such families survived in health and wealth for the entire period covered by the study. The Dymokes inherited not only the estates of the Norman Marmions by means of a fortunate marriage but also their duties as hereditary Champions of the Dukes of Normandy. They have continued to exercise their prerogative of challenging all comers at most coronations since, although the last time one appeared on horseback in armour was at George IV's coronation in 1820. They are still seated at a much-reduced Scrivelsby Court with 3,000 acres, and the present Champion served as High Sheriff of Lincolnshire in 1979. A number of Dymokes represented the county between 1372 and 1593, but only two emerged after 1660, the last ending his service in 1713. This was due to inheritance difficulties, a series of clergymen who unexpectedly succeeded to the manor and were disqualified by the cloth from election to parliament, declining wealth, and one Champion who became a hermit.

Table 2.2 Parliamentary service of all English elite families with at least one MP, 1660–1945

| | Fewer than 5 MPs | | 6 or more MPs | |
	N	%	N	%
Total Families	1,119	75.2	368	24.8
Total MPs 1295–1994	2,658	24.6	8,142	75.4
Total English MPs 1660–1945	2,095	31.1	4,632	68.9
Years Service as MPs 1660–1945	25,394	29.3	61,228	70.7
Total Peers 1660–1945	525	18.5	2,312	81.5
Years Service as Peers 1660–1945	9,873	15.7	52,888	84.3

The Nevilles of Eridge Castle were the only great noble family in the modern era virtually bereft of MPs. They are said to possess a male pedigree 'without parallel among English noble families'. The 1st Baron Bergavenny (1450) was a son of the Earl of Westmorland by a daughter of John of Gaunt. The 8th and 9th Barons both served in the Commons under Elizabeth I and James I, but religion barred further participation until the 2nd Earl conformed and became an MP (1784–85). Their estates were large (worth £30,000 p.a. in 1876), they served as lords lieutenant, gained a Garter, and were promoted to marquess in 1876, but they demonstrated electoral impotence unmatched in recent centuries by any other great dynasty.[12]

Most families with six or more legislators were either old and powerful or magnates in the making. Some accumulators of many MPs look more influential than they really were because they had secured a death-grip on a pocket borough. Tewkesbury, for example, was responsible for sending eight Martins and nine Dowdeswells to the Commons between 1660 and 1885. However, they *were* rich. The number of families able to sustain control over a single borough for more than a couple of generations purely through technical manipulation of the electoral system as opposed to ownership of extensive estates and high standing in landed society was negligible.

The 'six-plus' category contained many members of the greater gentry. Substantial landed families such as the Windhams of Felbrigg, Norfolk, who elected ten MPs between 1439 and 1859 and had an income of £13,000 in Bateman, were an example of this type. Similarly, the Mordaunts of Warwickshire managed to elect six baronets in a row for their county. The Wrottesleys were at Wrottesley by 1164 and elected eight MPs between 1460 and 1837, while the Curwens of Workington represented Cumberland in every century from the fourteenth to the nineteenth.[13]

The Grandees

At the apex of the social and political pyramid stood great clan-like families such as the Stanhopes described earlier. Between 1660 and 1914 a small group of dynasties presided above the rest of the parliamentary elite. It would be a mistake to conflate these leaders with all families who elected six or more MPs or the baronetage or even the peerage.[14] The colossi, who were informally called 'the grandees', did much to shape British high politics and culture over the last four centuries. Their dominance and durability lay not only in their commanding and disproportionate place in government and as patrons of the arts, but also because they owned much of the nation's wealth.

Grandee dominance was evident in the House of Commons, where often three or more members of a family would sit simultaneously. A number of these dynasties produced MPs in six successive centuries. Families such as the Cavendishes and

Lowthers accumulated more than six hundred years of service in the Commons as well as multiple seats in the House of Lords. Grandees largely engrossed highly sought-after prizes such as lord lieutenancies and Garters.

Establishing the precise number of grandee families is not easy. Estimates have ranged from 200 to 600.[15] For the purpose of this study I established a list based on the following categories: ten or more MPs, 1295–1994; 150 or more years service as MPs, 1660–1945; 150 or more years service in the House of Lords, 1660–1945; £20,000 p.a. or more income in Bateman;[16] and a combination of any two of the following – a Garter, a cabinet office, six or more MPs sitting for a single county, and a lord lieutenancy.[17] A number of important families did not fulfil every qualification. However, if one includes all families listed in at least three categories, a distinct group stands out from those who met fewer or none of the criteria. This elite company of 164 families was actually even smaller, if allied lines and clans are combined, when the total drops to 139.

A case can be made that some families do not belong on the list. The Aclands, though a potent force in Devon for many centuries failed to enter the House of Lords.[18] The Bagots were ancient and rich but never very prominent on the national scene after the fifteenth century. Other than tumbling down the steps of the throne at Queen Victoria's coronation, the appropriately named Lord Rolle rarely attracted much notice. On the other hand, some families are missing that probably ought to be included. They became extinct too early or entered the elite too late to be counted. The Lekes, Pulteneys and Veres were all grandees, but their lines failed soon after the Restoration. The Woods, Guests, Ridleys and Rothschilds were on the rise during the twentieth century. A few great Catholic families such as the Petres and Throckmortons should probably be counted as well. A fringe area encompassed the Devereaux Earls of Essex, the Hesketh-Fermor Earls of Pomfret, the Keppel Earls of Albemarle and the Edens. Finally some cadet lines of grandee families might qualify for inclusion by association, such as the Howard Earls of Effingham or the Earls Stanhope.

Many of the grandees bore names well known even to casual students of English history: Berkeley, Cavendish, Grenville, Grey, Grosvenor, Herbert, Manners, Montagu, Pelham, Russell, Seymour, Spencer, Stanley, Thynne and Townshend. Other dynasties are not as well known but were no less pervasive, persistent and power-hungry: Legh, Lowther, Onslow, Wallop and Willoughby-Bertie.

What evidence is there to demonstrate the special status of the families listed here as grandees? Although they composed less than one in ten of the families in this study, they enjoyed half of the income listed in Bateman for parliamentary families. They garnered 53% of all the years of service in the Commons 1660–1945 and 61% of the years in the Lords. They elected almost one-third (30%) of all the MPs included in this study between 1295 and 1994.

The English grandee families who dominated the higher reaches of honour and power were mostly very old in origin. Twenty-two held medieval titles. More joined the peerage in the first half of the seventeenth century than in any other comparable period and nearly half of all their first titles pre-dated the execution of Charles I. But these figures underestimate the antiquity of the families. The Earls of Carnarvon (1780) or the Earls of Yarborough (1794) appear to have achieved grandee status fairly late in the game, but they were younger sons of families with much older titles – the Herberts (first peerage 1551) and the Pelhams (1572). The Herbert title of 1551 is itself misleading because their estates passed via an illegitimate son from the medieval Earls of Pembroke. Three dukes on the list of grandees descend from bastard sons of Charles II. There was no long trek up the ladder from squire to baronet to duke for those families, although the comparatively recent dates of the peerages might suggest otherwise. One look at Lyme Park or Wollaton Hall makes it plain that although the Cheshire Leghs and Nottinghamshire Willoughbys came to their modest baronies rather late, commanding power and grandeur were present much earlier. Most of the grandee families were both old and rich before Henry VII came to the throne. To be sure, the Grosvenors, Lambtons and Leveson Gowers only entered the top class of wealth after the Industrial Revolution turned their properties into private mints, but these were old families already well established in medieval times. The estates of the Dukes of Devonshire extended to 100,000 acres at the beginning of the seventeenth century.[19] The Russells did well out of the Howland marriage in the seventeenth century and the London property boom in the eighteenth, but they were at Woburn from the time of the dissolution of the monasteries, peers by 1538 and county gentry long before that. The reason many of these families rose even higher in modern times is that they were already well positioned in the Tudor or Stuart periods.

The few families who did manage to attain grandee status without the springboard of ancient lineage were fortunate to accumulate very large estates quickly. Although they only acquired their fortunes in the late seventeenth or eighteenth centuries the Duncombes, Dundases, Smiths, Barings and Peels were all credited with estates worth over £40,000 p.a. in Bateman. It was possible to rise rapidly to the pinnacle of prestige, but this was very rare. Some other families entered comparatively late, but did not do so by pulling themselves up by their own bootstraps. The Bouveries, Huguenot merchants in the eighteenth century, married a Pleydell heiress, while the merchant Heathcotes gained their earldom by carrying on the Bertie line.

Almost three-quarters (70%) of the grandee families of 1660–1914 achieved gentry rank in medieval times, and 18% more gained that status before the death of Elizabeth I. Only twelve entirely new families emerged in the seventeenth century and six in the eighteenth. A number sent knights to France during the Hundred Years War and at least seven were descended in the male line from men who served during the

Agincourt campaign.[20] Some minor gentry clung to the same spot of ground for many centuries. However, it was peculiarly a characteristic of the grandees to be deeply rooted at an ancient seat. Only the Cadogans and the Percevals seemed to roam aimlessly about, the Flying Dutchmen of the English aristocracy. The Ashburnhams of Ashburnham, on the other hand, in a Victorian genealogist's breathless but accurate description were 'of stupendous antiquity'.[21] The Berkeleys of Berkeley, Chomondeleys of Chomondeley, the Comptons of Compton Wynyates, the Lowthers of Lowther and the Wallops of Wallop were seated at their eponymous places for very long periods. Not far behind were the Curzons at Kedleston, the Leghs at Lyme, the Molyneux at Sefton, the Stanleys at Knowsley, the Townshends at Raynham and the Wortleys at Wortley. Many other families, like the Aclands in Devon or the Bagots in Staffordshire, held land in their home counties from Norman times but did not settle at their modern seat until several centuries later. Nearly half (43%) of the grandee families were ensconced in one place for over five hundred years and 85% were owners of the same country house for at least three centuries.

Grandee families dominated certain great offices of state from the Restoration onwards. On accepting the Lord Lieutenancy of Ireland in 1885, the 4th Earl of Carnarvon noted that he became the fifteenth viceroy in his family if one counted on both sides.[22] Every Marquess of Salisbury in this century save one has sat in the cabinet: 1903–05, 1916, 1922–29, 1940–45, 1951–57, and (the present heir) 1994–97. This is a family that acquired its initial peerage under the Tudors and was producing politicians of the first rank in the sixteenth and seventeenth centuries as well as a formidable nineteenth-century premier. Between 1832 and 1955 four Greys and five Stanleys sat in the cabinet. The 14th Earl of Derby was premier of a government in which the 15th Earl served as Foreign Secretary.

In terms of cabinet membership grandee dominance peaked in Walpole's later years, during the Pelham administrations, Chatham's second ministry and under Lord North's premiership.[23] A slump occurred under the Younger Pitt, when grandees and their close male relatives dropped at one point to only one-third of the cabinet in 1804, but his ministries usually averaged over 50% grandees. (See Figure 2.2.) In the nineteenth century cabinets gradually grew larger, which diluted the grandee presence, but their numbers in absolute terms increased. They were assisted in their retention of the majority of the places in the cabinet by the influx of Scots, Irish and Welsh grandees. It was usual to see five or six magnates in an administration until 1805 and six to nine thereafter. During the early to mid-nineteenth century the grandees once again literally engulfed the chief offices of state. Grey's administration was three-quarters grandee in 1831 and in Peel's second ministry of the 1840s the proportion was four out of five. Even a peer from an old family thought Peel's 1841 government 'too lordly and aristocratic, for these days'.[24] Thus in the midst of the most serious social unrest during the century, Britain was most fully in the hands of grandee leadership. Throughout the late Hanoverian and Victorian years one finds Cecils, Greys, Russells and Stanleys not only among the leaders of the cabinet but serving as prime ministers. Nine premiers came from grandee families between 1721 and 1868 (71%), and they held office for all but fifty-eight years of that period, with Salisbury, Rosebery, Churchill and Home still to come. Although their presence dropped back to one-third of the cabinet under Gladstone in 1870, subsequent governments continued to draw heavily from the 164 families (and a handful of Scottish and Irish dynasties). It was not until Campbell Bannerman's administration in 1905 that Liberal governments relied less on grandees for their composition than Conservative ones, and a general decline set in. Bonar Law's government reversed the trend dramatically but briefly in 1922, and Churchill provided the last envoi with one-third of his final wartime cabinet composed of grandees in 1945.

Namier insisted that the great families never monopolized government, even at the peak of aristocratic rule in the eighteenth century. He pointed to the examples of the Walpoles and the Pelhams, who, he claimed, were only lifted to extraordinary heights in recent times.[25] The evidence presented in this chapter suggests otherwise. The grandees were clearly adept at acquiring wealth and power. They dominated the

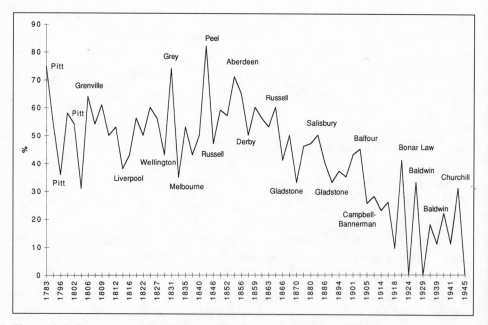

Figure 2.2 Proportion of cabinets composed of grandees and close male relatives (including Irish, Scottish and Welsh families), 1783–1945

cabinet and the premiership for much of the eighteenth century. New families were able to push themselves forward, and it is true that the Walpoles did not become magnates until Sir Robert's time. But the Pelhams had held high office in the fifteenth century and elected fifteen MPs before 1700. A Walpole was Bishop of Ely in 1302 and one sat as knight of the shire in 1315. Seven more members of the family were MPs before the first Prime Minister took up his post. Other families that did not achieve peerages until after the Restoration, such as the Waldegraves and Wallops, were already headed by great men centuries earlier. Sir Richard Waldegrave sat for Suffolk in twelve parliaments in 1376–90, was the son of a shire knight, and served as Speaker. He led a retinue of men-at-arms on Richard II's Scottish campaign and was a member of the king's council in 1393–97. The family entertained Elizabeth I at their seat in the 1570s and Sir William Waldegrave led five hundred men from the county for which he sat as shire knight to the Armada field at Tilbury in 1588. Two Wallops were elected shire knights in the early fifteenth century and they were reported to be the richest family in Hampshire in 1625.[26] These were important parliamentary dynasties ready to assume peerages when the House of Lords was enlarged.

Outflow from the Elite

The pages above have made plain that the high aristocracy was more ancient and smaller than many observers guessed. The core group of the elite also managed to hold on to large estates, great wealth and even some real power for longer than any other similar group in the modern world. Their exclusiveness and continuity over long periods was remarkable. But was this true of the parliamentary elite as a whole? Historians have long been interested in the extent to which the governing class was open to new entrants. Was England a closed oligarchy or an easy place for new men and ideas to rise and flourish. Much of the explanation for why the first modern society arose in England may depend on how frequently the walls of privilege were breached.

First let us turn to the outflow from the established elite (see Table 2.3). The rate of turnover indicates the degree to which the elite was flexible, casting out those unable to sustain parliamentary rank and opening up places for families on the rise. Some studies suggest very high attrition rates among the governing class during the Middle Ages both in England and elsewhere.[27] This was not just a phenomenon found in medieval life when tournaments, battles, plague and the headsman's axe all added extra danger to a nobleman's existence. John Cannon calculated that in 1700 over one-third of the peerage was of less than twenty years creation and four out of five titles were granted within the previous century.[28]

These high rates of turnover, however, are somewhat artificial – the product of applying anachronistic rules of succession.[29] The public scaffold and attainders did, of course, thin out the ranks of the elite. However, most dynasties ended more prosaically, splintering into fragments with multiple heiresses or staggering to a conclusion through a series of spendthrifts and wastrels who with eerie regularity failed to produce any successors. Variations in disappearance rates before 1660 are difficult to account for with precision.[30] One can speculate that they are related to demographic crises, but I have not found any correlation between upsurges in diseases such as the plague and the disappearance of parliamentary families.

Table 2.3 English parliamentary families who disappeared from the House of Commons, 1540–1959

Date	Five or Fewer	%*	Six or More	%*	Total	%*
1540–59	33	11.6	10	2.2	43	5.8
1560–79	23	8.4	7	1.5	30	4.0
1580–99	41	14.0	6	1.2	47	5.9
1600–19	26	9.2	6	1.2	32	4.1
1620–39	26	8.9	11	2.0	37	4.4
1640–59	28	8.4	12	2.2	40	4.5
1660–79	39	10.4	18	3.2	57	6.0
1680–99	64	16.0	26	4.6	90	9.3
1700–19	82	21.1	38	6.8	120	12.6
1720–39	48	14.4	21	4.0	69	7.9
1740–59	41	13.0	33	6.3	74	8.8
1760–79	60	18.9	37	7.5	97	12.0
1780–99	45	15.1	48	10.3	93	12.2
1800–19	46	15.0	35	8.2	81	11.1
1820–39	68	22.4	58	14.6	126	18.0
1840–59	66	25.0	46	13.5	112	18.5
1860–79	51	22.8	65	21.8	116	22.2
1880–99	75	37.0	65	27.9	140	32.2
1900–19	62	45.2	72	42.6	134	43.8
1920–39	36	45.6	40	41.2	76	43.2
1940–59	21	48.8	27	47.4	48	48.0

* The percentages are of the total existing elite in that category at that time.

After years of low turnover a sharp rise in disappearances took place during the 1550s. This was a result not of sickness but financial, dynastic and religious difficulties. Seven heads of elite families died without male heirs and left their estates to multiple heiresses. A few sold off land or showed other signs of financial distress that probably made it impossible for their heirs to continue as politically active gentry. By far the most significant factor in the political destruction of families was religion. One Protestant was hanged by Queen Mary for conducting active opposition to her policies and at least fourteen failed families were Roman Catholic. Others survived down to the present day, but their recusant status left them politically emasculated.

The rate of disappearance among parliamentary families remained remarkably steady between 1540 and 1680. Between 4 and 6% of the existing elite ceased to sit in the Commons every two decades. There was, however, an upwards trend from 1640. For the first time since the Middle Ages the failure rate moved dramatically in one direction. Between the Civil War and the Hanoverian succession it almost tripled, then dropped down again for the next half-century. Three of the four decades between 1680 and 1720 experienced the highest numbers of departures recorded since the fourteenth century. The years 1700–09 witnessed almost twice as many families disappear permanently from the Commons as the unusually high number in the 1550s mentioned earlier.

Two factors probably explain these figures. The first was the Civil War and its aftermath. While there was no immediate holocaust among the royalist gentry in the wake of deaths in battle, fines, sequestrations and indebtedness, none the less the rate of disappearances post-1660 rose in absolute numbers and in relative terms. In Lancashire, B.G. Blackwood found that the number of greater gentry who dropped out among leading families tripled after the Restoration. However, the unusually high proportion of Catholics and royalists in the county may exaggerate this phenomenon.[31] While comparatively few families met total ruin as a result of the Civil War, many were hit hard and encountered heavy financial burdens. This hampered the stability of even important dynasties and increased the likelihood that some would go under completely and others would be knocked out of the parliamentary elite. This can be seen in the data set out in Table 2.4.

Table 2.4 Portion of the English parliamentary elite who disappeared from the House of Commons before and after the Civil War

	1600–39	1660–99
N	66	118
%	8.6	13.6

The second factor leading to increased numbers of disappearances was the demographic crisis of the late seventeenth and early eighteenth centuries.[32] Failure of male heirs, which most historians point to as a much increased phenomenon during this period, was a significant but not overwhelming factor in causing permanent departures from the House of Commons. Many survived through the female line. Indebtedness and religion caused a larger number of families to disappear. The comparatively high failure rate in the early eighteenth century may be related to the intensification of political conflict during these years. The rate of disappearance of the 'five or fewer' MP families more than doubled between 1660 and 1720, reaching a peak never achieved before or afterwards. 'Six-plus' MP families also departed in rising numbers during the later seventeenth century, but the rate was about the same in 1700 and 1750. We have already noted the more transient nature of the families with five or fewer MPs. The failure rate among the less important members of the elite was always higher and often double the rate of the 'six-plus' families. The most acute period of disparity between these families was during the above-mentioned demographic crisis. (See

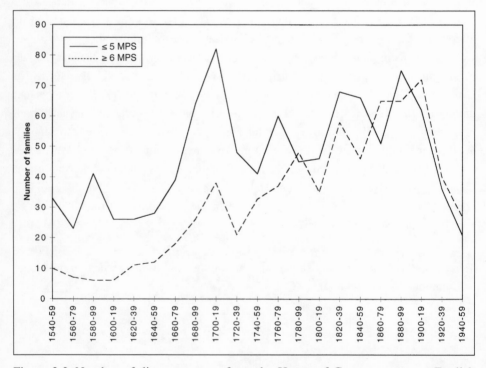

Figure 2.3 Number of disappearances from the House of Commons among English families with five or fewer and six or more MPs, 1540–1959

Figure 2.3.) It was among the new, less well endowed and rising families that mortality produced true havoc.[33]

Older families had more opportunity to generate cadet lines. They also paid careful attention to genealogical information about remote kinsmen in order to ensure the survival of their estates and titles intact. This, along with their greater resources, allowed them to outlast even bouts of sustained ineptitude, executions and confiscations. A number of famous titles were preserved in this way, most notably the earldom of Derby. Alert relatives were always on the lookout for estates going astray. For instance, Richard Norton (MP 1693–1705) of Southwick Park, last of a long line of MPs, left his estate to the nation for the benefit of the poor, hungry, thirsty, naked and sick. However, kinsmen from another elite family succeeded in overturning the will in their favour on the grounds of insanity.[34]

The failure rate averaged about 15% (per two-decade period) among the 'five and under' MP families from the Restoration to the Reform Act of 1832. Although there was some oscillation, the outflow from the elite was generally steady, making substantial amounts of room for replacements decade by decade. Once established, however, it took a great deal to dislodge a really rich family. The failure rate among 'six-plus' dynasties remained very low. Only 1 or 2% of this group disappeared every two decades from the 1540s to 1660. The rate continued to rise thereafter, but it was well below that of the lesser group. The first time more big families collapsed than modest ones in absolute terms was at the end of the eighteenth century, and the percentage of old families becoming defunct never exceeded the younger ones.

Much data has been collected by historians about the survival rates among the gentry and nobility. This topic is of interest to those who regard the presence of 'old' families as a source of stability and continuity in English society. Some counties seem to have had landed elites congealed with ancient blood while in others newcomers predominated. Different regions and centuries produced varied survival rates.[35] Leading scholars of landed society, however, such as J.V. Beckett and G.E. Mingay, argue for relatively rapid turnover among the landed elite since the seventeenth century.[36]

In order to compare the data on parliamentary families to that collected by other historians some adjustments have to be made to my data. The majority of families in this study dated their achievement of gentry status at about the same time as their first success in a parliamentary election. But for the purposes of comparing the antiquity of pedigrees, when I have come across clear evidence of establishment of a landed family, such as being pricked as High Sheriff or acquisition of a substantial estate (usually the site of the family's seat) pre-dating their first MP, I have used the earlier date.

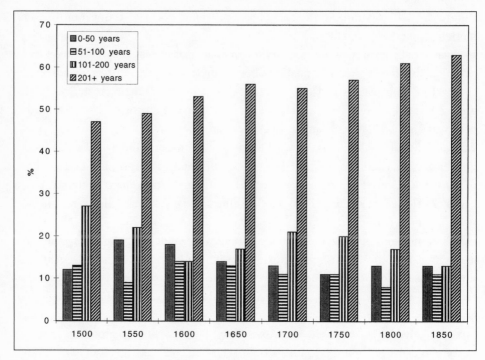

Figure 2.4 Length of time between date of achieving gentry status and last MP among the English elite, 1500–1850

One can see from Figure 2.4 that those who argue for rapid turnover rates seriously underestimate the continuity of the landed elite. Beckett describes an aristocracy almost wholly renewed in the eighteenth century, while my data shows that over three-quarters (78%) of families with one or more MPs post-1750 had entered the landed elite at least one hundred years earlier. That figure is not much different from the 72% of families of similar type a century before.[37]

One of the most striking features of my research is the stability in the percentages of newcomers, moderately well established and 'ancient' families over the centuries. After a steep but brief rise under Henry VIII, the proportion of families who had recently joined the elite remained stable at an average of about 13% for the three centuries after the execution of Charles I. (See Figure 2.4.) At any given time about one-seventh of the elite was new. The rate for families of fifty to one hundred years standing was also quite steady, never exceeding the range of 8 to 13% between Henry VII and Edward VII. The numbers for those with membership in the elite of a century or more was less fixed. Their number diminished during the socially mobile Tudor and early Stuart era, and rose during the eighteenth century before declining

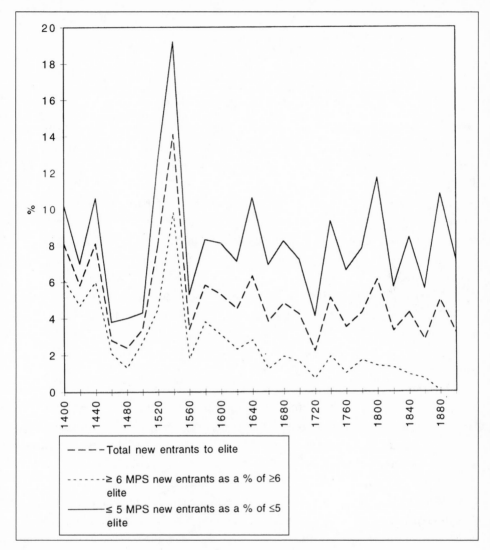

Figure 2.5 English parliamentary families – new entrants by date of achieving gentry status, 1400–1880

again in the nineteenth. It was this middle category that bore the brunt of a consolidation of electoral power in the hands of the magnates under George III and the impact of the Great Reform Act. While the entry rate for new families remained steady during this period and the old families continued to prosper, the 100 to 200-year-old families faded. What we see in Figure 2.4 is a steady turnover at the lower end of the scale and a solid, relatively unchanging central core. This is a point to which we will return in due course. For the moment let us look at the process of replenishment that created a sense of social mobility not perhaps as real as it seemed.

New Entrants into the Elite

In Warwickshire the number of gentry more than doubled between the mid-fifteenth and the mid-seventeenth century.[38] This large increase was not untypical of the continuous expansion of the landed class. The accolade of gentle birth was readily dispensed by the heralds. If income rose greatly, 'the rest would in time follow'.[39] Of course, the national population was expanding too. Landed property was always available for purchase. Although many estates passed by inheritance for centuries, others were constantly changing hands. By the mid-thirteenth century the land market could be described as 'vibrant', and it remained fluid thereafter.[40]

The evidence of the parliamentary elite suggests that new entrants were numerous throughout the fourteenth and first half of the fifteenth century. (See Figure 2.5 and Table 2.5.) Then a dramatic decline took place between 1460 and 1520. New entrants form only 3% of the contemporary elite in 1460–1520 as opposed to over 8% in the sixty years before and sixty years after this infertile period. The decline does not appear to be directly related to demographic factors. The disappearance rate among elite families dropped to its lowest point between the fourteenth and twentieth centuries during the years 1480–1520. Nor can the diminishing number of new families be attributed to less frequent summoning of parliaments. Nineteen were called in 1480–1520, while only sixteen met in 1440–80, when the new entrant rate was higher.[41] However, lacunae in lists of MPs during this period may mean the first entry of some families is artificially delayed. The explanation for the falling-off of new blood seems most likely to be related to economic and political factors. With the exception of the brief rise in new entrants in the 1420s and 1430s, when perhaps some families did well out of the military successes in France, the decline in the fifteenth century occurred during a period of economic decay and political instability. The lowest point of new entrants, when the growth of the parliamentary elite came to a virtual halt, between 1460 and 1520, coincides with the nadir of economic decline and the fall of rents and the uncertainties leading up to the slaying of Richard III at Bosworth. The explosive growth in the elite after 1520 is clearly linked with the reviving economy and the dissolution of the monasteries.

Another interesting phenomena revealed by the data in Figures 2.6 and 2.7 are the disjunctions between the dates of social origins and the date of first MP. From 1340 to 1380, for example, it took much longer for families who had acquired an estate and perhaps local office to elect members of the family as parliament men. On the other

Table 2.5 'New' English parliamentary families by date of entry* into the elite, 1380–1919

Date	Five of Fewer/Six or More		Total Elite	% of Total Elite
1380–99	28	52	799	10.0
1400–19	42	26	838	8.1
1420–39	29	21	859	5.8
1440–59	42	28	865	8.1
1460–79	14	10	844	2.8
1480–99	14	6	825	2.4
1500–19	15	13	828	3.4
1520–39	49	23	896	8.0
1540–59	89	55	1023	14.1
1560–79	24	10	1014	3.4
1580–99	39	22	1045	5.8
1600–19	38	18	1054	5.3
1620–39	34	14	1070	4.5
1640–59	53	17	1103	6.3
1660–79	35	7	1105	3.8
1680–99	42	11	1101	4.8
1700–19	35	9	1055	4.2
1720–39	17	4	956	2.2
1740–59	38	10	935	5.1
1760–79	26	5	892	3.5
1780–99	28	8	831	4.3
1800–19	42	6	786	6.1
1820–39	19	5	729	3.3
1840–59	24	3	630	4.3
1860–79	13	2	532	2.8
1880–99	22	0	438	5.0
1900–19	10	0	308	3.2

* Date of first achieving gentry status not date of first MP or peer.

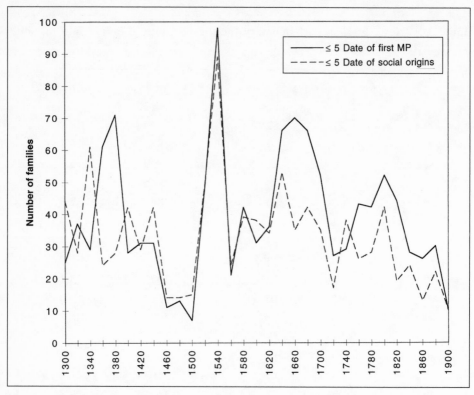

Figure 2.6 English parliamentary families with five or fewer MPs by date of achieving gentry status and date of first MP, 1300–1900

hand, between 1460 and 1560 there was more immediate admittance. Although one has to take account of the Tudor and Stuart habit of creating new borough seats, which alleviated the pressure of competition for entry into parliament, it does seem that the sixteenth century was marked by an easier social atmosphere and perhaps a need to fill up spots in the governing class as quickly as possible.

The barriers to social mobility were certainly lowered in the reign of Henry VIII. The upward surge is graphically displayed in Figures 2.5 to 2.7. The years 1520 to 1560 witnessed the single most remarkable expansion in the size of the elite in over seven centuries. From a rate of entry in the first two decades of the sixteenth century lower than that of any other comparable period between the Model Parliament and the death of Queen Victoria, the rate jumped to Himalayan proportions. More than one in ten of all parliamentary families entered the elite between 1520 and 1559. The only comparable period was 1640 to 1679, but that amounted to only three-quarters of the Tudor entrants and formed a considerably smaller proportion of the total elite at the time.

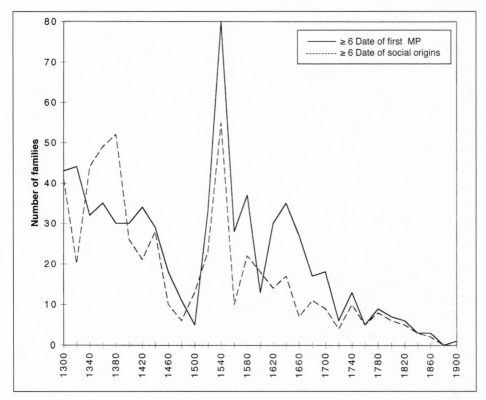

Figure 2.7 English parliamentary families with six or more MPs by date of achieving gentry status and date of first MP, 1300–1900

This finding broadly conforms with the prevailing orthodoxy about the expansion of the landed elite during the sixteenth century.[42] The dispersal of monastic land may only have hastened the process of emergence of new wealth that was already under way. The latter view is confirmed by the rapid expansion of the parliamentary elite in the 1520s before the dissolution commenced.[43]

However, my data does not accord with another assumption made by historians that a *new* elite was formed during this period.[44] Although the rate of entry as a proportion of the whole governing class was high, even at the peak period no more than 14% of the existing families were new. On the eve of the Civil War over half of the parliamentary families had medieval origins and almost three-quarters were over a century old.

Nor do the numbers support the contention that the expansion of the elite begun under Henry VIII continued robustly until the mid-seventeenth century.[45] The years 1560 to 1640 witnessed a serious slump in entrants. During the first two decades of this period new families entered the elite at a rate less than one-quarter of what it had been in the previous twenty years. Entrants averaged less than 5% of the elite in 1560–1640 in contrast to 11% in 1520–59. Moreover the total size of the elite remained relatively stable after 1560 until 1720, normally falling in the range of 1,000 to 1,100. Disappearance rates do not explain this plateau. They too were relatively stable from 1540 to 1680. The explanation is a drop-off in the entry of new families.

Contemporaries may have thought they noticed an increase in the size of the elite under Elizabeth I and the early Stuarts, but among the governing class this was largely illusory. A lot of country house building went on during this time, which perhaps made people think they were seeing an expansion.[46] The Stuarts' sales of honours may have enhanced the visibility of new families. A large number of grants of arms were also issued between 1560 and 1640.[47] But most of these must have marked arrivals at the lower levels of the gentry.

There is little unanimity among studies of the Civil War period when it comes to the impact of the time of troubles on new entrants to landed society. Some surveys suggest a reduced rate of growth in the elite during the later seventeenth century but not a decline. Others see a clear diminution in size. Stone found a variable result in his survey of country house owners in three counties. The number of new entrants fell dramatically in Northamptonshire, was down modestly in Hertfordshire, but up in Northumberland. He argues that a hardening of social attitudes tended to keep out new entrants and that there was a tailing-off of large fortunes made in national politics and administration.[48] Studies of Huntingdonshire and Lancashire show declines in the number of gentry after 1660, in Kent stability, and in Yorkshire increases. Peter Roebuck found access to the higher ranks of the gentry was more readily attainable, stemming in part from opportunities for aggrandizement available during the Interregnum.[49] A study of the Long Parliament seems to show that more families with previous MPs disappeared from national politics during the Civil War period than new families who came into the Commons for the first time in the 1640s and elected more MPs later.[50]

The last finding is the easiest to assess. Data on the parliamentary elite show it to be erroneous. This can be seen in Table 2.6. The rate of new entrants was clearly much higher than disappearances during this period. Indeed there was a general surge of new entrants after 1650 until the turn of the century. We have already seen that the Civil War did not destroy the old gentry, but the composition fines, debts and repurchase of sequestered estates did force many gentlemen to sell land. Newcomers had exceptional opportunities to establish themselves.[51] Eighty-two new elite families entered parliament between 1650 and 1669, the highest number for any two decades in the study except for the years of Tudor social mobility (1520–59). This high rate of entrance continued for four more decades. Most of it was, however, concentrated among the 'five or fewer' MP families. Comparatively few were able to sustain their membership in the elite over the long term, unlike the great families founded in the mid-sixteenth century. It is also worth noting that the overall size of the elite stayed relatively unchanged: 1,103 in 1640–59 and 1,101 in 1680–99. Departures balanced the flow of incomers.

Table 2.6 Impact of the Civil War on English parliamentary families, 1640–69

1640–49	20 families disappeared	19 entered Commons
1650–59	19 families disappeared	40 entered Commons
1660–69	16 families disappeared	42 entered Commons

Another important finding relevant to the century before the Civil War is the dramatic shift in the balance of membership in the Commons between individuals unconnected with other MPs on the one hand and legislators who were part of the parliamentary elite. Before 1529 probably little more than one-quarter of the lower house was 'dynastic'. In that year, however, well over half (57%) of MPs were drawn from families that were or would become 'parliamentary'. Many of these MPs were founders or sons of founders, so there was not necessarily any sense at the time that a major change was occurring. In 1584 two-thirds (67%) of MPs were drawn from the elite. Increasingly, parliament was the preserve of established families. The proportion dropped to 63% in 1601, but by the Long Parliament it was 79% (see Figure 2.1). For the next two centuries the elite composed over three-quarters of the membership of the House. The Stuart kings faced a legislature of increasing feistiness, conscious of its authority and stature in part because the parliament men more than ever before constituted the *established* national elite. Many of these dynasties had risen under Henry VIII, but by Charles I's reign they had been in the saddle for a century or more and were indistinguishable in confidence and assertiveness from more ancient stock. This shift in the nature of the membership of parliament made the king's task of coping with the Commons more difficult and perhaps helped give them the confidence to seize the initiative that most Tudor MPs lacked.

Historians have tended to regard the eighteenth century as a more stable period with less mobility into the elite. It has been argued that the rise of new families was restricted by limited availability of land on the market, and that it became particularly difficult to assemble a major estate. Most of the greater landowners, so it is said, were in place by 1700. Social mobility was silting up.[52]

More recent analysis of the eighteenth-century land market suggests that it was vigorous and estates were widely available for purchase by newcomers.[53] The first quarter of the eighteenth century was a particularly active period in building country houses, and there was another peak in 1760–1820. Habakkuk believes that for most counties the ratio of new to established landed families increased over time until the 1870s, though the magnitude of the change is unclear.[54]

Data on the parliamentary elite shows a continued flow of new families during the first two decades, and then a slump in 1720–39, perhaps as a result of the end of the wars on the continent, which had offered opportunities for military and administrative profit, and the stock market débâcle of the 1720s. Then there was a rise again, a modest decline and a surge in 1780–1820. (See Figure 2.5.) Ian Christie found a similar pattern in a study of non-elite MPs, who increased in numbers in 1715–40, declined at mid-century and rose markedly after 1760. He attributes the elevation in numbers under George III to the establishment of the commercial empire in India after 1763, the expansion of banking and the continued growth of the West Indian economy.[55] I would add the rising number of industrialists. New entrants were about the same proportion of the contemporary elite in 1760–1819 (averaging 4.6% per two decades) as they were in 1640–99 (4.9%) and higher than in 1700–59 (3.8%).

After 1820 a decline in the number of new entrants began from which the elite never recovered. The end of the Napoleonic wars and the subsequent economic downturn decreased opportunities to found new families for a time. After 1832 the extension of the suffrage, further electoral reforms and the spread of a more egalitarian spirit made it difficult to sustain hereditary hegemony in the Commons. Eventually, it became impossible for families who had four or five MPs to extend their parliamentary service and accumulate more because time literally ran out. Changes in the political culture made it hard even for great families to maintain parliamentary service after 1885.

New entrant families continued to be established through much of the nineteenth century. Well over a thousand and perhaps as many as two thousand country houses were built in 1835–1914. Until the agricultural depression late in the century, land became increasingly expensive, which meant fewer families could afford to purchase a substantial estate. This did not stop a few of the super-rich like the Rothschilds and Loyds from buying up chunks of whole counties.[56] But very few new families lasted.

Summary

Let us consolidate and summarize the findings about the size and composition of the governing class. It controlled four out of five of the seats in the Commons and most of the places in the Lords from 1660 to 1832, and was smaller that historians have hitherto imagined. Barely more than a thousand families from the reign of Edward VI to George II constituted the English political elite, which numbered no more than about 800 in the golden years of aristocratic rule in the late eighteenth and early nineteenth centuries (see Figure 2.8).

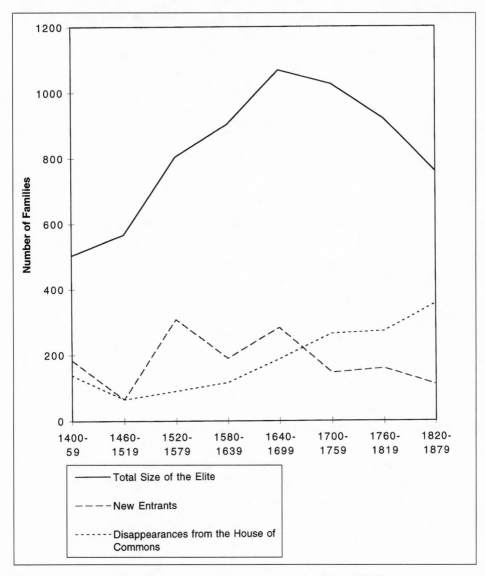

Figure 2.8 Total size of the English parliamentary elite, 1400–1879[57]

Historians have tended to underestimate the antiquity of much of the elite. About half
the families in 1640 with fewer than six MPs, and over two-thirds of those with more
than that number, were established before the Tudors came to power. A steady outflow
of families unable to sustain aristocratic leadership for financial and biological reasons
drained away and several surges of large numbers of new entrants took place,
especially under Henry VIII and in the mid-seventeenth century, when exceptional

63

opportunities were available for social mobility. The different categories within the elite remained remarkably stable over long periods. The proportion of new, moderately well established and 'ancient' families stayed steady from 1640 to 1832.

The years 1560 to 1640 were not as fertile a time for raising economic and social status as has been previously thought, and the slump in new entrants may have contributed to the tensions of Charles I's reign. Statistics based on country house ownership miss the consolidation of power into fewer hands during the second half of the eighteenth and early nineteenth centuries, a process that took place even though the economy was expanding. The control of parliament became the prerogative of such an exclusive band of families that the political system became vulnerable to attack from outside and was undermined from within by weakening confidence and the ideology of the great Whig families. The backlash against Wellington among his own supporters in 1830 may have been provoked as much by the perceived exclusion of the gentry by the magnates from electoral politics as by Catholic emancipation. The years 1640 and 1832 were both preceded by dramatic shifts in the composition of the elite.

Yet England never had a closed elite. Men from many walks of life – from pirates to harness-makers, apothecaries to sheep farmers, and former footmen to merchant princes – could dream of being granted arms and ultimately founding a parliamentary dynasty. At the lower levels of the elite, the turnover was rapid, which ensured that there was always room for newcomers at the foot of the ladder. The belief held by contemporaries and later observers that men were free to rise and were accepted rapidly into the elite was true from the Middle Ages onwards. Most authorities acknowledge that the lower one dips into landed society the more turnover one is likely to find. What is striking is that even in the rarefied layer of the governing class, the 'five or fewer' category of families was in a constant state of flux and renewal. On the other hand, a tiny apex of grandees was old and exclusive.

Chapter 3

The Penetration of New Wealth into the English Governing Class

The examples generally used to demonstrate that it was possible to rise high in English society from humble beginnings form a familiar litany. The De La Poles, fourteenth-century Hull merchants with a maternal descent from a family called Rottenherring, rose to an earldom with remarkable rapidity and a few generations later stood in line of succession to the throne. Henry VIII's man of business Thomas Cromwell, son of a Putney clothworker, took only a few years to become a great landowner and an earl. Historians also note the meritocratic navy as a producer of dazzling rags-to-riches stories, such as that of Viscount Torrington, who ascended from cabin boy to peer in the early eighteenth century.[1] But some of these examples are raised only to be challenged. John Scott, the 'coal fitter's son' who became the Earl of Eldon in 1821, was in fact the heir with his brother to a fortune of £25,000.[2]

Rapid rises from very humble beginnings were not uncommon. Many examples can be found among the founders of parliamentary families. Even great dynasties could start modestly. John Thynne, a younger son of a minor squire, went to London as a kitchen clerk in the royal household and by 1580 owned 6,000 acres at Longleat in Wiltshire. The Holles Dukes of Newcastle began with a baker in London, whose grandson was a merchant who purchased an estate in 1541. His grandson was an earl by 1624. The 1st Duke of Leeds was the great-grandson of a London apprentice whose initial step to wealth and power was the rescue of his master's infant daughter when she tumbled out of a window into the Thames from her father's house on London Bridge.[3]

England was also open to foreigners, as the rapid rise of the Caesars from Italy or the Barings from Germany showed. Huguenots were exceptionally successful and produced a number of great families. The grandson of a Portuguese Jew named Gideon, a West India merchant in the early eighteenth century, became a shire knight in 1770 and gained an Irish peerage in 1789. The Ricardos were brokers from Amsterdam. The first MP (1819) and eminent economist purchased estates and his sons settled down as landed gentry. Other Jewish families such as the Disraelis, Levys and Rothschilds rose high in wealth and also gained peerages and married into the established aristocracy.

These examples and hundreds of other cases do not prove that the English elite was *wide* open to men with luck or talent, but they do demonstrate that it was by no means tightly closed. This chapter seeks to answer the question, to what degree was the governing class composed of families founded by merchants and tradesmen as opposed to lawyers and judges, obscure upstarts rather than younger sons of established gentry, and adventurous entrepreneurs instead of government officials with a bureaucratic cast of mind? Many observers tend to see those who rose through office and the professions as closely akin to landed society in origins and values,[4] and so we will first examine the most traditional methods of entry into the elite.

Land

The largest source of new entrants into the governing class until the death of Charles I was the 'landed' category. (See Table 3.5.) Absurd claims to old pedigrees were commonplace. The Seymours were supposed to have descended from King Solomon and the Queen of Sheba. The Cliffords had Lady Godiva as an 'ancestor'. There was a tradition that the Puseys were granted Pusey in Berkshire by King Canute. The Gells claimed descent from a Roman soldier called Gellius, after an eighteenth-century discovery of a Romano-British pot on their estate allegedly inscribed Gelli.[5] On being told the lineage of the Lumleys, King James I exclaimed: 'Oh mon! gang na further. I maun digest the knowledge I ha' this day gained, for I did na ken Adam's ither name was Lumley.'[6]

Like the king's, our reaction to dynastic hagiography tends towards cynical hilarity. However, many of the families who were made out to be companions of Methuselah were authentically old, deeply rooted in the land. Among the knightly families in Warwickshire prominent in the twelfth and thirteenth centuries we find the following producing MPs in the nineteenth and twentieth: Shuckburgh (last MP 1804), Lucy (1830), Hastings (1831), Shirley (1880) and Compton (1911).[7] In Nottinghamshire, of the thirteen greater knights of the late fourteenth century one finds the Chaworths (last MP 1727), Cliftons (1869), Pierreponts (1900), Stanhopes (1905) and Markhams (1916), while the Nevilles and Willoughbys remained in the House of Lords.[8] The leading families of Cheshire in the fourteenth century included Egerton (last MP 1906), Stanley (1950) and Grosvenor (1964). Of 118 Lancashire families with acreage enough to qualify for inclusion in Bateman's *Great Landowners* in the 1870s, twenty-five were landed gentry before 1464.[9] Out of a list of fifty-seven leading Gloucestershire gentry in modern times, sixteen were of medieval origins.[10] In total, 183 families listed in the volumes covering the years 1386 to 1421 of the *History of Parliament* elected at least one MP post-1660.

66

Few English families have a proven descent (male or female) from Saxon times: the Ardens, who derived from a Saxon Quisling and never amounted to much in modern times; the Trelawneys of Cornwall, a prolific parliamentary family; and the Berkeleys, earls and marquesses, in residence at Berkeley Castle to this day.[11] At least thirty-four families in this study made undocumented claims to Saxon ancestry. Most of these are dubious, but the Derings, Hampdens and Trefusises are probably genuine.[12]

In the decades following 1066 the Normans killed, exiled or dispossessed most of the Anglo-Saxon elite, but a number of Norman families almost certainly married Saxon heiresses and hence the bloodlines and ownership of long-established families survived among the elite.[13] The Audleys, Greystokes, Nevilles, Osbaldstons, Stanleys, Stonors, Tichbornes, Towneleys and Traffords, for example, probably did have some Saxon lineage.[14] The Tracy estates in Gloucestershire passed via a French count solely by descent from a date before the Conquest until the modern era.[15] Even a conservative estimate lists three hundred or so, probably more, modern gentry families with Norman ancestry, though few enjoy an unbroken line of male succession. There are fifty-seven English families in this study with pedigrees that pre-date 1100. Crowcombe in Somerset and Glyndebourne in Sussex have not been bought or sold since the Conquest, and the Okeovers were at Okeover from about 1100 to 1955.[16]

The only proved male pedigree from a Domesday tenant still on the original estate in modern times is that of Earl Ferrers, although the descendants of the Stafford Dukes of Buckingham, who were tenants in chief in 1086, continued to hold important estates until recently. The Percys too descend from a Domesday tenant in chief and were at Leconfield by 1087.[17] Parliamentary families with MPs post-1660 whose landed status reached back before 1400 were numerous.[18] Families who fought at Poitiers, Crecy, Otterburn, Agincourt, Pinkie and Bannockburn elected MPs into the twentieth century.

Many ancient 'landed' families undoubtedly derived their fortunes from sources other than knightly service and the careful husbandry of estates. If we could follow in detail the accumulation of their fortunes, everything from legal expertise and local office-holding to pillage and theft would come into view. The most recent historian of the Stanley family acknowledged that they acquired much of their vast land holdings through 'double-dealing and unprincipled behavior'.[19] War and marriage were keys to success.[20] The latter was always a vital means of leverage. Violence and crime gradually declined.

When record-keeping improved and fuller documentation survives we can see more clearly how rising by 'landed' means was done. The Grenvilles, Pierreponts and Spencers advanced themselves by amassing thousands of sheep. Cautious husbandry raised families such as the Archers of Umberslade, Drydens of Canons Ashby, Leighs of Northcourt and Reynells of East Ogwell. Much depended on the period and region. In fifteenth-century Warwickshire there is little evidence of successful peasants moving into the gentry, while in sixteenth-century Yorkshire kulaks buying more and more land were the greatest source of recruitment for the landed elite. In the north country prosperous farmers leased under-rented holdings to peasants and invested the profits in more land.[21] The pattern one sees repeated over and over again is of small landowners raising themselves by shrewd exploitation of every available means to extract value from their estates, including proto-industrial production. The Kayes, who were franklins at Woodsome under Richard II, purchased the manor in Henry VII's reign, and added piecemeal to their estates, accumulating property over a lengthy period. They were industrious, businesslike and enterprising: they developed

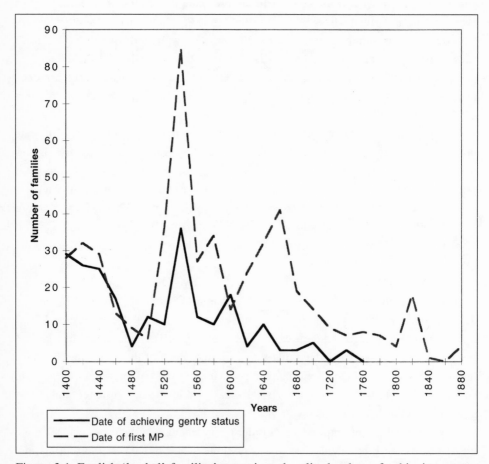

Figure 3.1 English 'landed' families' entry into the elite by date of achieving gentry status and date of first MP, 1400–1899 (per two decades)

unproductive land, mined for coal, operated fulling mills, and set up iron forges, salt pans and alum works. It took four generations to build up an estate worth £1,000 a year. Their first MP was elected in 1610, and a baronetcy was achieved in 1642. By 1876 they had an income of £10,000 p.a.[22] Playing the land market proved highly remunerative as well. Acting as an estate steward could give a man training and opportunity to become a landowner in his own right, as was the case with the Buxtons, Groves, Wilkinsons and Williamses.[23]

One of the most striking findings of this study is the continuity and antiquity of families with landed origins: 84% of all 'landed' entrants to the English parliamentary elite 1295–1945 achieved gentry status before 1480. A further 10% had their social origins in the 1480–1599 period, which means that virtually all of the 'landed' entrants had established themselves as country gentlemen before the Stuarts succeeded to the English throne. If one measures entry date by *first MP*,[24] half (49%) entered before the rise of the Tudors. One quarter of first MPs came to Westminster in 1480–1599 and a further large proportion entered in the years immediately after the Restoration, as Figure 3.1 shows. The large upward spike in the sixteenth century was due partly to the inrush of old families who now regarded being Members of Parliament as important, a process made easier by the enlarged number of constituencies, and partly to the expansion of incomes owing to land purchases at the Dissolution. The final small burst of entries occurred in the years after 1800, probably funded by rising agricultural incomes during the French wars.

G.E. Mingay thought that the sixteenth and seventeenth centuries were an age of great opportunities for yeomen to rise to gentry status, if they were bold, lucky and shrewd. Lawrence Stone believed 'thousands' of families rose from the yeomanry into the gentry in the late sixteenth and early seventeenth centuries by farming and using improved techniques.[25] This was undoubtedly true among the modest gentry, but families who rose to great estates and to the point of being able regularly to elect MPs by the accumulation of land from the profits of agriculture, property speculation and marriage alone were rare. Less than 16% of such families achieved the feat under Tudor and Stuart sovereigns. Stone's new owners of large country houses from 'landed' backgrounds during the same period, who composed slightly over two-fifths of all his entrants in these years, are a much larger group than the 'landed' families gaining their first foothold as members of the parliamentary elite. (See Table 3.1.)

The 'landed' category produced 40% of the English governing families in this study.[26] This is an impressive proportion, but it is important to remember that the vast majority of these families rose to gentry status before the end of the Middle Ages. After Bosworth most families did not rely on agriculture to gain entry into the governing elite.

Table 3.1 Comparison of the percentage of English new entrants from 'landed' backgrounds by date of first MP and first ownership of a large country house, 1400–1879*

The highlighted percents on the left under each date come from this study, and the percents on the right from Table 6.2 in the Stones' *An Open Elite?*

1400–1579**		1580–1639		1640–1699		1700–1759		1760–1819		1820–1879	
42.9	29	**31.7**	45	**27.1**	35	**17.1**	27	**9.6**	41	**14.9**	42

* Note: the Stones' data comes from three counties: Hertfordshire, Northamptonshire and Northumberland.
** The Stones' category is for all pre-1579 families in their study. I begin with entrants after 1400.

Office

Royal, noble and public service lifted families to greatness. Personal favour with the monarch or great magnates could lead to rich rewards. The 1st Earl of Dysart, for example, rose from parson's son to peer as whipping boy and friend of Charles I.[27] However, there was no equivalent in England of gaining nobility by ownership of office, a principal route to advancement in France. For every success story there were other new men who failed to gain a foothold and older families ruined by the expense of court life. On the other hand, few methods were better guaranteed to create wealth rapidly than military contracts. One can see in Figure 3.2 the close congruence between date of entry into the social elite and date of first MP among 'official' families. If one compares the graph to other figures in this chapter, one can see that these two variables are more closely tied here than in any other category. Of course, it was natural for men on the make in administrative positions to seek entry into the Commons. None the less, office was a fast track to success. Much could be done legally with inside information and by skimming off interest during periods when public funds were held in privately managed accounts. Embezzlement was a hardy perennial in public service. An added advantage to office-holding was the cornucopia of decorations and titles likely to be emptied over those with personal access to the sovereign and his close advisors and the opportunity to achieve advancement of the state's interests, which brought fame and dignity.

Holding office was one of the earliest ways, other than through military service, by which a new man could raise himself to elite status. Of course, many such individuals did not found families because medieval state servants were often celibate churchmen.

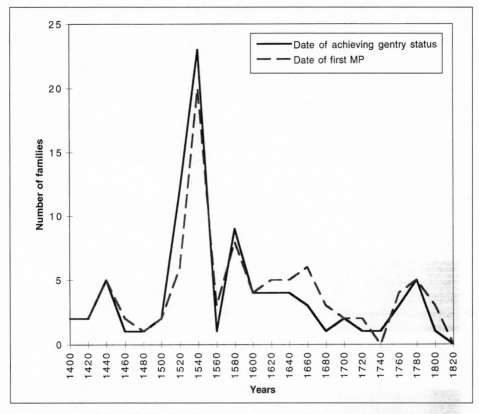

Figure 3.2 English 'official' families' entry into the elite by date of achieving gentry status and date of first MP, 1400–1839 (per two decades)

However, in the thirteenth and fourteenth centuries laymen began to rise from quite humble backgrounds, including mercantile origins, to became manorial lords, great landowners and even earls through government service. The new Lancastrian nobility was composed of the official class: Bardolf, Cromwell, Hungerford, Say, Sudeley and Tiptoft.[28]

The stepping-stone to such opportunities often consisted of local office-holding and serving as a counsellor or 'minister' to one of the great magnates. Acting as coroner, royal forester, constable of a castle and the like gave men access to leases, land and opportunities for graft as well as the possibility of being drawn into the royal household. Being a noble servant not only offered many of the same chances but also gave access to the elite marriage market. In Aylmer's study of the king's servants in the seventeenth century, among government officials of the second rank, transfer from private to royal service seems to have been the commonest single mode of recruitment.

Noble service in the Middle Ages could lead to very rapid advancement and acquisition of estates. Thomas Hasilden, controller to the household of John of Gaunt, was soon a knight of the shire and was succeeded in that rank by two of his sons in 1384–1406. William Herbert, a Welsh squire, raised himself to a barony in 1461 by uninhibited ambition and a grasping nature. In less than ten years of royal service he became an English magnate. Rises could be assisted or carried further both by the traditional route of marriage or by other means. The founder of the Morleys of Halnaker, Sussex, was an Exchequer official but also an ironmaster on the side.[29] Noble service died out as a method of advancement into the elite, unless one counts estate agents and stewards, by the time of the Civil War. The Hollands, retainers of the Howards under Elizabeth I who elected their first MP in 1621, were among the last of this type.

Figure 3.2 shows that the sixteenth century was a golden age for those rising by office. Even relatively modest posts could produce fortunes of thirty or forty thousand pounds or more.[30] It was a bloody game for major players such as Wolsey and Thomas Cromwell, but magnates with ancient lineage could die messily as well. Religious conflict made the world at the top especially dangerous at mid-century, but the new civil administration created by the Tudors gave many men an opportunity to found families. Historians have written of a new 'service aristocracy' founded on office in the central government during this period. A rough survey of about one hundred of the most important courtier country houses in the first half of the century shows that only about one-third were inherited and two-fifths were obtained by gift or grant/purchase from the Crown. The Stones list 'office' as the source for 44% of their pre-1579 category of families rising into the elite.[31]

The latter figure greatly exceeds the percentage of 'official' families entering the parliamentary elite during this period. The sixteenth century was a fertile time for such families, but, as a proportion of the entire elite, 'office' was never the largest source of recruitment. Some celebrated dynasties that might be thought to have emerged through 'office' were in fact raised into the parliamenatry elite by other means. Sir John Russell served Henry VIII in a number of important official capacities, was made a peer and acquired large blocks of church lands after the Dissolution. But the family rose as merchants in the fourteenth century, purchased estates gradually in the 1300s and 1400s, and elected their first MP for Melcombe in 1340. A Russell was knight of the shire for Dorset in 1472.[32] The grandfather of the first Cecil peer was the younger son of a poor Welsh squire, and began as a yeoman of the guard to Henry VII. He managed to purchase an estate near Stamford and was elected MP for the borough in 1504. His son was a royal page at the Field of the Cloth of Gold, extended the estate by purchasing Burghley and was also an MP. *His* son became Lord Burghley, Elizabeth's great minister. The family rose in royal service, but they had become members of the governing class and MPs before the first peer was born.[33] Other

Table 3.2 Comparison of the percentage of English new entrants from 'official' backgrounds by date of first MP and first ownership of a large country house, 1400–1879

The highlighted percents on the left under each date come from this study and the percents on the right from Table 6.2 in the Stones' *An Open Elite?*

1400–1579		*1580–1639*		*1640–1699*		*1700–1759*		*1760–1819*		*1820–1879*	
6.9	44	**7.5**	19	**4.1**	13	**2.3**	15	**6.0**	8	**0**	7

families such as the Arundells, Carys, Knollyses, Pauletts and Sidneys rose high in Tudor government, but they had entered the elite in earlier generations.

Stone's figure for 'office' drops off later in the sixteenth century, but he continues to measure a higher proportion entering the elite in his sample than this national survey in subsequent sixty-year periods. Aylmer and Habakkuk also believe that office-holding ceased to be a contributor to social mobility in the seventeenth century.[34] Like election as an MP, achieving an official position had become the marker of arrival at gentility and confirmation of it, not something that helped one to get there in the first place. Most of the large sinecures went to families who were already important and influential, until 'Old Corruption' was finally swept away.[35] The one exception (aside from legal offices, for which see below) was the Paymaster Generalship, which lifted Amherst, Cadogan, Chandos, Fox, Marlborough and Walpole to great heights of wealth, although even in these cases some were secondary rises from already established families. Despite mushrooming numbers of civil servants after 1688, only a few eighteenth-century officials of humble origin such as Addington, Bradshaw and Rose founded parliamentary dynasties.[36] In modern times a handful of political families rose in public service, such as the Foots, Hardies and Hendersons, but there were no more stories of men such as the silversmith Peter Taylor: son of a Wells grocer and orphaned at thirteen, he made £400,000 in four years as Deputy Paymaster General in Germany in the 1750s by arranging the exchanges in currencies to his advantage and by paying the army in light coin.[37]

The Professions

From the Middle Ages onwards there was a steady influx of upwardly mobile professionals, but the status of the professions varied over time, as did the hierarchies within them, and the methods of admission and sources of recruitment. Enhanced complexity of social differentiation characterized the period 1580 to 1680. From the mid-sixteenth to mid-seventeenth century, the legal profession, for example, was fundamentally reconstituted while the same period saw the appearance of a university-educated elite at the head of the nascent medical profession and the rise of several wholly new groups such as architects, school teachers and university dons. Increasing numbers in the learned professions, a rapidly expanding officer corps and more formal systems of regulation and organization appeared after 1680. The professions grew strikingly in self-confidence and material well-being in the early Hanoverian period, with even more explosive growth in the nineteenth century.[38] It is worth looking at each profession separately, before examining the category as a whole and comparing it to other groups and to the findings of other studies.

Not until the sixteenth century can we discern career officers in the army and navy making their way into the elite as a distinctly separate category from 'land', although many of these were younger sons from already established families. The surprise is, considering the large number of army and naval officers who began to sit as MPs after 1660 (one in ten or more of all MPs), how few succeeded in raising their families permanently into the elite if they were not already members.[39] The army produced a few new men, but Amherst, Burgoyne, Churchill, Gage, Monck, Stanhope and Wellesley all came from families who had previous MPs. Stone argues that from the late seventeenth century in times of war the army and navy were a principal means of entry into the elite, and Rubinstein has shown that until the end of the Napoleonic Wars many men made large fortunes in the national defence.[40] Most of these families, however, failed to sink roots. The quasi-piratical prize system in the navy could create great fortunes almost instantly, yet even in the senior service only a handful of base-born admirals managed to found long-lasting elite families, and most of the really successful ones had connections in the peerage to begin with.[41]

Only a tiny proportion of the parliamentary elite derived from military service. Even at the peak of imperial conflict between 1760 and 1819, when one-third of all military entrants who were to found parliamentary dynasties did so, they formed only 8% of all entrants achieving gentry status during those years. The percentage of all new families coming from military backgrounds in 1640–99 was 5 and in 1700–59 it was 4. Since three-quarters of all military entrants came into the elite during these years, one can see that their numbers were not a principal source of recruitment. Only thirty-eight governing families sprang primarily from the profession of arms between 1520 and 1869.

The medical profession fits uneasily into any analysis of social structure in English history. Only a small proportion of doctors ever achieved incomes on a scale that could lead to entry into the governing class, and many practitioners were no more than barbers or apothecaries. None the less, it is a mistake to dismiss the early top members of the profession as automatically debarred from reaching high rank even though their methods were crude and regulation of medical education and practice non-existent. Royal doctors had amazingly successful careers.[42] They were regularly created baronets from the reign of Charles I. Among new baronets 3% were doctors in 1649–1707 and this rose to 7% in the nineteenth century. By the latter period top practitioners could make £10,000 p.a.[43] However, only eight parliamentary families in this study rose from a medical background.

A few other professions produced a handful of parliamentary families. The founder of the Adam family of architects made money both in his practice as well as through ordnance contracts. Three generations of Dugdales were heralds in the seventeenth and eighteenth centuries, although fortunate marriages also assisted their rise. The Butlers of Trinity College, Cambridge, were a formidable academic line, producing headmasters, dons, civil servants, clerics and a major politician in the mid-twentieth century. A journalist became the first MP in the Hurd family in 1918, and they have since elected several more members to parliament, gained a peerage and most recently held the Foreign Secretaryship. These and a handful of other examples, most of them after landed society was in decline, are the only 'minor' professions to produce families that achieved parliamentary status.

Both Stone and Habakkuk found that the Church produced little social advancement to the elite level, and this study confirms their judgement. A few medieval prelates were able to lift their nephews into higher positions, most notably the Kempes of Kent, but only six Tudor and four seventeenth-century clerics managed to found lasting dynasties. Considering the incomes enjoyed by some bishops – in the nineteenth century the Archbishop of Canterbury received £20,000 a year – it is a puzzlement that more top clerics did not establish elite families. Moreover, some prelates exercised significant electoral patronage. The explanation probably lies in the fact that many bishops only gained promotion late in their careers, and the aristocracy used its influence to secure many of the lucrative mitres for younger sons.[44]

When one talks about the professions providing new families for entry into the elite, one is largely speaking of the law. This profession lent itself to parliamentary life. The place, season and time of meeting of the Commons suited most lawyers, and the knowledge gained by judges and barristers through their political and legal work gave them unusual opportunities to exploit the land market, 'network' with the influential and marry well. In the fourteenth century it is estimated that 7–8% of MPs were connected with the law. In the fifteenth and sixteenth centuries one in five MPs was a lawyer, though this proportion dropped back to 11% in 1614. It remained in the range of 10–15% from the Long Parliament until the mid-Victorian period. Lawyers comprised one of the largest (and sometimes *the* largest) identifiable status and occupational group in the House of Commons next to the landed gentry.[45] The legal profession contributed at least two hundred families to the English parliamentary elite as well as raising many more from modest circumstances to great landowners.

As with other categories, of course, one has to be careful. Sons of landed families were educated in the law, and lawyers performed non-legal functions or used other means to acquire fortunes. Indeed, most lawyers who founded parliamentary families did so through a combination of income streams that could include (in addition to legal or judicial fees) investments, inheritances, marriage, office, money lending, profits from farming, noble service, land speculation, fraud, acting as electoral agents and the like. Sir Robert Bowes (MP 1539) was a lawyer and border warrior who spent his career alternating between the court room and the battlefield. John Eston (1545) was a London lawyer and grocer.[46] Among those holding high legal positions only the Lord Chief Justices and Lord Chancellors usually had opportunities to make great fortunes.[47] However, provincial attorneys also made up a sizeable proportion of purchasers of landed property.[48] Identification of some legal new entrants is made difficult by the fact that landed families sometimes continued to produce lawyers, even among eldest sons, for generations after entry into the elite. The Lutwyches were at Lutwyche Hall by 1418, but all three of their MPs in 1586–1734 were lawyers.[49]

Historians debate about the proportion of lawyers who already enjoyed gentle backgrounds as opposed to those who were recruited from further down the social scale.[50] It is certain that some men rose from humble circumstances to great heights through the law. In the sixteenth century Nicholas Bacon, son of a yeoman, spent £37,000 on land purchases and more on house-building and estate improvements. Sir James Ley rose from modest beginnings to a judgeship and earldom in the early seventeenth century. The 1st Earl of Hardwicke (1754) was sired by a provincial merchant.[51]

Some of the greatest families in the kingdom were originally raised up by the law. The father of the first Sir Winston Churchill in the early seventeenth century was a lawyer and Deputy Registrar of Chancery. He purchased an estate and married a small heiress of the knightly Winston family. Sir Winston was also a lawyer and his nephew was Attorney General to the Duke of York and Master of the Rolls. The Cavendishes began with a judge under Richard II. The first Howard lawyer, the son of a yeoman, was elected an MP in 1295 and made Chief Justice of the Common Pleas in 1297.[52]

There is a general assumption among historians that a *steady* influx of lawyers into the landed elite took place over the centuries.[53] As one can see from Figure 3.3 the entry flow was not consistent. In the period 1400 to 1519 about one in ten of all new entrants to the parliamentary elite were from legal backgrounds. Stone found much the same thing.[54] Rapid growth among lawyers did not come until the sixteenth century. However, as a proportion of all entrants not much change took place, because this was a period when the gross numbers of entering families rose rapidly. No single source of

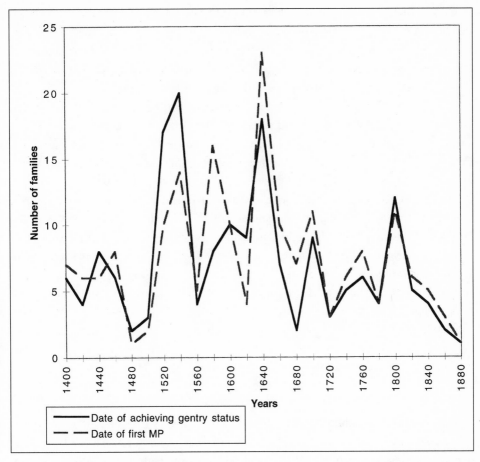

Figure 3.3 English 'legal' families' entry into the elite by date of achieving gentry status and date of first MP, 1400–1899 (per two decades)

recruitment within the profession emerged. In the mid-Tudor period a little less than half the new legal families were founded by judges, but there were also London barristers, attorneys general, politicians and successful provincial attorneys, many of whom speculated shrewdly in monastic land.

Although the number of barristers expanded rapidly during the second half of the sixteenth century and the first half of the seventeenth, no comparable increase in the proportion of legal entrants to the parliamentary elite developed.[55] The rate of growth among such families slowed after the accession of Elizabeth I. Only four legal families rose in the first two decades of her reign compared to twenty in the previous twenty years, and seventeen in the same length of time before that. In the last decades of the sixteenth century and the early Stuart period the rate of entry averaged five or so a decade, with a second burst in the troubled years 1640–59. This was not matched in official or other professional groups. Of the eighteen lawyers who founded families in the period, only three were judges while fourteen were barristers or provincial attorneys. Several were prominent figures in the parliamentary cause. The dangerous mid-sixteenth and mid-seventeenth centuries were the most fertile periods for lawyers to rise, although it is interesting to note (Figure 3.3) that legal families who grew rich between the 1520s and 1560s did not gain such immediate acceptance into the parliamentary elite as did those who attained their wealth in the days of Pym and Cromwell. The mid-Tudor lawyers or their sons or grandsons often did not achieve (or did not desire?) admission to the Commons until the last years of Elizabeth's reign.[56]

Barristers' fees rose two or threefold in real terms in the second half of the seventeenth century, yet the rate of new entrants to the parliamentary elite from the law slackened after 1660. The eighteenth century witnessed an average of only two or three a decade. More 'legal' baronetcies may have been granted in the period 1660 to 1720 than before or later and Stone believes legal office was an especially fertile source of new elite families. He is supported by other historians who argue that the law offered one of the best opportunities for upward social mobility in eighteenth-century Britain. But data on the parliamentary elite shows only one decade, 1710–19, that produced more than three new entrants from the legal profession.[57] It was still possible for Lord Chancellors to do spectacularly well, as Hardwicke's and Eldon's fortunes showed, but the rate of entry had slowed to a trickle.

The last spike in the graph came in the first three decades of the nineteenth century, a period when the number of barristers nearly tripled.[58] Between 1800 and 1831 seventeen new entrants arrived, a much higher number than for any other thirty-year period since the Restoration, and it was never matched again. Fourteen of this group ultimately gained peerages, although none acquired property on the old scale. No legal family which rose after 1800 had an income listed in Bateman higher than £7,138 p.a. This was due to a variety of causes: the end of 'Old Corruption', opportunities to find other types of secure investments, and less time than previous entrants had enjoyed to fish the marriage market for heiresses. Lord St Leonards was the last Lord Chancellor (1852) to purchase an estate large enough to qualify for inclusion in Bateman. Of the seventeen families, there were three provincial attorneys who married well, two Lord Chancellors, two agents of magnates, two legal officers of the Crown, four judges, one courtier, one diplomat and two judges in India.

The proportion of legal families among all entrants to the parliamentary elite rose to nearly 13% in 1640–99, but dropped slightly in the period 1700–59 and rose to 14 in 1760–1819. However, the latter figure is misleadingly high. Absolute numbers were falling. The proportion went up because the number of 'landed' entrants had dropped so dramatically.

Halévy proclaimed that in the early nineteenth century, 'Nothing was beyond the reach of a successful barrister; there was no office or title to which he might not aspire.'[59] It is true that lawyers from very humble backgrounds, such as Edward Sugden, could still rise into the landed aristocracy in a single generation, but fewer and fewer such cases occurred. After 1830 only a handful of the most able and lucky lawyers founded new parliamentary families and that was largely because life peerages could not be created for them. Hence their progeny continued to sit in the House of Lords, but rarely with a suitable estate to support them. The percentage of judges owning land dropped precipitously as the century wore on.[60] A few notable exceptions proved the rule. Lord Selborne, Lord Chancellor in the 1870s, made a fortune as a barrister and judge, and set up as a country gentleman, purchasing an estate and building a house in the late 1860s at a cost of £155,000, but his family descended from rich eighteenth-century London merchants.[61]

Lawrence Stone and Geoffrey Holmes argue strongly that we should direct our attention to the great increase in the importance of the professions in English society in the late seventeenth and early eighteenth centuries. According to Stone's figures, nearly half (46%) of all new entrants into the landed elite in 1700–59 came from fortunes founded in government office or the law.[62] Table 3.5 shows that this was not the case with the parliamentary elite. Moreover, office and the law provided far greater numbers in absolute terms (though not proportionally) to the new entrant category in the sixteenth and first half of the seventeenth centuries than later. From the Middle Ages until the end of the Victorian period, office and the professions combined only once exceeded 30% of all entrants in any given sixty-year period. In later years few legal families amassed the wealth necessary to found a long-lasting parliamentary dynasty. Only business activities were capable of turning out huge fortunes in large numbers from the eighteenth century onwards.

Business

In the Middle Ages some urban merchants and tradesmen founded parliamentary dynasties and represented their towns over three or more generations. However, from the twelfth century rich and distinguished members of the bourgeoisie were becoming landed and entering the aristocracy. London merchant families began to attain knighthoods in the thirteenth century and sometimes even became barons. The wars of that period produced military contractors and government financiers who could make large amounts of money and earn royal gratitude. Urban magnates began to think of themselves as gentlemen and purchased landed estates to secure social advancement. The heralds were authorized to grant arms to London and provincial merchants from the fifteenth century onwards. Big London fortunes such as those of the Greshams, Kitsons and Seymours provided regular recruits for the nobility and gentry.[63]

If one discounts members of the gentry and professional men with commercial interests, 15–20% of all MPs were businessmen in the later Middle Ages and Tudor period. The proportion declined to 9–12% in the seventeenth century, and rose to 10–15% in the eighteenth. Numbers started mounting steadily from the late eighteenth century onwards.[64]

During the Middle Ages only a small proportion of the City of London merchants and an even tinier number of those from Bristol, Exeter, Hull, Norwich and York produced substantial landed families. However, as time progressed more and more important parliamentary families owed their origins to trade both in the provinces and in the metropolis. In the fifteenth century a big merchant's capital could easily surpass that of the wealthiest lawyers, and in amounts and numbers of individuals this remained true throughout the period of this study. Merchant tycoons proliferated.[65] Between 1386 and 1579 law and office provided less than one in five (18%) while business produced more than one in four of new entrants (27%).

Figure 3.4 shows a significant drop in new business families between 1460 and 1520. From an average of almost seventeen per decade in the later fourteenth century, the numbers dropped to fewer than five per decade in 1470–90. There were only two entrants in 1500–09, the lowest recorded number between the accession of Edward II and the First World War. This accords with a period of low economic growth and population decline discussed in Chapter Two. The economic crisis hit business harder than land.

A strong revival came after 1520. The number of new business entrants rocketed upward. By the mid-sixteenth century it was unusual for a merchant of great standing who had a son not to invest in estates. An unprecedented thirty families entered in the decade 1550–59: the highest number of commercial entrants in the six hundred years between 1310 and 1910. One-fifth of all business entrants between the Conquest and modern times entered the gentry in the Tudor period. As with the professions, the early years of Elizabeth's reign witnessed a radical falling-off in new entrants, followed by a recovery in the 1580s. From then on the numbers began to rise again until 1700, with the peak decades being the 1620s and the 1690s. Unlike the lawyers, who had entered the gentry in the Henrician boom but only later gained acceptance to parliament, the businessmen generally entered the Commons soon after making their fortunes until the post-Armada years when a serious delay began to develop. This was reversed in the mid-seventeenth century, again a different trend than that found among lawyers. However, all categories experienced an exceptionally swift social acceptance during Henry VIII's reign.

Several patterns emerge in the origins of the business entrants during the Tudor period. Clothiers did particularly well, especially in the 1550s. However, founders of parliamentary families came from almost every conceivable type of background. Grocers, fishmongers, merchant tailors, privateers, shipbuilders, tanners, wine

Figure 3.4 English 'business' families' entry into the elite by date of achieving gentry status and date of first MP, 1400–1899 (per two decades)

merchants, drapers, goldsmiths, coal fitters, ironmasters, army victuallers, mercers and gunpowder manufacturers all succeeded in establishing elite dynasties. They were spread out in terms of geography, although often the most successful commercial men moved from a small provincial town to London to expand business opportunities before returning to the countryside to buy an estate. Big towns like Norwich and lesser ones such as Chesterfield, Dorchester, Fowey and Tiverton produced a share of new entrants. Even small town merchants began to send their sons to Eton and to marry country gentlemen's daughters. Bristol merchants, an observer complained in 1571, 'attain great wealth and riches, which for the most part they do employ in purchasing of lands, and by little and little they do creep and seek to be gentlemen'.[66]

The mid-seventeenth century witnessed rapid growth of parliamentary families of commercial origins, the largest entry of any twenty-year period. Business fortunes were increasingly derived from overseas commerce and big finance. In the eighteenth century global warfare created gigantic fortunes that could rapidly raise a family to grandee status, but there were also innkeepers, revenue farmers, money lenders and saddlers.

With the exception of the sharp economic downturn in the 1730s, business entrants averaged twelve or thirteen new families per decade throughout the eighteenth century. Studies of London aldermen seem to suggest that fewer City businessmen were leaving commerce and investing in land after the Civil War and after the middle of the eighteenth century. My own data tells us nothing about the proportion of successful men who converted their fortunes into land during this period. It is entirely possible that an increasing number found other safe means to invest and that more rich men's sons and grandsons began to constitute permanent City dynasties. However, recent research suggests that aldermen are not necessarily a typical sample of all successful businessmen, and that a substantial number of great merchants or their sons continued to buy large landed estates and send their sons into parliament.[67] What the data on business entrants to the parliamentary elite shows is that significant numbers of commercial families continued to enter well into the nineteenth century, most of whom became landed. They also formed an increasing proportion of all entrants (see Table 3.5). The market price for estates continued to be driven up by increasing demand.[68]

For the eighteenth century the heightened differentiation in economic activity and more plentiful research materials make it possible to analyse the sources of commercial wealth in greater detail. We can break down the numbers of entrants into separate categories with more confidence. The 'West Indians', for example, were a comparatively new category. Although some planters acted as if they were English landed gentlemen temporarily living in an exotic locale, even when they were not engaged directly in mercantile pursuits, they were neck deep in the slave trade. Many combined landed and business activities, even if few were purely commercial men. The rise of John Bromley was so precipitous that 'the obscurity of his origins became the stuff of legend'.[69] What is not in doubt is that great fortunes could be made, as the incomes of the Beckfords or Edward Morant, who received £20,000 p.a. from his estates in Jamaica in the mid-eighteenth century, suggest.[70] A number of such families gained peerages – the Bromleys as early as 1741. The Freeman-Thomases eventually achieved a marquessate.

The gradual return of creole families took place throughout the later seventeenth and eighteenth centuries. The peak decade for the establishment of West Indian families within the parliamentary elite was the 1740s, when three entered simultaneously. For the rest of the period they averaged one or two a decade between 1660 and 1820 though there were gaps, especially during the second half of the eighteenth century. West Indian MPs never formed a large source of new families. When one removes those who were already members of the elite before acquiring estates abroad and the men who were primarily London merchants with secondary interests in the West Indies, only thirteen governing families can be called West Indian in origin.

Though celebrated for their wealth as well as their vulgarity, nabobs were also not fertile in producing parliamentary families. This was not for want of trying, and a number of men made concerted bids to become founders, but only seven Englishmen of the East left a lasting elite dynasty behind them. Others of nabob origin enjoyed a secondary rise that benefited from the infusion of Indian riches. The largest fortunes were made in the decade after Plassey (1757) and the inrush of nabob MPs came in the 1760s through the 1780s. Most nabobs or their heirs sold up quickly.

The odd scrivener or two managed to found a parliamentary family in the medieval and Tudor periods. One fifteenth-century gentleman, appropriately named Scriven, was MP for Shrewsbury in 1407. He inherited a manor and the family produced several more MPs into the late seventeenth century. Some goldsmiths and usurers might also be considered paleo-bankers in the sixteenth and seventeenth centuries. The Ducies derived from a banker to Charles I, but the founder was equally engaged in mercantile activities. It was after the Restoration that important families whose fortunes were largely based in banking began to establish themselves, such as the Childs, Duncombes, Hoares and Vyners. Service banking expanded as the pace of commercial and industrial growth quickened during the eighteenth century, especially, as Figure 3.5 shows, during its last decades. Bankers peaked as a proportion of all new entrant families at one in ten in the period 1760–1819. Six families entered in the single decade of the 1790s. Not all came from London, as the Smiths' rise in Nottingham demonstrated. The Becketts were from York, the Handleys from Newark and the Rounds from Colchester. The business continued to provide the foundation for a dozen more new families in the nineteenth century, the last being the Fabers, who elected their first MP in 1900.

Brewers lived in a twilight zone – less respectable than bankers but superior to other industrialists. They fall into a peculiar category, shared perhaps with builders, mustard-makers, shipowners, distillers, cigarette manufacturers and newspaper tycoons. Historians differ about the extent to which social acceptance was conferred on them by the landed elite.[71] Technological change in the industry in the early eighteenth century lent itself to mass production and economies of scale. By mid-century some brewers had become really rich, well before the textile industry got off the ground. Perhaps the agricultural connection helped to make social intercourse with

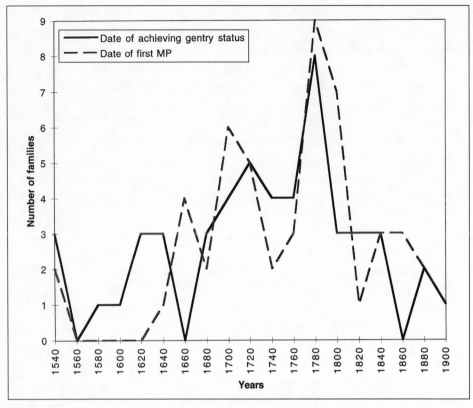

Figure 3.5 English 'banking' families' entry into the elite by date of achieving gentry status and date of first MP, 1540–1919 (per two decades)

the landowners easier. As with bankers, brewers and distillers continued to be associated with their businesses long after they were established in landed society.

The Tates were the first family with significant interests in brewing to become a landed parliamentary family (first MP 1487). The Ridgeway Earls of Londonderry (created 1623) were launched by an early Tudor brewer. Robert Smallwood (1545) was regularly styled a 'gentleman' and married a knight's daughter.[72] The Parsons (1685) were London brewers who purchased an estate under Charles II, while the Tufnells (1640) produced beer in Southwark and became landed by 1710. The big expansion in the number of important brewing families came between 1740 and 1820, a period which witnessed a steady flow of one or two a decade. Nineteenth-century brewers, though many of them were rich, were less likely than banking families to found parliamentary families.[73] The notion of a 'beerage' – Victorian peerages going to lots of brewers – is mythic. Banking families gathered far more titles and very rich brewing families such as the Whitbreads gained no honours. Brewers were absent from the grandees, unlike industrialists such as the Peels or the banking Barings.

Few families rose to parliamentary status from backgrounds such as distilling, contracting, shipowning, railways and newspapers. Only the Nicholsons (first MP 1866) rose wholly in the liquor business. Builders were very rare: Papillon (1674) and Cubitt (1847). Shipowners such as the Furnesses and Runcimans did rise very quickly to social acceptance and great wealth, but such cases were also scarce. The most successful railway family, the Brasseys, ended with grand country houses and an earldom (1911), but were almost alone in entering the elite solely on the basis of steam locomotion. Newspapers produced large fortunes very late, and the intimate connection of the business with politics helped to raise a few families such as the Berrys and Harmsworths rapidly.

Finally, we turn to industry. Two quasi-gentlemanly activities were mining and iron-making. Few new families entered by the former method, and, of these, tin and copper producers were more common than coal extractors. Minerals, in the main, raised landed families higher but did not establish them in the first place. Ironmasters were a different matter. This field was perhaps the most commonly entered both by new men and older landed families. Iron manufacturing raised one family to grandee status, the Foleys (1659), and given more time the Guests (1826) would have no doubt followed them. A number of important modern politicians were sponsored by wealth made in steel, including Baldwin and Whitelaw.

It was the textile industry, however, that not only formed the early focus of the industrial revolution but also produced a significant number of landed families in the eighteenth and nineteenth centuries. One of the first MPs to be a partner in a Manchester cotton firm was Samuel Touchet (MP 1761–68), but his family failed to sustain a presence in parliament. By the turn of the century many of the names famous in the history of the industry were entering the governing elite: Peel (first MP 1790), Arkwright (1813), Feilden (1832) and Pease (1832). In 1870 over 20% of the great landowners of Lancashire derived their wealth from the textile industry.[74] The gentry produced twenty-nine MPs in the county in the period 18–59 while cotton men held thirty-one.[75]

Later in the nineteenth century other industries began to fund parliamentary dynasties: printing, hosiery, carpets, glass, agricultural implements, brick-making and armaments among them. The first 'industrial' peer is said to have been Lord Belper in 1856. However, this is misleading. The Jacobean Robartes were tin-smelters. The Foleys were still making iron when their barony was conferred in 1712. John Strutt, who was apprenticed to his uncle, a substantial miller, had a son who was made a peer in 1821.[76]

The entry of industrial families into the landed and parliamentary elite became significant in the last two decades of the eighteenth century, when the early giants in the field began to purchase big estates and elect MPs. The rush came between 1820 and 1859 when twenty-four industrial families elected their first MPs. (See Table 3.4.) The next few decades, however, perhaps as a result of the depression in the business cycle in the 1870s, produced only one manufacturing parliamentary dynasty, the Chamberlains (1876). The pace picked up again in the 1880s and 1890s.

W.R. Rubinstein asserts that Britain's economy was primarily a service and commercial one, not dominated by manufacturing even at the height of the industrial era. He bases this proposition on research which seems to show that the great fortunes of the nineteenth century were earned in commerce, finance and service to the state, rather than in coal, iron and textiles. He further argues that this was reflected in the fact that industrialists were proportionally under-represented in political circles. Martin Wiener, Geoffrey Ingham and Lawrence Stone also believe the new elite was primarily composed of bankers and merchants and not industrialists. This idea supports the theory that signs of self-assertion by industry which would have radicalized and modernized English society were successfully opposed by a City–Bank–Treasury nexus, and that 'gentlemanly' culture enervated the British business elite. Jonathan Clark argues that Britain was closer to the continental regimes in its pre-industrial, non-industrial composition of the elite until as late as the 1870s.[77]

These assumptions about sources of recruitment are not supported by my study. As can be seen in Tables 3.3 and 3.4, industry (excluding brewing, shipping lines, railways, food production, cigarette makers, etc.) produced over one-fifth of all business entrants to the political elite in the early nineteenth century and nearly half during the mid-century. If one includes other commercial men who were not strictly financiers or merchants the proportions are between one-quarter and one-third and almost two-thirds (63%) respectively. Though industry and mining declined in the later nineteenth century, the total from the manufacturing and steam-driven sector remained over 60%. Harold Perkin and David Spring are right to challenge the Rubinstein/Stone thesis.[78] Moreover, these figures do not include Scotland and Ireland. Rubinstein himself admits that a disproportionate number of Scottish wealth-holders in 1870–1914 were chiefly engaged in manufacturing and industry.[79] Ireland did not produce many manufacturers, but there were some important ones such as the Guinnesses, Harlands and Mulhollands. English banking and mercantile fortunes of great proportions were still being made in the nineteenth century, such as those of the Loders, Loyds, Mathesons and Morrisons. However, industry was overtaking commerce and banking as the real generator of new entrants to the ruling class as early as 1820, and industrialists had been buying land extensively since the later eighteenth century.

Table 3.3 Number of English parliamentary families deriving fortunes from business (by date of achieving gentry status), 1700–1899

Origin of Fortune	1740–1779		1780–1819		1820–1859		1860–1899	
Finance and Commerce	40	78.4%	33	68.7%	16	37.2%	13	39.4%
Brewing and Ships, etc.	6	11.8%	6	12.5%	6	14.0%	9	27.3%
Industry and Mining	5	9.8%	9	18.7%	21	48.8%	11	33.3%
Total	51		48		43		33	

Table 3.4 Number of English parliamentary families deriving fortunes from business (by date of first MP), 1700–1899

Origin of Fortune	1740–1779		1780–1819		1820–1859		1860–1899	
Finance and Commerce	37	77.1%	47	77.1%	19	36.5%	15	33.3%
Brewing and Ships, etc.	7	14.6%	3	4.9%	9	17.3%	17	37.8%
Industry and Mining	4	8.3%	11	18.0%	24	46.2	13	28.9%
Total	48		61		52		45	

An Open Elite?

John Cannon has described the eighteenth-century House of Commons as 'one of the most exclusive ruling elites in human history'.[80] This is a rather difficult statement to assess, since we have no easy means of making comparisons with other cultures across the millennia. Ian Christie has shown that a large and increasing proportion of the eighteenth-century Commons was composed of 'new men', and in addition many MPs were only a generation or two away from plebeian origins.[81] Perhaps that constitutes 'exclusivity' in comparison to other elected assemblies, but the emphasis on quarterings at the Hapsburg Court and on lineage among the Japanese *daimyo*, for example, make one wonder whether Cannon has not overstated his case.

Even more sweeping assertions about the exclusivity of the English elite come from the pen of Lawrence Stone. His renown as a scholar makes his judgements influential. His data on country house ownership in Northumberland and Northamptonshire in

1540–1880 show that the presence of business entrants was always 'negligible', while in Hertfordshire, close to London, there were more, but he sees them as 'merely transients'.[82] He believes businessmen did not buy as much land nor aspire to the trappings of gentility in the way that men from more genteel backgrounds such as office and the professions did. He argues that the theory of a substantial circulation of elites from land into trade and back into land is not borne out by the evidence. 'The traditional concept of an open elite – open to large-scale infiltration by merchant wealth – is dead.' No more 'than a thin trickle' of merchants were buying country houses and sustaining the status and prestige of landed gentlemen. 'The unity of English elite society was a unity of the land and the professions, only marginally of the land and businessmen, and not at all of land and industry.'[83]

This attack on the 'open elite' thesis is the most formidable and influential ever made. Though scholars who have spent their careers studying the English governing and mercantile classes have expressed serious reservations about his methodology and findings, many historians have accepted the idea of a closed elite and incorporated Stone's work into their publications.[84]

Stone's thesis rests on the finding that over a 340-year period only one-third of the new entrants in his sample were businessmen: 40% in the home county of Hertfordshire (where many sold out very soon after purchase in any case), 24% in Northumberland and 14% in Northamptonshire.[85] Of course, others than myself have already noted that what amounts to one-third of his sample is actually quite a high figure for penetration to the upper reaches of a traditionalist landed aristocracy and more than enough to justify the term 'open'.[86] While Stone sees the Stuart century, especially after 1660, as a period of exclusion when the boundaries of the elite became far less porous, my data reveals commercial wealth flowing ever more freely and swiftly into the ruling class.[87]

Table 3.5 shows how important a contribution the world of business made to the renewal and expansion of the elite. If one counts by the date of social origins, the figure for the total proportion of business origins of all parliamentary families from 1400 to 1879 is 56%. Notice the importance from the very beginning of business entrants. Also contrast the proportions of business entrants compared to the professions. Table 3.6 shows, contra Stone, that businessmen were not significantly more liable to quick disappearances from the elite than 'official' or 'professional' families. The data show that most business families were as stable as those derived from other non-landed sources.[88]

Stone acknowledges that many 'parish' gentry who were later able to purchase a country house large enough to qualify for inclusion in his study may have originally entered the gentry via business, and that most of his 'landed' entrants had non-landed wealth in their backgrounds. In Hertfordshire only 5% of his elite families were

Table 3.5 Percentage of new entrants to the English parliamentary and country house elites by social origins, 1386–1879[89]

In each column the figures in bold print are from my study and the figures on the right are taken from the Stones' *An Open Elite?*, Table 6.2

Origin of Fortune	1386–1579		1580–1639		1640–99		1700–59		1760–1819		1820–79	
Land	**47**	29	**51**	45	**32**	35	**32**	27	**19**	41	**13**	42
Office	**7**	44	**7**	19	**4**	13	**2**	15	**8**	8	**0**	7
Law*	**11**	10	**15**	16	**22**	16	**17**	31	**26**	11	**19**	8
Business	**27**	17	**25**	19	**42**	36	**49**	27	**46**	41	**68**	43
Unknown	**8**		**.6**		**.6**		**0**		**1**		**0**	

* Includes the other professions, but three-quarters were lawyers or judges.

Table 3.6 Years between first and last MP for all English parliamentary families by social origins, 1400–1879

	1–50 yrs	51–100 yrs	101+ yrs	201+yrs	T %
Land	10.0	12.5	20.4	57.1	100
Office	11.4	33.3	30.5	24.8	100
Law	23.9	23.9	26.5	25.7	100
Business	22.5	28.8	29.5	19.2	100

landed for more than three generations without some non-landed source of wealth. In Northamptonshire 23% were purely landed. If one looks at the fathers of purchasers of houses, Stone's data show a picture that 'more closely approximates to the traditional paradigm about the English landed elite'.[90] The acceptance that there was always a strong infiltration of commercial entrants among the middling and lesser gentry suggests that the Stone thesis rests on insubstantial foundations. The Springs put it best: 'An open gentry is an open elite.'[91]

How can Stone's conclusions and my findings be so far apart? First, as noted in Chapter One, Stone's sample of country house owners dipped deeper into the gentry than did the parliamentary elite, so to some degree we are looking at different elites. However, since Stone and most other observers agree that one finds higher rates of social mobility the further down one moves on the social scale, one expects to find *fewer* business entrants at the rarefied level of the governing class. But just the reverse is the case. Other studies have also concluded that a large and steady turnover took place in the landed elite, much of it recruited from the world of business.[92] Stone's idea of using country house ownership to identify the elite was an ingenious one, but he underestimated the flaws of such a method of measurement. His system of calculating the size of ground plans was open to serious errors.[93] Even assuming the sizes of the houses were correctly calibrated, the proposition that a house over a certain size was automatically connected to a large landed estate, while smaller houses had smaller estates, has little objective or statistical basis of support. Architectural experts such as Colin Platt and Malcolm Airs note that the evidence for the sixteenth and seventeenth centuries shows size and expenditure on country houses varied over time and among families far more than Stone assumed. While certain families spent heavily and built prodigiously, many others constructed more modest dwellings. The record of poor landed families who clung to large houses and new rich who lived in small ones is there to see for anyone who browses through books on architectural history. Servants' quarters peregrinated about, causing different footplates to emerge in different periods. Building manias could lead men to spend more on houses than they could afford – and thus created a false image of their true wealth and standing.[94]

Another problem with the Stones' work relates to multiple ownership of houses and possession of estates in several counties, as the list of twenty houses owned by the Montagu family of Northamptonshire, acquired at different times and by different methods, suggests.[95] Barbara English's study shows how fraught with complex stories of inheritance, mysterious arrivals and dramatic disappearances even a small selection of estate histories can be.[96]

Equally risky was Stone's decision to use only three counties in his study, and the choice of the three, even he admits, was probably unrepresentative.[97] It has long been known that Hertfordshire had few old families, which was not true of some other home counties.[98] Historians have also noticed that it was easier to make fortunes rapidly and in larger amounts in port towns such as Ipswich or Bristol than in inland cities such as Northampton; since the majority of English counties have access to the sea, this makes his choice of a landlocked midland shire as typical of rural England dubious.[99] Stone admits that to generalize from the experiences of three highly divergent counties is almost meaningless, yet throughout his book he speaks of the *national* experience, sometimes using evidence from only *one* of his counties.[100] The absence of an industrial shire such as Lancashire, Staffordshire or the West Riding, and of a coastal county such as Suffolk, Somerset or Devon, and the inclusion of Hertfordshire instead of Surrey or Kent, not to mention the total unsuitability of Northumberland, renders many of Stone's general conclusions open to serious doubt.[101]

The statistical data presented above have shown the extent to which the governing order was open to men rising from a variety of backgrounds. What this analysis cannot do is show how fully the business community formed a self-conscious class or penetrated into the culture of the parliamentary elite.[102] But the diversity of evidence over different centuries, from different regions and relating to different levels within the elite shows that the notion of landed exclusivity in terms of recruitment is false.

The statistical data on parliamentary families do show that there was a symbiosis between landed society and wealth created in business, focused in parliament, which served as a mechanism to confer acceptance on the freshly minted families and to integrate new and old money. Both types of wealth were largely represented there from the Middle Ages until the First World War. One of the great contributions of the *History of Parliament* is to unveil the robust and acquisitive governing class heavily engaged in capitalistic agriculture, foreign export and industrial development. Landed society grasped early on the fact that success for their country and grandeur for themselves lay in promoting English economic interests beyond the seas. Their pursuit of a commercial foreign policy was not necessarily imposed upon them by a powerful bourgeoisie. No doubt some blimpish twits sat in the Commons, but most of the landed gentlemen could comprehend the essentials of the situation for themselves. A ruling class does not have to listen to the voices outside its ranks in order to serve interests other than its own. Of course, it did not hurt to have a constant inflow of men with commercial backgrounds entering their councils and county communities. It is hard to believe that this did not contribute to the stability of the established property-owning elite in England and also promote interest and support from the ruling class for commercial legislation and foreign policy.

A number of leading historians have noticed the 'close and surprisingly harmonious relationship between a landed ruling class and a broad commercial community'.[103] Parliament provided the skeleton on which the social organism metamorphosed through changing stages in politics and the economy. It legitimated the authority and leadership of the landed class but fused it with new money and new men. The robust sense of self-importance of the Commons and its mixed composition helped merge the untitled great landowners and the big bourgeoisie, preventing the concept of three separate estates developing in England.[104]

The aperture into the elite was like a Dutch door that was more widely open at the bottom than at the top. This created an illusion of greater social mobility than actually existed. It was well known that not just the recently risen Bouveries, Peels and Smiths (Carrington) sprang from business backgrounds. The Russells began as wine merchants; the Hobarts were country attorneys; the Foleys were ironmasters; the Robartes were in the tin trade; the first Fox began as a footman; the Lascelles were slave owners; the Spencers were sheepmasters; Clive was a nabob; the Eliots were practically pirates. Although attempts were made even in the best houses to concoct false pedigrees, the origins of many families were too well known to conceal and other families never made the attempt. It was impossible to imagine rising to ducal status in a single bound, but it was not beyond reason to hope that one could place a son's foot on the next rung of the ladder that led there. The knowledge that there was no system of quarterings and that wealth ultimately counted for more than lineage was a tremendous incentive to excel. A false consciousness that society was more egalitarian than was actually the case proved useful in maintaining stability.[105] A belief in social mobility requires only a few instances to make it credible. Self-delusion is commonplace.

However, the 'five or fewer' category of parliamentary families was genuinely open. If one lifted the roof on the apparently genteel assembly of country gentlemen at Westminster, one found a steady flow of *ci-devant* hatters, coal fitters, bankers and lord mayors. Moreover, the laments of the established elite who deplored the influx of newcomers into the elite were not *cris de coeur* but clichés, ritualistic mantras. It is rare to find evidence of serious men of affairs among the governing class making snide remarks about newcomers. Two of the most celebrated instances of crass snobbery that erupted in the House of Lords – Lord Arundell's insult of 1621 directed at the 1st Lord Spencer for his sheep-pen origins and the Duke of Grafton's 1779 sneer at Lord Thurlow's plebian ancestry – boomeranged with crushing retorts from the original targets.[106] An Elizabethan country gentleman of Norman ancestry noted with approval the well-bred qualities 'and other actions fitting a gentleman well affected to his God, Prince and Country' displayed by the son of a newly landed neighbour whose fortune had been made as a merchant.[107] The 8th Duke of Argyll, a Victorian grandee, whose lineage was genuinely lost in the mists of time, noted that the English aristocracy 'never had any vulgar prejudice against "new men"'. Sir Lewis Namier, who was a master of eighteenth-century social nuances, believed that energy and wealth were always respected by aristocratic society: 'Trade was never despised.'[108] Acceptance into the elite for those able to establish a hereditary presence in either house of parliament was usually rapid. The old nobility did not feel threatened because they could be promoted higher in the peerage, and the new entrants only wished to emulate them and sought acceptance and approval, which actually heightened the security and authority of older families. This in turn strengthened the whole aristocratic system by bringing in fresh ideas, defusing tension arising from social climbers and making the old families feel safe. The stream of business entrants into the elite flowed through the course of English history, broadening and deepening as it went.

Chapter 4
Wales, Scotland and Ireland

The geography of Britain is exceptionally varied. Widely different landscapes and ecologies exist in a narrow compass. The histories of Wales, Scotland and Ireland matched the platforms on which they were set, producing unique cultures. England's comparatively large size and imperial temperament imposed increasing uniformity on its neighbours, although historians disagree about the rate of homogenization, the extent of backwash in the English homeland owing to conquest and absorption, and the degree to which a genuine merger of the disparate nations was ever accomplished. The contradictions of interpenetration are reflected in the characters of the Welsh, Scottish and Irish elites. This chapter examines the separate origins of the parliamentary elites of the two kingdoms and the principality that shared the British archipelago with the aggressive, indeed overwhelming, English state. Did integration merge the aristocracies or were the distinctive characteristics of each country preserved by leading families who may have taken on an 'English' patina but retained native cores? One test of the extent of assimilation is to analyse the type and rate of new entrants to the different elites. The political families in Wales, Scotland and Ireland clearly took their shape in drastically different ways, but if there was a merger then at what point did they begin to become a *British* elite? Were they open or closed? Did they respond similarly to the challenges of the industrial age, rising nationalism and democracy?

Wales

During the Middle Ages the leading families of Wales did not practise primogeniture. Although the convulsions of the late medieval period considerably reduced the numbers of the old feudal aristocracy, it was the partability of inheritance that led to the fragmentation of princely and noble houses. It is estimated that by the time of the Union in the mid-sixteenth century some three-quarters of the population, mostly small peasant proprietors, were 'bonheddig' – men with gentle pedigrees. Genealogies were of vital importance and more emphasis was placed on lineage by a wider proportion of the population than anywhere else in the British Isles.[1]

This unusual situation was transformed by the decline of gavelkind inheritance between the fourteenth and seventeenth centuries which led to the gradual consolidation of land into larger estates owned by individuals and not clans, and by the establishment of Welsh parliamentary seats in 1542. After the mid-sixteenth century a new means of asserting status by election to parliament made it possible for established and ambitious families to reinforce their mastery over their communities and to lift themselves above the broad plateau of Welsh landed society.[2] Nowhere else in the British Isles was the gap in wealth between families with MPs and those without greater than in Wales. Among those listed in Bateman in 1883 the average income of parliamentary dynasties was well over three times as high as that of non-elite families.[3] In England and Ireland the ratio was closer to two to one and in Scotland less than three to one. Because few peerages were granted to Welshmen subsequent to the Union and the dilution of ancient pedigrees was so ubiquitous, election to the Commons played an especially important role in gaining social recognition. Repeatedly electing parliament men became the mark of leading families. Being knight of a shire carried more prestige in Wales than it did in Ireland, Scotland or England.[4]

The Welsh elite rapidly adapted to the English parliamentary system and eagerly sought seats. This phenomenon occurred at the same time as the expansion of landed participation in parliament by the English governing class, which reinforced the increasingly patrician nature of the lower house under Elizabeth I. The Welsh quickly branched out to sit for English seats as well. This was necessary because only one knight sat for each of the thirteen county seats (except for Monmouthshire) and thirteen boroughs were single member constituencies as well. Wales had considerably fewer seats *per capita* than England. The electorates were tiny. Five counties had fewer than 1,000 voters in the eighteenth century, with a total of 21,000 for the whole country.[5]

The Welsh parliamentary elite were willing to use coercion, intimidation and violence on a greater scale than their English counterparts to ensure electoral obedience. The status stakes were high. Fewer contests took place than across the border in part because in some counties one family was indisputably the most powerful and in others because the lesser gentry were more subservient and feudal loyalty was more ingrained. Some families put up spectacularly long shows of dominance. Welshmen called such claims to electoral preferment 'hereditary'. Forty-one Herberts sat for Wales as MPs between 1542 and 1895.[6] The Mostyns represented Flintshire continuously from 1747 to 1837. Individual magnates often enjoyed exceptionally long tenures of up to sixty years in the Commons.

About eighty families dominated Welsh political and social life. They elected 542 MPs (227 before 1660 and 332 in 1660–1945) with 4,545 years of combined service between 1660 and 1945. Very few Welsh families produced MPs for Irish or Scottish seats, although seventy MPs sat for English constituencies between 1660 and 1945. Although the population of Wales was tiny in comparison with England (*c.* 325,000 compared to 5,000,000 in the late seventeenth century), the number of elite families as a proportion of the population was even smaller. Out of all English and Welsh elite MPs and peers in the post-Restoration period the latter produced 4% of the total, considerably less than the approximately 6 or 7% Wales represented in the joint populations. Years of service was closer at 5%. Some of the under-representation was due to the fact that a few Scottish families, such as those of Lords Bute and Cawdor, inherited property in Wales and sat for Welsh seats, and some families, such as the Pembrokes and Beauforts, whose estates were originally largely Welsh established themselves as principally English in orientation and residence. Native elite families filled nearly four-fifths of all Welsh seats in 1660 and the proportion stayed above 74% from the Restoration to the Reform Act of 1832.[7] A number of the remaining seats were filled by English or Scottish elite families with estates in Wales. Sometimes above 90% of the Welsh representation was in elite hands.[8] The proportion was over 80% as late as 1865.

Nearly half (44%) of the Welsh elite families elected three to five MPs, though they produced an average of only 16% of all Welsh elite MPs. Most of these families constituted the greater squirarchy beneath the magnates. Among the 'six-plus' families about one in five produced more than fifteen legislators.[9] This magnate group's share of the total number of elite MPs was very large, ranging above 40% in the late seventeenth and early eighteenth centuries and again in 1780–1832. They elected 60% in 1830, the peak period of dominance of the parliamentary representation of Wales by magnate families. Of course, the big dynasties were at a disadvantage in producing larger numbers of MPs vis-à-vis ancient English families because the Union only took place in the mid-sixteenth century.

The Welsh elite was distinguished from its counterparts in the other kingdoms by a number of special characteristics. Its members clung longer to traditional practices and met with less of a challenge from middle-class urban elites who hardly existed in Wales until the nineteenth century. Bards still wandered from mansion to mansion as late as 1720 and some gentle families did not adopt a surname until the same period.[10] As one might expect, the lineages of the parliamentary families were mostly quite old. Some claimed descent from Roman emperors, Trojan warriors or the sons of Noah, and it was said that the Trevor genealogy soared 'into the clouds like Jack's beanstalk, and a body climbing it to the top might find himself in Eden garden'.[11]

Because pedigrees were so important in Welsh society, for legal as well as social reasons, modern scholars are inclined to give some credence to princely descents from the 900s or earlier. The Trevors seem genuinely to derive from a tenth-century

Table 4.1 Example of a Welsh parliamentary family

MOSTYN

Peter Mostyn MP Flintshire 1545; Flint Boroughs 1558	**Younger Son**
William Mostyn MP Flintshire 1554 1554 1572	**Head**
Sir Thomas Mostyn MP Flintshire 1572	**Head**
Sir Roger Mostyn MP Flintshire 1621	**Head**
John Mostyn MP Anglesey 1624; Flintshire 1640–43	**Younger Son**
Sir Thomas Mostyn, 2nd Baronet MP Caernarvon 1679–81	**Head**
Thomas Mostyn MP Flint Boroughs 1698–1702; Flintshire 1702–05	**Younger Son**
Sir Roger Mostyn, 3rd Baronet MP Flintshire 1701–02; Cheshire 1702–05; Flint Boroughs 1705–08; Flintshire 1708–13; Flint Boroughs 1713–15; Flintshire 1715–34	**Head**
Sir Thomas Mostyn, 4th Baronet MP Flintshire 1734–41, 1747–58	**Head**
John Mostyn MP Malton 1741–68	**Younger Son**
Savage Mostyn MP Weobley 1747–57	**Younger Son**
Sir Roger Mostyn, 5th Baronet MP Flintshire 1758–96	**Head**
Sir Thomas Mostyn, 6th Baronet MP Flintshire 1796–97, 1799–1831	**Head**
Edward Lloyd, 1st Baron Mostyn MP Flint Boroughs 1806–07; Beaumaris 1807–12; Flint Boroughs 1812–31; HLds 1831–54	**Head**
Edward Lloyd-Mostyn, 2nd Baron Mostyn MP Flintshire 1831–37, 1841–42; Lichfield 1846–47; Flintshire 1847–54; HLds 1854–84	**Head**
Thomas Lloyd-Mostyn MP Flintshire 1854–56	**Eldest Son**
Llewelyn Lloyd-Mostyn, 3rd Baron Mostyn HLds 1884–1929	**Head**
Edward Lloyd-Mostyn, 4th Baron Mostyn HLds 1929–45	**Head**

ancestor and acquired their seat at Brynkinalt in the eleventh century. The Kemys family were Normans in Gwent by 1091. The Pryses of Gogerddan have been prominent in Cardiganshire politics and society for nine hundred years.[12] Emphasis on lineage also meant that kinship ties were often stronger than in England. A 'Welsh cousin' could be quite a distant relative connected only by marriage. These clan-like webs were, however, of political substance.[13]

The proportion of Welsh elite MPs from families holding gentry status since the Middle Ages (pre-1485) was very high, running over 80% from the Restoration to as late as 1870. There were periods, especially the second half of the eighteenth century, when this dropped to about two-thirds but then rose again. Far fewer English and Irish MPs after 1660 came from medieval families. The Scottish elite produced many MPs of ancient lineage, but in the early eighteenth century, again after 1800, and between 1840 and 1900 the proportion of Welsh MPs with medieval social origins exceeded even that of the Scots.

In the 1870s, 672 individuals owned estates of over 1,000 acres in Wales.[14] Incomes were usually much lower than in England. A county member in the sixteenth century might hold lands worth only £10 a year, substantially below the level of most English shire knights.[15] In England two-thirds of the great landowners listed in Bateman were members of the governing class, while in Wales only a little more than one-third elected three or more MPs. The main beneficiaries of Reformation land redistribution were the old families. In the seventeenth and eighteenth centuries the big estates in Wales continued to be enlarged at the expense of smaller ones.[16] In Wales, the more ancient one's pedigree, the more likely one was to be rich and have political authority.

Peers were scarce in Wales, and few Welshmen ever received the orders of the Garter, Thistle or Patrick.[17] Only about a dozen families stood out above the rest of elite society like high rock formations on a flat mesa. If the same criteria applied to create the list of English grandee families in Chapter Two are used for Wales, only five families qualify: Bulkeley, Hanbury-Tracy, Morgan, Williams Wynn and Wyndham-Quin. None met the mark in all five categories. A reduced standard of 150 years' service combined for peers and MPs makes more sense in light of regional conditions, and since only a handful of families gained Garters or cabinet posts, two or more lords lieutenant seems enough to qualify for category three. This modification adds seven more families: Mansel, Mostyn, Owen, Pennant, Phillips, Vaughan (Carbery) and Wynne. Even with these dispensations the system misses some Cymric dynasties who ought to be counted in terms of their status as magnates *in* the principality. The Myddeltons, Pryses, Rices and Vaughans (Lisburne) should be added. The Baileys, nineteenth-century ironmasters, were making a strong showing at the end but had insufficient time to gain momentum.[18] The dropping-away of many lesser gentry and the consolidation of the larger estates tended to produce an elite with a unique profile, unlike that found in England or Scotland.

About one-quarter of all Welsh MPs between 1660 and 1830 came from the twelve grandee families. This was a higher level (25% compared to 19%) than the English top elite families achieved in the seventeenth century, and is comparable to the English rate in the first half of the eighteenth century. However, the Welsh grandees garnered nearly one-third of all Welsh seats in the second half of that century, seven points higher than their English counterparts. Except for the period 1754–90, the twelve Welsh families were usually behind the Scottish grandees, who more consistently achieved an average above one-quarter of all the Scottish seats from 1715 to 1830.

The Welsh elite was unusually stable even outside the circle of grandees. Thirty of the eighty families elected their first MP before 1560, and half had done so by 1600.

Many of those who did not elect an MP until later came from long-established landed dynasties. If one counts families who retained a continuous name and residence even when their estates passed through an heiress, the turnover rate among the Welsh elite shows hardly any unusual disturbance during the 'demographic crisis' of the late seventeenth and early eighteenth centuries. Only four Welsh families with three or more MPs before 1660 failed to produce MPs afterwards. Between 1660 and 1860 no more than six elite families disappeared in any two-decade period, a peak falling in 1700–19, but six also departed in 1760–79 and five in 1800–19 and 1840–59. Only two disappeared in 1740–59 and 1780–99.[19] If one uses the date of first MP for new families, the peak decades were 1660 to 1679 when six new families entered; there was only one in the last part of the seventeenth century, with two in the early 1700s, four in 1720–39, and two in 1740–59. If one counts entry by the date when a family achieved social prominence through landholding and lineage, only three elite families were 'new' between 1660 and 1800.[20]

Historians paint a somewhat contradictory picture about the importance of lineage in marriage partners and in the admission of newcomers to the established Welsh elite. Some have portrayed a ruling class that placed far more importance on ancestry in the selection of mates than their English peers, while others see Welsh society, at least from the sixteenth century, as an 'open elite' with 'no prejudices against commerce or industrial exploitation'. Philip Jenkins notes, 'It is remarkable to see how easily the new industrialists were absorbed into the existing social structure,' as JPs, MPs and in marriage.[21] During the Middle Ages hostility existed between the native princely families and the newly arrived Anglo-Norman elite, and this lasted into the sixteenth century.[22] But by and large frequent marriage oiled integration and absorption. New entrants to the parliamentary elite after that period were few and far between. Most of those who did manage to found new families gained fortunes in business and were accepted quickly, but there were not many of them.

Office-holding and the professions produced relatively few new entrants. Welshmen on the make were liable to leave for England, such as the founder of the Cecil dynasty, or Henry VII for that matter. Normally governmental and military service by Welshmen was not a conduit into the elite in any period.

The Church produced two families: the Baylys and the Barlows sprang from the loins of bishops. No family made their fortune as physicians or in any similar profession. The law produced only seven families.[23] Welsh attorneys could rise from quite humble backgrounds to gentry status.[24] The editor of the *History of Parliament* for 1790 to 1820 noted that John Edwards, a prosperous attorney who was elected shire knight for Glamorgan in 1818, was accepted into the landed elite with a rapidity 'probably without parallel' in the rest of Britain.[25] However, most lawyers claimed princely or noble descents, although in the case of the Williamses of Gwernyfed the family had sunk to yeoman status until the decline was reversed by one who became an MP in 1584 and judge of the King's Bench.[26] The total of 15% of the Welsh elite coming from official or professional backgrounds was consistently much lower than the English experience.

Only one family in the Welsh elite acquired a fortune as West Indian planters (the Pennants of Penrhyn), and none as nabobs, clothiers, tradesmen, brewers or shipowners. One banking family, the Lloyds (though gentry in fifteenth-century Wales), rose in Birmingham and London and have been counted as an English family for the purposes of this study. However, some of the most important parliamentary families in Wales did arise from business backgrounds. The Laugharnes of St Brides, Pembrokeshire, were merchants in the later Middle Ages. The Myddeltons were modest gentry lifted to spectacular wealth by a grocer in London during the reign of James I. They purchased Chirk in 1595 and became the largest landowners in Denbighshire. The McLarens were founded by the son of a farmer apprenticed as a draper who became an enormously successful merchant in the mid-nineteenth century; they purchased Bodnant and acquired a peerage, electing seven MPs between 1865 and 1974. But as with office and the professions the contributions of business in creating new families was modest – no more than 10% of the parliamentary elite. It is surprising that few new families emerged from the industrial growth of the eighteenth and nineteenth centuries. Those that did, notably the Guests and the Vivians, quickly established themselves as English and are counted as such. The Hanbury family was heavily engaged in the iron industry in the seventeenth and eighteenth centuries, and the Baileys were made by coal and iron. The Bruce family (originally Knight) became wealthy businessmen engaged in steel and railways in the mid-nineteenth century, and gained a peerage in 1873. They had been gentry, however, who purchased the estate which produced the mineral wealth that made them really rich in 1747, a century before coal was discovered there.[27]

Perhaps it was the sense of security imparted by demi-royal lineages and exceptional control over the electoral system which made the Welsh elite appear welcoming to the few new families able to penetrate into their midst. This sense of command was being silently eroded, however, from as early as the seventeenth century. As the big estates were enlarged at the expense of the smaller squires, the great landowners became more remote and Olympian figures. The lesser gentry who served as social buffers in England largely disappeared in Wales, and the magnates and their tenantry drifted apart. London politics and society drew the parliamentary elite away from Wales physically.[28] Although some historians point out that in the sixteenth and seventeenth centuries the Welsh elite actually strengthened their position by leading their country into the world of English speech and accepting the Reformation, this advantage began to dissipate as they detached themselves from the values and language of the national culture. Some members of the elite continued to speak Welsh until the mid-eighteenth century and even later, but education and marriage became increasingly an English experience for them. 'Welsh' became a synonym for 'drunken, ignorant, and superstitious'.[29] The growing strength of Methodism and other nonconformist sects in the eighteenth and nineteenth centuries created a wide gulf of misconception and ultimately made communication between the elite and the people difficult.

This model of cultural divorce has been challenged by Matthew Cragoe in his study of the Carmarthenshire elite from 1832 to 1895.[30] He argues that landowners remained more popular than has been assumed and agriculture was less commercialized. His work is a useful corrective to the exaggerated picture of neglect of Welsh culture by the native elite that in part derives from anti-aristocratic propaganda spread by radicals for political purposes. The grip retained by landed society on the electoral system actually strengthened, as the data on the number of seats held by the grandees indicates. The Welsh electorate in the nineteenth century remained tiny. Due to lack of contests only 546 people voted in 1826 and none in 1830.[31] Unlike in England, where the crazy-quilt franchise gave many sections of society a voice even in the unreformed system and where there was a strong sense of common interest between the landed elite and both tenants and businessmen, the Welsh electoral structure created an almost colonial atmosphere with the arrogance and bitterness that such environments can breed.

The 1832 Reform Act left the political control of the elite largely unimpaired in the counties and had only a limited effect in the boroughs. Even so the percentage of Welsh seats filled by the elite dropped to 69 in 1835, although there was a recovery to 81% by 1865. Some landowning families previously barred from Westminster by the dearth of constituencies in the principality gained election when the counties were given two seats. Only 4,352 Welshmen went to the polls in 1859, but the rise of a powerful radical movement fuelled by class resentment and religious enthusiasm made 'landlordism' and the Anglican religion of elite culture the central issue in Welsh politics in a way that never emerged in England and that was more akin to the Irish experience. The elite responded with coercion and some evictions.[32] The Second Reform Act of 1867 nearly doubled the franchise in Wales. Some electorates in Welsh boroughs increased by 250%, and the total number of voters topped 112,000 by 1871.[33] The massive industrialization of the south also menaced landed supremacy. Modern Welsh nationalism was budding. In 1865 fourteen of the fifteen county seats were held by landed aristocrats. In 1868 this fell to eleven and in 1880 to nine. A similar decline took place in the boroughs.[34] The percentage of seats held by the elite dropped from over eighty to sixty in 1870, forty-eight in 1880 after the passage of the Ballot Act, and fifteen by 1895. The political disappearance rate among the Welsh elite had averaged 4.4 families per two decades from 1660 to 1859, but now it leapt to

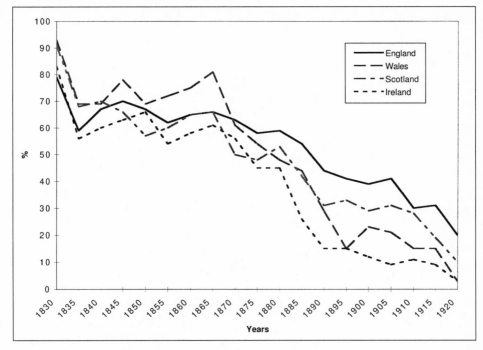

Figure 4.1 Proportion of English, Welsh, Scottish and Irish seats in the House of Commons held by members of the parliamentary elite, 1830–1920

a dozen between 1860 and 1879 (nine of these after 1865). Eight more faded in 1880–99, and one-quarter of all the elite families vanished from parliament in the years immediately after the Second Reform Act. New entrants virtually ceased after 1820. Few traditional elite families survived the 1885 election, which carried off even Sir Watkin Williams Wynn in Denbighshire. Virtually all were gone by the 1890s.

Not surprisingly, many Welsh landlords began to sell their property on a scale unparalleled in England. After the First World War big landed estates largely disappeared. In recent years only a handful of substantial ones remained.[35] The Tory party evaporated as a viable force in Welsh politics, and unlike in England, Scotland and Northern Ireland, members of the elite almost never entered the electoral process in the twentieth century, or when they did, like the 7th and 8th Lords Dynevor (MPs 1910–35), they sat for English constituencies. In 1923, when the 7th Earl of Lisburne stood for Cardiganshire where his family had been a dominant force for centuries, he came in third place and never ventured into politics again.[36] Some signs during the 1940s and 1950s suggested old animosities were being forgotten, but unlike in Scotland this movement had no political legs.[37]

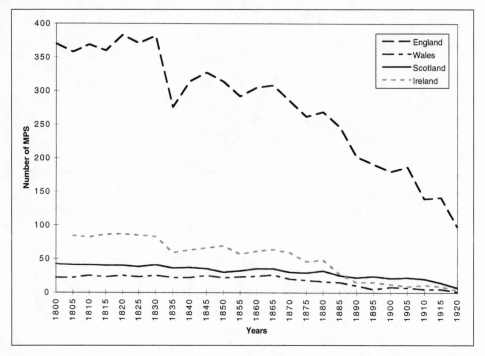

Figure 4.2 Number of MPs sitting for English, Welsh, Scottish and Irish seats in the House of Commons who were members of the parliamentary elite, 1800–1920

Scotland

Though an ancient institution first mentioned in Scottish records in 1235, parliament was never as important north of the Tweed as it was to the south. The Scots, however, developed unique institutional structures, although these have been thinly explored by historians. Both a parliament and a convention of estates (in which only the burghs – not always the same ones as in parliament – were represented) functioned independently with overlapping responsibilities and meetings interspersed with each other. Parliament was unicameral, developed a peculiar form of steering committee, incorporated ministers of the Crown *ex officio*, and remained peripatetic until settling permanently in Edinburgh in the 1630s.

The original council consisted of great nobles and churchmen, but burgh representatives were summoned with increasing regularity in the fourteenth century. The gradual emergence in the fifteenth century of a titled, parliamentary peerage separated this group more clearly from the lesser barons. Becoming a lord of parliament henceforth gave special standing to certain families.[38] Those landowners who did not qualify for this mark of honour became known as lairds. Poor attendance among this estate led in 1587 to the creation of elected shire commissioners who could act as representatives of their brethren.

Parliament was never a forum for continuous debate. Although during the fifteenth century a tradition of annual meetings arose, this gradually lapsed. Meetings in the sixteenth and early seventeenth centuries were spasmodic and short. The centre of public life lay elsewhere. After the departure of James VI for London in 1603 and the disappearance of a Scottish Court, however, parliament emerged as the central national institution and began to resist royal policies successfully. A large new hall near St Giles Kirk was begun in 1632 (completed in 1639), which symbolized this change. During the 1640s parliament was freed from the executive control of the Lords of Articles and mobilized Scotland for war. Compared to most continental assemblies in the seventeenth century parliament became a remarkably powerful institution. In 1639 Sir James Balfour spoke of 'this grate parliament Long wished for. . . . for setling all things both in kirke and stait'. The nobles used parliament to direct the fate of the nation in the critical months between October 1659 and April 1660. Government control was further reduced after 1689. Meetings became more frequent and the house became lively, even rowdy.[39]

Serious consideration was given by James VI and I to a union of the Scottish and English parliaments. Cromwell briefly did merge them. Debate about possible changes continued on and off during the Restoration period. This is not the place to discuss the motives of either the English or Scottish politicians in the final consummation of the kingdoms. There is ample controversy, and much finger-pointing still goes on.[40] The Union of 1707 extinguished the life of the Scottish parliament, and the landed elite was more or less incorporated into the Westminster assembly if not into the English social system. After 1707 Scotland sent forty-five MPs to London, and only sixteen representative peers.

Recent research indicates that the Scottish parliament demonstrated more vigour and independence than was once assumed. The 'Riding', when members processed to and from Holyrood Palace to the meeting place on opening and closing days, produced intense acrimony over status and precedence. Precarious finances and declining kinship bonds encouraged some peers to take a closer interest in the control of patronage, which could be enhanced by influence in parliament. Much of the legislation passed during the seventeenth century concerned landownership, which was of obvious concern to the elite and gave them opportunities to strengthen their economic and political position.[41] During the eighteenth century access to the English and imperial patronage system made a seat in the British parliament even more alluring.

Lords and their eldest sons were debarred from sitting in the Scottish parliament as burgh or shire commissioners. A few younger sons in the sixteenth century were elected and then later succeeded their brothers in the family titles. New lords were not normally seen in parliament before their elevation. All this began to change, however, after 1600, which indicates both the rising importance of the institution mentioned earlier and its increasing inclusion of the social and political elite. Although this rise in the status of parliamentary membership developed later than in England, it is worth remembering that it was only in the fifty years preceding James VI's accession to his southern throne that the English nobility began to pour into the House of Commons in large numbers. During the first half of the seventeenth century 15% of the new Scottish lords sat in parliament before gaining a title. This rose to 38% between 1650 and 1699 and 83% in 1700–07.[42] Members of peerage families frequently sat as shire commissioners after 1587 and also began infiltrating burgh seats as well.[43] However, the phenomenon remained relatively limited until the Glorious Revolution, when a Scottish version of the 'invasion' of the burghs began.[44]

An increase in the number of elective commissioners vis-à-vis nobles added prestige and conferred more power on the growing Scottish 'commons'.[45] In 1662, 61% of all Scottish elective commissioners were from elite families. This proportion waxed and waned over the remainder of the century, ranging between 45 and 57%. By the closing period of the institution up to three-quarters of the commissioners came from elite families.[46] The Scots were also learning about the importance of parliamentary participation in England. In the thirty years after the Restoration eleven heirs to peerages and two younger sons sat at Westminster.[47]

The English House of Lords ruled in 1711 that Scots nobles with English titles could not sit in the upper chamber. The decision was not reversed until 1782. Hence only sixteen elective slots were open to competition among the whole peerage. Moreover, the eldest sons of Scots lords were debarred between 1707 and 1832 from sitting in the Commons for a Scottish constituency, although they could sit for an English seat after 1800. This left the Scottish peerage and their eldest sons in a kind of 'Catch-22' position. Parliamentary participation had become a *sine qua non* of aristocratic leadership before the Union, and the dramatic reduction in places for lords and their heirs produced resentment, some of which may have contributed to the violent episodes of 1715 and 1745. Nevertheless, out of 261 Scots MPs between 1707 and 1760, sixty-four were sons and brothers of peers.[48] After 1782 many Scots lords gained British honours, which gave them a hereditary right to sit in the upper chamber.

The failure of many lesser landowners to take a seat in parliament automatically, which was their right before 1587, indicates that some did not value a place in the legislature very highly. Nevertheless, the Reformation Parliament was attended by over a hundred small barons.[49] Once the new system was established not only was there an ample supply of lairds to fill the shire seats, but also they began to spill over into the burgh representation. Younger sons of landowners often became merchants and lawyers, and many of them sat for towns as genuine representatives of the commercial interests of their place of residence. However, some of these men stayed closely associated with landed families, acquired estates and rose high in royal service. Despite the fact that urban constituencies were controlled by self-perpetuating town oligarchies, in the seventeenth century lairds began regularly to sit for burghs even though this was against the law.

Nearly one-quarter of the burgh commissioners in 1660–1707 came from governing families, most of whom were landed. Six of these commissioners also sat for a shire. The system of paying burgesses broke down after 1688. In the last years of the Scottish parliament after 1702 the percentage of burgh representatives from parliamentary families rose to sixty-one. Seven shire elections were disputed in 1648. More were contested after 1660 and for the first time a committee to deal with controverted elections had to be established in 1678. The awareness of the opportunities offered by a seat in parliament achieved expression in the persistent demand for increased shire representation. The number of elective commissioners rose over the course of the seventeenth century: from approximately 99 in 1639 to 151 by 1706.[50] At the Union, the lairds won the exclusion of the eldest sons of peers from sitting at Westminster because the seats had become highly prized by untitled families.[51]

The overall proportion of commissioners from elite families, shire and burgh combined, was 56% during the last six decades of parliament's existence, 89% among shire representatives alone. Only a handful of families with three or more commissioners were from merchant oligarchy families. After 1660 virtually all elite families were landed or had become so by the time of the first commissioner's or MP's election. This gave the Scottish landed class (lords and commissioners) a commanding position in the unicameral parliament unequalled in England despite the large number of burgh seats in Scotland.

During the Union negotiations the landed elite used its influence to distribute the new smaller number of constituencies between shire and burgh in a ratio of two to one in their favour. A new system of grouped burghs contributed to the further weakening of urban interests and most burgh seats fell into the hands of aristocratic patrons or political managers such as the Earl of Cromartie or the Duke of Argyll.[52] From 1707 onwards Scottish seats became more firmly dominated than ever by elite families, and the paucity of openings made them more valued and exclusive marks of rank. In 1710, 82% of MPs sitting for Scottish seats came from governing families and this percentage rose as high as 95 in 1775. The average proportion of elite MPs lay well above 80% until the Reform Act of 1832.[53]

Scottish electorates had been highly restricted since the fifteenth century. In 1715, 284,000 men voted in England but only 2,700 in Scotland, although the populations were in a ratio of roughly five to one. Even in the early nineteenth century the total county electorate stood at 2,000 to 3,000, with only two constituencies over 200. Cromartyshire had six voters and Bute twelve, eight of whom were members of the Marquis[54] of Bute's family. At least half of the electors attending elections in Argyllshire in the early eighteenth century were Campbells who still paid heed to the clan chief's wishes.[55] Great Scottish families often dominated shire elections over many centuries. Almost twice as many elected six or more family members for a single county than did their English counterparts. If one adds cadet lines this performance was even more extraordinary. For example the Dukes of Argyll elected seven MPs for Argyllshire in 1700–1885, but a further five close cadets also sat, and more remote kin as well. In 1801, 1,280 people had the right to vote in burgh elections out of a population of 409,000. A single by-election in a large English constituency such as Westminster or Nottingham would bring more electors to the poll than all of Scotland at a general election in the eighteenth century.[56] Venality was rampant, fictitious voters were created; spoils, patronage and threats were the language of politics. For most of the first half of the eighteenth century the 2nd and 3rd Dukes of Argyll could deliver two-thirds of the Scottish MPs to the government as lobby fodder. The political managers tended to sweep the board in the election of representative peers as well.[57]

But this picture can be exaggerated. As is the case with England, recent research on unreformed Scottish politics suggests that there was more life in the electoral system than has traditionally been assumed. It took delicacy and hard work to sustain an interest, and most voters could not be treated as mere bargaining chips. A good deal of 'desperate electioneering' took place, and campaigns could cost thousands of pounds. Between 1790 and 1820 the rate of contested elections was higher than it was in England. Sometimes no national political manager held sway. At other times he could be challenged and defeated.[58] Moreover, as the statistics in this study show, the social backgrounds of Scottish MPs in the eighteenth century were not what one might expect of mere automatons or lackeys.

Thus, although the Scottish parliament was clearly inferior in importance to the English one, from 1600 and especially after 1660 seats for Scottish constituencies were sought by the landed elite. The great landowners outside the Highlands identified their own status with being a lord of parliament and during the seventeenth century untitled landowners placed a higher and higher premium on membership. One cannot, however, speak of the full congruence of the Scottish social and economic elite with the circle of parliamentary families until after the Restoration. This means some important dynasties accumulated far fewer MPs than their English equivalents. Also, the dividing line between parliamentary and non-parliamentary families was higher on the social scale in Scotland than in England because the number of seats available as a proportion of population was smaller. In 1750 Scotland had fewer than four MPs for every 100,000 of population, significantly worse than the Welsh ratio and less than half that for England, although this disparity was compensated for to some degree by Scottish aristocrats sitting for non-Scottish seats.[59] On the other hand, there were proportionally more gently bred landowners in Scotland than in England. So a smaller proportion of the whole landed elite were included among the parliamentary families. The power of the political managers and the small size of the electorate makes the use of the Scottish parliamentary system less accurate as a method of measuring social status than for England. Against this it can be said that Scottish peerages and baronetcies were more evenly distributed among the great landowners than south of the border, making titled Scots more fully identical with the top economic and political families.

Estimates about the size of the landed elite in Scotland vary. In the old Scottish kingdom honours and titles enjoyed a much wider distribution than in England. In 1707 Scotland, with a population of one million, had 154 peers while England, with over five million, had 164.[60] In addition some 10,000 individuals bore titles of chiefship or were lairds with territorial designations. Evocative honorifics such as Lochiel, Swinton of that Ilk, Lockhart of the Lee and The Mackintosh of Mackintosh are still in use today. Even in the south kin connections were of consequence. This 'noblesse' formed a patriciate greater than any in Europe in proportion to its population.[61]

Most gentle families were not large landowners. As in late medieval Wales, armies of the pedigreed lived in obscurity and even poverty. Only a small proportion held sway over large territories and aspired to regional or national leadership. After the Reformation a sizeable number of families remained Roman Catholic. Some of these disappeared completely in the Hanoverian triumph. Others, including a number of earls of important lineage, fell into irreversible economic decline.[62] A core group of about 1,500 families held virtually all the land in the kingdom from the seventeenth to the twentieth century. More of the country was owned by the elite than elsewhere in the British Isles: up to 92% of land was held in 1,000 plus acre estates compared to 56% in England. In the nineteenth century there were about 800 Scottish landowners with sizeable estates. Various estimates of the economic elite based on acreage put the total number of leading families at between 100 and 350.[63] Three-quarters of the income from the Scottish estates of over 3,000 acres worth more than £3,000 p.a. belonged to 227 members of the parliamentary elite in 1883.[64]

This study, using the three MP/peer line of demarcation, produced a total of 370 elite families in Scotland between the Middle Ages and 1945.[65] About a dozen of these were predominantly urban burgess dynasties and a few more emerged in the late nineteenth or early twentieth century and remained exclusively professional, political or commercial in orientation. About 350 were or became landed proprietors. In total, 336 of this elite elected at least one commissioner/MP between 1660 and 1945. Altogether the Scottish parliamentary elite produced 1,866 commissioners or MPs. Very few Scottish families elected MPs for Welsh or Irish seats. However, 240 Scottish elite MPs sat for English constituencies.

When one compares the totals of elite MPs and peers in England and Scotland (8,613 to 1,882) and electoral years of service in parliament (86,622 to 11,807) in 1660 to 1945, the ratios are roughly comparable to population size, although Scots lords and MPs served proportionally fewer years per person than their English counterparts because the Scottish parliament met more irregularly, and for nearly a century after the Union lords with Scottish titles could only enter the House of Lords as elected representative peers. The latter had to be rechosen at each general election.[66] The average number of years of service *per MP* for all Scottish elite families was considerably lower than in neighbouring parts of the British Isles.

The large number of cadet lines created a different configuration of types of family in the Scottish elite compared to the English and Welsh. The fertility and longevity of the nobility in Scotland in the late Middle Ages were unusually robust. Male lines enjoyed a very low extinction rate. Cadets were established to ensure succession and to bolster local power. For example, fifty families of landowning Forbeses arose from four sons of Sir John, the Blacklip, Forbes between the fourteenth and sixteenth centuries, a rate that was exceeded by the Gordons in the same county of Aberdeenshire.[67] The tangled webs of these descents sometimes defy belief. The succession to the Earldom of Mar is of dizzying complexity.[68]

The decision whether to include the numerous cadet lines with clans in the associated family category, which formed only one in ten of the English families but one-quarter of the elite in Scotland (though a much smaller proportion of individual MPs and peers) is complex. On the one hand, even distant kin relationships were of greater importance in Scotland than in England, especially in the Highlands, and this tradition lasted longer than elsewhere in the British Isles. Kindred cohesion was intimately involved with military action, the distribution of political power and the control of land even in the late seventeenth century. Clan chiefs led regiments into the field in the Bishops Wars of the 1640s and as late as 1715 and 1745. The Campbell Chief granted Ardkinglas, Argyllshire, to a younger son in 1396. The cadet line kept up an intimate connection with the Earls and Dukes of Argyll, had their young sons live with the chief's household, and sat in parliament for Argyllshire with the chief's assistance in 1646–49 and 1693–1734. When the 9th Laird was attainted in 1662, Argyll secured the restoration of the estates to the 10th.[69] After careful study of all

MPs in the second half of the eighteenth century Namier and Brooke found that 'the Scottish M.P., to a much higher degree than the English, regarded himself in the House more as a representative of his family than his constituency'. On the other hand, many Campbells or Mackenzies were only very remotely related to the clan chiefs of that name. Others had no blood relationship at all, but took the clan name out of solidarity. Thousands of these families held little or no land, and were mere humble followers of their lords. The clan system began to break down in the seventeenth century and was largely smashed by the mid-eighteenth.[70] Therefore, cadet families with fewer than three MPs/peers were only counted as associated families when the blood connection to the main line was well documented, acknowledged by both clan chief and the subordinate family, and they held the status of lairds with a significant landed estate.

These cadets were only a segment of the associated family's MP group. A number of noble Scottish families elected few or no commissioners or MPs, especially before 1707. The Earls of Erroll, Hereditary High Constables of Scotland (1314, peerage 1444), so far as is known, never sent a commissioner to parliament or an MP to Westminster. The Earls of Wigtown (cr. Lord Fleming 1451?), and the Barons Gray (1445?) and Barons Forrester (1633) were similarly placed. The Earls of Newburgh (1660) elected only English MPs although a Scots family. The Earls of Home (1473) elected their first MP in the main line in 1931. Of course, these families qualify for inclusion in this study because of their titles, but some greater lairds do not appear because of their equally barren electoral histories.

Great Scottish families often elected their first family member to parliament long after becoming clan chiefs or acquiring a peerage, which was the reverse of the case in England. The McLeods of Dunvegan were clan chiefs by 1260 but had no commissioners until 1640. Even the Dukes of Argyll, lords by 1445 and eventually profuse generators of MPs, did not elect their first until 1700. However, it is important to note that while a handful of great families produced few MPs, such as the Earls of Airlie and the Kennedys of Cassillis, most powerful lords and lairds did increasingly become committed to electing family members to parliament, especially after the Union.[71] The Earls of Wemyss, who were ancient and rich, elected their first commissioner in 1596, but they made up for lost time later. It was rare to find Scottish families with large landed incomes having fewer than three British MPs. Some titled families, however, specialized in becoming representative peers, which became their principal means of gaining access to political influence.[72]

When the Scottish parliament still existed, its unicameral structure enabled the head of a family to look after dynastic interests without the necessity of an electoral delegate. After the Union the cost of travel to and living in London was sometimes too great a drain on family resources for more than the *pater familias* to attend. In any case the legal exclusion of eldest sons of peers meant that they could not use experience as an MP as a preparation for public life in the way that their English and Irish counterparts could. While in England over a hundred families elected three or more MPs simultaneously in the same session of parliament, only twelve did so in Scotland, and five of these were during the last fifty years of the old Scots assembly.

Political misfortune resulted in under-representation among some families. The Camerons of Lochiel, who were credited with 126,000 acres in the 1870s (although their income was only £10,000 p.a.), elected one MP (1868–85). They fled to France after the Jacobite defeat in 1715 and were 'out' again in 1745. The 22nd Chief was born and raised abroad during the later eighteenth century. The Mackintosh Chief was also credited with over 100,000 acres in the 1870s. The family stayed loyal to the Stuarts, although they did not participate in the '45. The 25th Chief, when a younger son, moved to Canada and was elected a member of the legislative council of Upper Canada early in the nineteenth century. The 28th stood for Inverness-shire in 1890 and lost.[73] Other leading Jacobites went into exile for long periods, such as the Drummond Dukes of Perth or the MacDonald chiefs, direct heirs of the Lords of the Isles, though Ranald MacDonald, 20th Chief of Clanranald, was an MP from 1812 to 1824. However, his estates had been sold, and he sat for an English constituency. With the exception of the Homes and Kennedys, most of the noble families whose titles survived into the nineteenth century or beyond with few MPs had fallen on hard times. The Earls of Erroll lost most of their lands, abandoned their house to the elements and finally departed for Kenya, dissipation and disgrace.[74]

A large proportion of distinguished families fell into the 'five or fewer' MP category, which consisted of nearly half (46%) of the Scottish parliamentary elite. The McLeods of Dunvegan managed only five. Their finances became rather shaky in the eighteenth century. The Lords Kenmure and Cathcart totalled only eight years' service between them. A higher proportion of peers are found in this category than in the same level in Wales, Ireland or England. While nearly a third (30%) in Scotland held titles, only a little more than one in ten of the English (14%) and Irish (12%) families were peers.

The 'six-plus' MP category includes many of the great dynasties of Scotland. A few families did not produce many MPs but made up for this deficit in gaining frequent election as representative peers.[75] Those with fifteen or more MPs composed most of the historic national families, such as the Dukes of Argyll, Atholl, Buccleuch, Hamilton and Queensberry. Many of these dynasties had comet tails of cadets streaming behind them, some rising high in their own right such as the Hamilton Dukes of Abercorn and Earls of Haddington. Two-thirds of them elected an MP in the twentieth century, an amazing show of strength which will be further considered below.

Table 4.2 Examples of members of the Scottish parliamentary elite and family relationships*

RAMSAY

<u>David Ramsay</u> Cmr for small barons 1609	**Head**
<u>David Ramsay</u> Cmr Kincardineshire 1612, 1625, 1630	**Head**
<u>William Ramsay</u> Cmr Montrose 1617, 1617, 1621	**Younger Son**
<u>Sir Gilbert Ramsay, 1st Baronet</u> Cmr Kincardineshire 1639–41, 1645–46, 1661–63	**Head**
<u>Sir David Ramsay, 4th Baronet</u> Cmr Kincardineshire 1705–07; MP Scotland 1707–08; Kincardineshire 1708–10	**Head**
<u>Sir Alexander Ramsay, 5th Baronet</u> MP Kincardineshire 1710–13	**Head**
<u>Sir Alexander Ramsay-Irvine, 6th Baronet</u> MP Kincardineshire 1765–68	**Head**
<u>Sir Alexander Ramsay, 2nd Baronet</u> MP Kincardineshire 1820–26	**Head**
<u>Sir Alexander Ramsay, 3rd Baronet</u> MP Rochdale 1857–59	**Head**

The Ramsays of Balmain, Kincardineshire, were briefly lords of parliament in the late fifteenth century, but the title was forfeited.

DALRYMPLE

<u>James Dalrymple, 1st Viscount of Stair</u> Cmr Wigtownshire 1672–74, 1678, 1681; Ld of Parlt 1690–95	**Head**
<u>John Dalrymple, 1st Earl of Stair</u> Cmr Stranraer Burgh 1689; Ld of Parlt 1700–07	**Head**
<u>Sir David Dalrymple, 1st Baronet</u> Cmr Culross Burgh 1698–1702, 1703–07; MP Scotland 1707–08; Haddington Burghs 1708–21	**Younger Son**
<u>William Dalrymple</u> Cmr Ayrshire 1703–07; MP Scotland 1707–08; Clackmannanshire 1708–10; Wigtown Burghs 1722–27; Wigtownshire 1727–41	**Younger Son and father of 4th Earl**
<u>George Dalrymple</u> Cmr Stranraer Burgh 1703–07	**Younger Son**
<u>John Dalrymple, 2nd Earl of Stair</u> Ld of Parlt 1707; Rep. Peer 1707–08, 1715–34, 1744–47	**Head**
<u>John Dalrymple</u> MP Wigtown Burghs 1728–34	**Brother**
<u>John Dalrymple, 5th Earl of Stair</u> Rep. Peer 1771–74	**Head**
<u>William Dalrymple</u> MP Wigtown Burghs 1784–90; Irish MP Duleek 1796–97	**Brother**
<u>John Dalrymple, 6th Earl of Stair</u> Rep. Peer 1790–1807, 1820–21	**Head**

John Dalrymple, 8th Earl of Stair MP Midlothian 1833–34; HLds 1841–53	**Head**
John Dalrymple, 10th Earl of Stair MP Wigtownshire 1841–56; HLds 1864–1903	**Head**
North Dalrymple, 9th Earl of Stair HLds 1853–64	**Head**
John Dalrymple, 10th Earl of Stair HLds 1903–14	**Head**
John Dalrymple, 12th Earl of Stair MP Wigtownshire 1906–14; HLds 1914–45	**Head**
Hew Dalrymple MP Wigtownshire 1915–18	**Younger Son**

The Dalrymples were small lairds in the fifteenth century who rose through the efforts of a lawyer and politician in the seventeenth. They owned over 100,000 acres in 1883 and are credited with 45,000 in the 1990s.

* Includes dates of commissioners to the Convention of Estates.

Most of the great families owned mammoth estates.[76] Of course, many of these holdings contained vast stretches of moor, bog and unproductive land. Incomes rarely matched the grandeur of the acreage. None the less, the Scottish grandees were very grand indeed. Many were of ancient lineage and were often clan chiefs. They were accustomed to a key role in national politics, and enjoyed immense social prestige. Though the peculiarities of Highland independence, Jacobite attainders, and low numbers of pre-1660 Commissioners makes the system used by this study to measure grandee status in England less effective in Scotland, most important families were captured in the list without the adjustments necessary in the case of Wales. Forty Scottish families qualify for the designation grandee by the method used in Chapter Two.[77] By adjusting a couple of categories to allow for later election of first Commissioners/MPs and the elective peer system and using a less rigorous standard for the acquisition of 'prizes' such as government posts and Thistles, nine further families can be added to the list.[78] Only a small number of possible candidates are then left out, usually due to the same factors that excluded English families: Roman Catholicism or extinction in the eighteenth century. Otherwise this list is largely the top elite of Scotland in the seventeenth, eighteenth and nineteenth centuries. Roughly fifty or so magnate families were prominent in medieval Scotland, and although there was some turnover as the centuries progressed, about fifty formed the dominant core in later periods as well.[79]

Most of the grandees were earls or above in rank. Over half were named in charters or titled before 1300, and all but eight were well established by 1500. Although largely excluded from high office in the century after the Union (except for the Scottish Secretaryship), grandees dominated the cabinet positions held by the Caledonian elite in the nineteenth and twentieth centuries. Four achieved the premiership (Bute 1762–63; Aberdeen 1852–55; Rosebery 1894–95; Home 1963–64). Grandee families on average produced over one-quarter of all Scottish MPs in 1715–1820, reaching a high point of 28% in 1754–90. This average was consistently higher than that achieved by the English and Irish grandees and was exceeded only for a couple of decades in the later eighteenth century by the Welsh.

One might assume, based on the often violent conflicts which punctuated Scottish history, that turnover among elite families must have been frequent. Historians suggest that Norse warriors and Anglo-Norman knights displaced members of the native elite in the early Middle Ages and that landed society was more fluid and enjoyed greater social mobility in the late medieval period than many societies elsewhere in Europe. The peerage was apparently depleted by political conflict in the mid-fifteenth century. The great sixteenth-century boom in the feuing (perpetual leasing) of ecclesiastical lands, the large number of elite deaths at the battle of Flodden, and the rapid expansion of the peerage under James VI and I (forty-one peers in 1585, ninety-two in 1625) continued to promote turnover. The economic and political traumas of the seventeenth and eighteenth centuries sent many old families to the wall and led to the consolidation of land into fewer hands. Edinburgh and Glasgow produced lawyers and merchants who built fine classical country houses and sought to emulate their superiors. It is claimed that there was more new money than old in the seventeenth century, and about one-third of the land in Scotland changed hands during the period.[80]

This picture of an elite in a constant state of renewal contrasts with the longevity of the grandee families and the ancient roots of lairds. The data in this study suggests more stability than turnover among elite families. During the last five decades of the old Scottish parliament 85% of the elite commissioners had medieval social origins. Between 1707 and 1832, when the percentage of Scots MPs from elite families never dropped below 82 and usually ran over 90, well over three-quarters came from families with medieval origins, rising at times to over nine out of ten, not declining below two-thirds until after Queen Victoria's Diamond Jubilee. For much of the period between the Restoration and the early twentieth century a greater proportion of Scottish elite MPs were of ancient lineage than legislators from any other region of the British Isles.[81]

One explanation for the apparent contradiction between historians' perceptions about turnover and the data in this study is that most new Scottish peers were drawn either from cadet lines of the great houses or from long-established landowning families. A study of baronets shows that extinctions of these titles were rarer in

Scotland than in England, and, as we noted earlier, the attrition rate among medieval magnates was also lower. Many Scottish peerages could pass through the female line, a device that preserved a number of ancient earldoms. Female primogeniture was practised, which helped to keep estates intact. Scottish peerage law permitted titles to pass through *ancestors* of the first holder if directly descended lines died out, and the resignation and regranting of titles was also allowed. Jacobite families often managed to get their attainders reversed, and if smaller lairds went under in the eighteen and nineteenth centuries, it was often the established magnates, not new families, who benefited through purchase of their estates. Those who gained new titles through government service and even commercial careers frequently came from old families. On the whole the nobility remained highly exclusive. Few truly 'new men' ever broke into the ranks of the parliamentary peerage.

The rate of disappearance from parliamentary participation by elite families shows only two dramatic surges between 1660 and 1945.[82] The first was caused by the Union, which drastically reduced the number of seats available to those who were ambitious for parliamentary election. Eighty-seven families, one-quarter of the elite (24% of all the Scottish dynasties in this study and over one-third of families with at least one MP in 1660–1945), disappeared from electoral participation between 1660 and 1707 – thirty-seven of them between 1700 and 1707, twice the number of any other decade in Scottish history. Most of these families came from the laird class. Gentry who could not sustain the expense of electoral competition were squeezed out or disappeared in the catastrophe of 1715. On the other hand, only four of the wealthier and more important families disappeared between 1660 and 1707. Departures from the Westminster parliament remained at a very low rate, averaging 5.7 per decade until 1832. The second wave of disappearances followed the Great Reform Act with seventeen families gone in the 1830s and forty-one more before the next instalment of reform in 1867. Many of those who withdrew from the electoral arena came from the more distinguished families.

New entrants to the elite in Scotland are not effectively measured by using the date of first peer or commissioner/MP for the reasons already discussed. The most dramatic period of expansion of the elite using such figures was between 1560 and 1699. In this period, 216 families achieved parliamentary status at a rate of about fifteen per decade. This contrasts with an average of one or two a decade during the previous century. The 1440–69 period was fertile on a smaller scale: a time when the parliamentary peerage was formed and many of the first permanent titles were distributed. After 1700 the rate of new entrants was comparatively low, with only forty-four in the whole of the eighteenth century and a relative handful (twenty-seven) in the nineteenth. However, if one uses the date of first recognition of a family achieving gentry status, over half (62%) of the elite was already established before

1400. Thereafter the flow of entrants was modest and declined further beyond 1500. Only twice after that date did it reach ten in a two-decade period (1560–79 and 1580–99) and often numbered no more than one or two every ten years.

The misty origins of ancient Scottish dynasties offered even greater opportunities to propose fictitious ancestry than was possible in England. The Urquarts of Craigston traced themselves through 130 generations to Adam. The Leslie Earls of Rothes were said to derive from Attila, King of the Huns, and Theodosius the Roman Emperor via a Hungarian nobleman who attended the Anglo-Saxon Princess Agatha. The Graham Dukes of Montrose claimed descent from a Caledonian chief who in the fifth century broke down Agricola's wall where the gap called Graham's Dike lies. The Menzie clan chief in the later nineteenth century was said to be sixty-second in a line beginning in 300 BC.[83]

Not only was this outrageous fabrication, but many later concoctions were equally false. The Davidsons' claim that they had held Tulloch Castle, Ross, since 1300 was fiction. They acquired it in 1762. Even clan chiefs invented heroic ancestors to bolster their authority, and ironically some undoubtedly ancient Celtic families began to claim Norman ancestors in the sixteenth century. Documentary evidence for grants of lands and titles rarely exists before the reign of William the Lion (1124–1214).[84] None the less, the Sinclairs and MacDonalds were almost certainly descended from ninth-century Viking lords. The Declaration of Arbroath (1320) lists over a dozen major barons whose descendants were still large landowners in the twentieth century.[85] The Stewarts became kings in the fourteenth century and spawned a number of distinguished families via illegitimate royal progeny from Robert II to Charles II. The Sutherlands and Douglases were earls by 1235 and 1358 respectively, while the Crawfords, who gained their first title in 1398, were magnates very early. MacLeods were at Dunvegan by 1200, Roses at Kilravok by 1297, Kennedys at Cassillis by 1367 and Lyons at Glamis by 1376.

Three-quarters (78%) of all families in the Scottish parliamentary elite were landowners during the Middle Ages or rose through activities directly related to landed proprietorship at a later date. This gave the Scots by far the most exclusive aristocracy to be found in any region of the British Isles, more so even than in Wales and much greater than in England. However, as with the English elite, medieval families who emerged as territorial magnates often acquired land by methods that were not directly related to mere husbandry. Royal and noble service and marriage to heiresses undoubtedly underpinned many ascents. Other families benefited from official, legal and commercial activities as well. The Balfours of Balbirnie were lairds worth less than £2,000 p.a. in the 1770s and raised themselves by innovative farming and mineral exploitation to parliamentary status with an income of nearly £8,000 by 1813.[86]

Non-landed occupations were always a route up for younger sons, but office yielded surprisingly few important families. One of the best known was the Primrose family, who were connected with the Revenue Department in the seventeenth century, and capped their rise with a judgeship in 1661, eventually becoming Earls of Rosebery. Sir Lawrence Dundas sprang from the ancient family of that name, but his father was an Edinburgh woollen draper and the son rose as an army contractor in eighteenth-century England. The family took up residence in Yorkshire and acquired estates there, entering the grandee category. The other Dundas peerage also came in part through politics and office, but the Viscounts Melville had always been landed (first commissioner 1612) and gained fame and a fortune in the law. Most of the noblesse of the robe were recruited from families who were already well-established landowners.

The professions attracted many younger sons. Scotland possessed a strong military tradition. Every Home laird of Paxton died in battle or as a prisoner between 1413 and 1576. Army and navy careers were a mainstay for many families after the Union opened up the opportunity for service in the imperial system. Even earlier, however, the Wood family (first commissioner 1560) was founded by a sea commander to James III. The Middletons were modest gentry until the 1st Earl became Captain General of the Forces in 1653 and a lord in 1660, though his career never produced sufficient riches to sustain a great title. In fact this case was a portent. Though many sons went off to serve the empire and some even gained peerages, fewer than six Scottish elite families founded parliamentary lines based on military careers (of the modern type). The Church was even less fertile in producing fortunes (only two), though the Calvinist manses of Scotland bred founders of fortunes in other fields. One family of architects and one surgeon, who was as much a merchant as a doctor, entered the elite.

Law may at first sight seem the most promising alternative source of parliamentary families after land. Scotland was a country where education was highly valued, and one could rise rapidly in the profession. The Lords of Session commanded great respect and acquired titles for their lifetimes. The first Foulis, for example, was the son of a skinner. He became a Lord of Session in 1526. The family elected seven Commissioners between that year and 1707, were created baronets and still held their estates in the late nineteenth century. The Livingston Viscounts of Kilsyth and a few other prominent families also raised themselves through legal careers, but surprisingly few elite families ascended in this way. No Scottish counterparts existed of the great landed families in England such as the Cokes and Yorkes, who began without gentle antecedents and rose as judges and Lord Chancellors. Perhaps the closest equivalent were the Earls of Stair, but the Dalrymples had long been a landed family. The Duffs began as small lairds, and it was a lawyer in the seventeenth century who put them on the map. However, he founded the fortune that would eventually support a dukedom on successful land speculation not at the bar.

The Scottish legal system was much less accessible to new men than the English one. In the seventeenth and eighteenth centuries the profession was increasingly dominated by the sons of families who were already landed. By the 1670s more than half of all advocates were the sons of lairds or higher. Almost one in five of their fathers had titles. In the following century landed origins rose to encompass 96% of entrants to the Faculty of Advocates, over half of whom were the sons of titled families or greater lairds.[87] Fewer than six new parliamentary families rose through the law after the mid-eighteenth century. Less than 8% of the Scottish elite can be said to have risen from humble beginnings to elite status through office and the professions. This is half the proportion in Wales and only a bit more than one-third of that in England.

After the fluidity and 'openness' that some historians believe existed in the sixteenth and seventeenth centuries, it is argued that conventions developed which prevented younger sons of nobles and gentry from going into trade.[88] This perception led Namier to judge that in Scotland lineage always played a much greater role than money in the selection of governing families.[89]

It has already been established that most of the leading families in Scotland had old roots, but it is not clear that any special prejudice existed against business backgrounds in elite society or that off-shoots of ancient lines did not found new fortunes in commerce. Some historians disagree with the picture of a 'closed' elite and argue that outside the titular nobility Scottish landed society from the sixteenth century onwards was diverse in origins. Much intermarriage took place between the gently bred and burgess and industrial families. Men who had made their fortunes in a wide range of activities purchased estates. It is argued that no social gulf existed between old families and urban wealth.[90]

Even as early as the fifteenth and sixteenth centuries younger sons established businesses in burghs, such as the Scrymgeours of Dundee and the Learmouths of St Andrews, and this continued in the following centuries. The Malcolms of Poltalloch, Argyllshire, had a charter for their estate dating to 1562 and purchased Duntrune Castle in 1792, but it was as merchants in the nineteenth century that they acquired great wealth and a peerage. To be sure some of the involvement by landed families in business was forced by circumstances such as estate forfeiture and impoverishment. The Setons of Touch saved their estates in the eighteenth century when one became a nabob, and careers in India were the making of a number of younger sons, most notably a cadet of the Balfours of Balbirnie mentioned above, whose estates at Whittinghame were purchased in 1812 with £300,000 made in the East.[91] This line produced the ineffably aristocratic Prime Minister Arthur Balfour. West Indian businesses and plantations restored a number of families to prosperity.

However, landed society did not provide all the recruits for the commercial life of Scotland. A number of important families rose from humble birth. The Napiers, Barons Napier and Ettrick, emerged as wool merchants in Edinburgh in the fifteenth century, purchased Merchistoun, elected their first Commissioner in 1563, and became barons in 1627. The Hopes were possibly of French origin and established themselves as merchants in Edinburgh by the 1560s, when they first entered parliament. A lawyer gained them a baronetcy in 1628. Large estates were purchased surrounding their seat at Hopetoun, which became one of the most magnificent houses in Scotland. The Mathesons made a fortune in China, which was converted into estates worth nearly £50,000 p.a. The great Atlantic trade centred in Glasgow transformed the landholding patterns of nearby counties such as Kirkcudbrightshire, and produced several rich parliamentary families including the Oswalds of Auchincruive, worth £42,000 p.a. in the 1870s.[92]

Industry and banking, which played such a significant role in helping to form the English elite, did not do so in Scotland. Four out of five (79%) families with commercial backgrounds were merchants not manufacturers or financiers. Business produced only 15% of all elite families in Scotland, a proportion similar to that in Wales and much lower than in England. Only one mercantile family, the Hopes, achieved grandee status.

We are left with the contradictory picture of an elite with few 'new' families and yet open to careers in and marriage with commercial wealth; an aristocracy intimately involved in political intrigue, few of whom rose via government service; a legal system that conferred great prestige on judges and lawyers with a few families raised up by the law; an old elite constantly renewed by business; a tightly woven, small patriciate with a narrow gate of entry which rapidly accepted newcomers when they did penetrate inside and remarkably adaptable both in restoring lost fortunes and providing political leadership even late in the day.

The resilience of the Scottish governing class can be seen in its performance after 1832 (See Figures 4.1 and 4.2.) The muddled drafting of the Scottish Reform Act ended many old malpractices but opened up whole new vistas for abuse. The revised system could be easily manipulated despite an electorate increased in size thirteen-fold. The Tories feared Scotland was lost forever, but although they never did as well in the cities again, they regained ground in the counties by means of evictions, manufacturing fictitious voters and through traditional landed influence. In the burghs Liberal aristocrats were often able to nominate candidates. Thus Scotland's electoral structure seemed to remain less responsive to social, economic and demographic developments than elsewhere in Britain. A study of the social backgrounds of Scottish MPs from 1832 to 1868 shows that over 80% were recruited from landed society. More than one-third were connected with the nobility.[93]

The findings of this study, however, indicate a greater impact made by the reform legislation than historians assume. In 1830, 91% of the Scottish seats were held by members of the parliamentary elite. In 1835 this fell to 68%, a figure fourteen points lower than any since the Union and thirty points below that of 1795. A slight recovery, to 70%, came by 1840 and as late as 1865 it was still 66%. Two-thirds is a substantial proportion of a parliamentary delegation; much of what has been written about the defects of the reformed system is obviously accurate. But in Wales the percentage of seats held by the elite in 1865 was 81 and in England 66, the same as in Scotland, though the Scottish Reform Bill is always held up as a more corrupt and inferior measure than the neighbouring version. Moreover, the Scottish drop of 23 percentage points between 1830 and 1835 was higher than the English 20% in the same years. The Scottish Reform Act may have permitted considerable undemocratic activity and kept the Scottish representation predominantly in the hands of nobles and lairds, but its effect in reducing the ability of the traditional political families to get elected was more dramatic and forceful than anywhere else in Britain.

Another assumption made by historians and not entirely borne out by the data on elite families is that after the passage of reform power went to the large landowners at the expense of the gentry. Undoubtedly the Dukes of Sutherland and Argyll still dominated their counties (no contested election took place in the former's eponymous shire between 1790 and 1885). The 12th Duke of Hamilton is said to have kept Bute conservative until his death in 1895.[94] But the proportion of the Scottish parliamentary delegation from families with fifteen or more MPs fell consistently from 1780, when it was nearly one-third (31%) to 18% in 1830, 11 in 1840, 9.4 in 1850 and 7.5 in 1860. It is instructive to look again at the English experience. In 1830 'fifteen-plus' families produced 28% of all MPs while in 1860 this was down only a few points to 24%, over three times the proportion held by the big families in the Scottish elite. The percentage of Caledonian MPs from families with five or fewer MPs, who were more likely to be small landowners or new families, was 27 in 1780 and 30 in 1860. The number of MPs with medieval social origins also declined after 1832. During the eighteenth century this figure had usually been above 80% and sometimes over 90. It began to fall after 1800 and dropped from 78% in 1830 to 66 in 1860, while it actually rose in England from 40 to 43% during the same years. The greater and older families in England by contrast did better than their brethren in Scotland in the years immediately following the 1832 reform.

The Second Reform Act gave Scotland a much larger electorate and a few more seats, though well below what their proportion of the total population of the British Isles entitled them to. In 1869 one in three adult males had the vote and the number was rising. The size of the electorate made it impossible to manipulate in the old way except in a few places, although 1867 left many abuses. The Marquis of Lorne and

Lord Colin Campbell, sons of the Duke of Argyll, sat for their county from 1868 to 1885 'quite in the old style'. However, the aristocracy was losing contact with political opinion in the urban areas. The famous battle between Gladstone and the Earl of Dalkeith in Midlothian in 1880 ended in a defeat for the Buccleuchs.[95] The elite's share of the Scottish seats dropped to half in 1870 and two out of five (42%) in 1885.

The Third Reform Act was a severe blow to aristocratic rule. By 1890 less than one-third of the Scottish seats were still in the hands of parliamentary families and a number of those were held by the new business elite. Yet now the strengths of the Scottish patriciate began to tell. They still composed 30% of the Caledonian delegation at Westminster in 1905 and although there was a dip to 10% in 1920 they fought back to 19%, which was achieved in 1925, 1935 and 1945. One in five Scottish MPs still came from a family with more than three MPs/peers, and most of these were from families with six or more. The English elite also managed 19% in 1925 and kept 17 or 18% through the Second World War, but during this period a much greater proportion of the Scottish elite MPs came from *old* landed families.

The extraordinary survival of large estates in Scotland late into the twentieth century helps to explain aristocratic success at the polls. Control of 100,000 acres or more gave families influence and prestige hard to match in a smaller if richer estate south of the border. Urbanization and industrialization were concentrated in the Forth-Clyde valley which left much of the rest of Scotland agricultural and rural. Of course, not all was rosy in the countryside. Many old families sold off their land owing to indebtedness. The Highland clearances, dissolution of kinship bonds, game laws, bad feelings arising out of the religious Disruption of 1843, the increase in small independent farmers after the break-up of some big estates, and the general trend towards the capitalization of agriculture polarized rural districts, and caused a gulf of misunderstanding between landlords and tenants that led to great hostility. Some lords and lairds responded to populism among the crofters with coercion and evictions. Crofter candidates entered the electoral field.[96]

Yet some owners of big estates not only continued to play an influential role in political associations, but also the economic power of their giant holdings may actually have increased. The sales of estates slowed or halted. The issues exacerbating relations between the elite and the populace diminished. Some of the great peers and clan chiefs played a prominent role in imperial service as proconsuls and military leaders. Lord Lovat led commandos on to the beaches in Normandy on D-Day accompanied by his own piper. This act of bravado signified the unusual character of Scottish culture. It is not so much the pipes and kilts, but an elite inextricably linked with the national heritage in ways absent in Wales or England that give the names Campbell, Hamilton and Stewart a special resonance. It was an everyday fact, for example, that on Lord Lovat's estates a majority of inhabitants were called Fraser.

Names are a far more potent and emotionally charged force than is often realized. In the later twentieth century tribal memories, rising national feeling, a group of progressive and unashamedly aristocratic landowners and the survival of enormous estates helped sustain aristocratic status in ways that did not develop south of the Tweed. For example in the 1970s and 1980s only fifteen lords lieutenant in England were drawn from the established nobility, while in Scotland nearly half came from the old guard. The Royal Company of Archers, an honorary bodyguard to the monarch of 400 members, includes most of the heads of the hereditary elite families and gives them an exclusive and official social association without parallel in England. Expulsion from the corps is still used as a means to punish disloyalty to elite values.[97]

Land continued into the late twentieth century as the crucial contributor to survival. Over one-third of land was still held by 121 estates larger than 20,000 acres in the 1970s. In the 1980s 10% of the nation belonged to thirteen individuals, the most concentrated pattern of landholding in Europe.[98] Not only does the Duke of Buccleuch still possess a quarter of a million acres, the Atholl Murrays 148,000, and several other peers 100,000, but some families have actually increased their holdings between 1970 and 1990, such as the Marquis of Bute and the Earls of Cawdor, Dalhousie, Rosebery and Wemyss. Though the vast acreages of some of the Highland estates may create an inflated idea of their value, a number of the clan chiefs and nobles are rich even by English standards.[99]

Forty Scottish elite families elected one or more MPs after 1919, eighteen of them after the Second World War. Eight noble MPs were elected in 1935, the highest number since 1880. The Sinclairs, driven from Caithness in 1885, produced an MP for the county in 1922–45. Among the leading families with MPs in the mid-twentieth century were: Anstruther, Cochrane, Fraser, Hamilton, Hay, Home, Hope, Kerr, Lindsay-Crawford, MacLean, Maitland, Murray, Ramsay, Scott, Sinclair and Stuart. A number of Scottish peers have remained active in politics at the ministerial level, most notably the Earl of Home, but also Viscount Thurso, the Master of Elibank, the Earl of Ancram, the Earl of Caithness and the Earl of Selkirk. A younger son of the Marquis of Linlithgow was created a peer in his own right in 1964, and the Hopes have produced four twentieth-century MPs. Over four-fifths of politically active families possessed pre-seventeenth-century origins compared to less than two-fifths for the English. It is not an insignificant indicator of continued self-confidence that the high aristocracy of Scotland has married regularly into the royal family, including unions with the daughters of Queen Victoria and Edward VII. Two other great families provided brides for English princes. The longest-lived and most beloved British queen of the twentieth century was born a Lyon of Glamis. The electoral destruction of the Tories in 1997 swept away the remaining aristocratic MPs, but a few reappeared in the new Scottish parliament including a brother of the Duke of Hamilton.

Ireland

The tortured history of landholding in Ireland presents dramatic contrasts with the more stable development of property ownership in England and Scotland. Moreover the history of the Irish parliament is less well known and often misunderstood. Records are fragmentary for membership before 1660, and even the histories of older Irish peerages are obscure in ways unknown across St George's Channel. As in Scotland, many Irish families important in the eighteenth and nineteenth centuries accumulated little or no parliamentary experience before the Restoration. Unlike their Caledonian brethren, however, many Hibernian nobles not only had no parliamentary histories, but no pedigrees at all. Among the Gaelic lords, on the other hand, some families enjoyed chiefly lineages of great antiquity.

The Irish parliament emerged, like the English and Scottish ones, out of meetings of the king's council. There is no evidence of elected representatives before 1297. By the reign of Richard II an Irish House of Lords as a distinct entity was emerging, and the first complete writs of summons exist for 1375. Meetings were infrequent, and parliament, which was largely confined to the Pale in any case (eleven counties were represented in 1578 and full conquest was not achieved until 1603), rarely functioned as a regular instrument of government until the seventeenth century. Few parliaments were called under the Tudors.[100]

Until near the end of its life the Irish parliament never achieved full constitutional equality with its Edinburgh or Westminster cousins. No Irish legislation could reach the statute book without prior consent of the English Privy Council. Moreover, the Irish representatives could only approve or reject bills, not amend them.[101]

Because 'Old English' (descendants of Anglo-Norman families who arrived during the Middle Ages) recusants managed to block much legislation in the 1585 meeting of the Commons, the Lord Deputy in 1613, Sir Arthur Chichester, moved to prevent a recurrence by creating forty new Protestant boroughs. This reform had several interesting effects. First, during the seventeenth and eighteenth centuries every town of any size in Ireland was officially represented in parliament, unlike in England, although many of the boroughs were little more than hamlets and were easily manipulated by an owner or patron. The dominance of the Protestant Ascendancy was ensured both by this manoeuvre and by the exclusion of Roman Catholic peers and voters from parliamentary activity and elections for much of the eighteenth century. On the other hand, the government was unexpectedly and repeatedly challenged in the parliamentary arena both by MPs who were more Protestant than the king and by an increasing sense of Irishness among the settler families as they became rooted in their adoptive country.

During the second half of the seventeenth century the Irish parliament became a more dynamic and assertive institution. After 1692 the Dublin assembly reached its full complement of members. It met more frequently, and became a regular part of the machinery of government. Until the reign of George III elections were normally precipitated by the death of the monarch. Irish MPs and peers became the high priests of the Ascendancy. As expenditures outran income, the government was increasingly dependent on parliament for supply. Enormous efforts were made to secure compliance with London's policies. Control over the appointment of bishops, creation of a Garter substitute in the form of the Order of St Patrick in 1783, and fresh infusions of peers helped to make the Lords relatively compliant. The Commons proved more of a challenge, and repeated outbreaks of 'patriotism' made the work of the rulers in Dublin Castle difficult. Dangling peerages could have a useful effect in the Commons. An irate Earl of Drogheda accused the members of the lower house as early as 1666 'of all wanting to be lords'. Until 1793 Irish MPs were not obliged to resign their seats on acceptance of a government place, as was the case in England after 1707. This made the distribution of patronage easier and more efficient. The orgy of title-mongering during the death throes of the Irish parliament and establishment of the Union in 1800 is well known, and prompted the Viceroy, Cornwallis, to call the Irish elite 'the most corrupt people under heaven'. The celebrated 'undertaker' system, somewhat similar to the activity of the Argylls and Dundas in Scotland, orchestrated by Lord Deputy Capel, the Earl of Shannon and Speaker Conolly relied heavily on patronage and votes were 'delivered' for the government.[102]

The Ascendancy elevated membership in the Irish parliament to the highest level of importance because their security as a class rested much more immediately on the control of the constitutional structure of the state than was the case in Scotland or England. They practised an alien religion and owned estates largely gained by dispossessing the native population. Social and economic inequality seemed more natural and irreversible on the other side of St George's Channel than it did in Ireland. For several centuries the Irish elite suffered nightmares which did not disturb the sleep of rich men in England, except perhaps briefly during the height of the French Revolution. Mastery of the island required a commitment to the use of every means of oppression available.

All of this has led to much tongue-clucking among historians about the deviant and depraved character of Irish MPs when compared with their Westminster counterparts, and the assumption is often made that only men willing to be poodles could so demean themselves as to join such an artificial and subservient institution. J.H. Plumb's judgement that the Irish parliament 'was utterly servile' is a typical specimen of a widely held view. Of course, there is some truth in the charge that after 1660 the Irish elite gorged themselves on the state's resources like 'beasts released on to spring pastures after a hard winter'. But if the Dublin legislature was little more than a bewigged Mafia and a 'noisy sideshow', it would be uphill work to use its membership to measure the size and composition of an aristocracy.[103]

'Corruption' was widespread on both sides of St George's Channel during the eighteenth century. Moreover, the Irish elite produced enlightened, progressive landlords and politicians just as the English aristocracy did. The Irish parliaments of 1634 or 1692 were anything but compliant or unimportant. Early in the eighteenth century the Crown recognized the Dublin assembly's right to initiate legislation, and during the reign of George III, especially after 1782, most Irish bills started in Dublin instead of emanating from the Privy Council in London. The 'undertaker' system was only partially successful and ended soon after mid-century.

Control of seats was not as monolithic as is sometimes portrayed.[104] To be sure some electorates were very small. Knocktopher had one qualified voter in 1783, Rathcormack seven and Baltimore eleven. In the later half of the eighteenth century peerage families controlled numerous boroughs and some county seats, and this continued even after the Union.[105] On the other hand Carrickfergus had 2,000 voters in 1739. Twenty-two open boroughs often produced ardent and expensive contests. As in England, even the most closed boroughs required care and attention to keep loyal. Local sensibilities had to be deferred to. Once the franchise was restored to Catholics after 1793 even more delicacy was required of candidates. Borough conflicts led to great bitterness among inhabitants. Many landlords did not choose to force their tenants to vote against their wishes, although the threat of eviction always lurked. Loyalty was often offered to family members but not necessarily to nominees unconnected by blood to a patron.[106]

None the less, many boroughs stayed obedient for long periods. This meant that some Irish MPs enjoyed extraordinarily long tenures, and Dublin produced proportionally more politicians with long service than England and far more than Scotland (although part of the reason for this was the long intervals between elections when the lives of parliaments were tied to the reigns of sovereigns). Thomas Bligh sat for Athboy from 1715 to 1775 and John Blennerhasset for County Kerry and Tralee from 1709 to 1775. Some counties were dominated by a single patron, although when this was the case usually only one seat was claimed exclusively for the family. After the Union two-thirds of the surviving seats were county ones, as was the case in Scotland.

Much abuse was heaped on the social pretensions of the Irish nobility and gentry. Horace Walpole sniffed at the Earl of Kildare's elevation to the Leinster title in 1766 as 'a pinchbeck Dukedom'.[107] Certainly many Irish gentlemen were both poorer and less sophisticated than their counterparts in England, but one also sees the cloven hoof of ethnic prejudice at work here. To consider unworthy of a dukedom a man so well bred, distinguished and rich as the chief of the Geraldines was more than just a little light snobbery. Walpole was belittling a nation. To be sure Irish peerages did not confer the same status as an English title – in England. But even there, English families were raised above the ordinary run of gentry and baronets by gaining an Irish peerage, and in Ireland a barony or better not only gave membership to the most exclusive social circle in the nation, but also conferred power and distinction.[108] After the Union the peerage voted (by postal ballot not at a meeting as in Scotland) for twenty-eight representative peers to sit at Westminster. In 1886 two-thirds of the Irish peers held British titles. Thus a large majority sat on equal legislative terms with their English counterparts. Moreover, Irish peerages continued to be created, unlike Scottish titles, although the process was an exclusive one. In addition Irish peers without British titles could sit in the Commons for non-Irish seats, a notable example being Lord Palmerston, a practice continued into the 1990s by the 6th Earl of Kilmorey, another advantage denied the Scots.

The nationalistic constitutional aspirations focused in the Dublin assembly were authentic; indeed, so much so that it was considered too dangerous to be allowed to continue. The Union of 1800 extinguished the existence of a potential threat to English interests. On 1 January 1801 the Dublin parliament came to an end against considerable opposition from both within and outside the chambers.

During the eighteenth century and even more so until late in the nineteenth the Irish peerage and those holding a seat for an Irish constituency in the Commons either in Dublin or Westminster were by and large the top layer of the economic and social as well as the political structure of Irish society. Roy Foster notes that as in England 'politics were an affirmation of status'. It is probable that by the later eighteenth century all landed proprietors worth £15,000 p.a. or more, with exception of Thomas Conolly and perhaps collectively the LaTouches, were peers, and no man with a rent roll of under £5,000 a year could hope for a title.[109] Three-quarters (76%) of the income of owners of 3,000 acres with more than £3,000 p.a. in the 1880s was possessed by the elite. The average income of non-parliamentary families was a bit less than half that of the governing dynasties.[110] New peers usually passed through the House of Commons first. When one takes into account those who succeeded as minors or for other reasons could not be elected to the lower house, virtually all eligible peers, new and old, sat in the Commons first as did many of their close relatives. After the Union, when the number of seats was reduced, one-third of all Irish MPs were the sons of Irish peers.[111]

The inchoate state of Irish landholding, political and religious turbulence and missing documentation in the sixteenth and seventeenth centuries makes it impossible to use membership in the Irish House of Commons as an indicator of social pre-eminence before 1660. The first contested elections we know about did not occur until that decade. After that social and political status became largely identical. In 1733, when the 6th Earl of Abercorn was ousted as a patron, he considered it an 'indignity' that anyone should 'endeavour supplanting us in a borough which must belong to me and my family'. A historian of eighteenth-century Ulster believes the real measure of a family's influence and membership in the upper elite 'was their control of boroughs'.[112] County elections were often hotly contested and led to duels. It is said that when George IV asked one hair-trigger squire who would win a Galway election, the latter replied: 'The survivor, Sir.'[113]

The earliest recorded offer of money for a seat was £100 in the Dingle election of 1714. Arthur Dobbs of Castle Dobbs spent more than £1,000 gaining a borough seat in 1727. Buying and selling electoral office was a well-established practice by the reign of George II and prices rose rapidly. County elections could be expensive. Robert French of Monivea spent £1,320 on a by-election for County Galway in 1745. He stood again in 1753 and during these eight years his electoral spending reached the equivalent of two years' rental on his estates. In the late eighteenth and early nineteenth centuries the Marquesses of Downshire and Londonderry spent as much as £60,000 a piece on electioneering in County Down. The latter nobleman was financially embarrassed for the rest of his life. The Dowager Marchioness of Downshire and her son spent nearly £200,000 on the purchase of land at uneconomic rates of return further to increase their political clout. Though this was an extreme case, county elections could cost £15,000 to £20,000 in the 1820s. In the later eighteenth century borough seats sold for £2,000 to £3,000 per election and for up to £15,000 outright. At the Union the government paid £1,260,000 in compensation to owners of disfranchised boroughs. Even after 1800 there was still a market in seats. The Irish elite paid dearly for high status.[114]

In many parts of Ireland the gentry were more thinly scattered than in England and sociability brought them to Dublin where the season at the 'Court' of the Lord Lieutenant merged with the sessions of parliament. The magnificent Parliament House which stands in the heart of Dublin illustrated, as had the new meeting place erected in Edinburgh, that the governing class saw parliament as a central institution, and that membership had become a principal means of asserting their rank.[115] The luxurious amenities provided in the new building erected in the 1730s made it seem more of a club than a place of business. Indeed its dining facilities, library, meeting rooms and central location made membership in the Irish parliament a necessity for those interested in entering the inner circle of Society. After the Union Dublin lost some of its lustre as a social centre, although the Castle retained a 'season'. The top elite now entered more fully into London life, where some families, such as the Ponsonbys, had already long been established. *Entrée* into the imperial parliament signified high social stature and became more prized than ever.

126

Estimates about the size of the Irish elite are just as complicated and confusing as those for the English ruling class. Some estimates for the eighteenth-century landed elite run as high as 5,000, but that figure includes many small holders. Other historians have put the number of significant Protestant families in the eighteenth century at about one thousand. This may be low. Mark Bence-Jones counted over two thousand country houses, though some of these were modest in scale, especially by English standards.[116] In the new Domesday survey of the 1870s, 303 owners held estates of 10,000 acres or more, one-third of the agricultural land in the kingdom. A total of 438 held 5,000 to 10,000 acres and 1,225 had 2,000 to 5,000 acres.[117] The size of the gentry seems to have been increasing during the eighteenth century as incomes rose and land that came on the market was snapped up. The nobility also increased in size. In 1585 there were twenty-four peers. The first two Stuart kings created eighty new ones. By 1692 the nobility consisted of 126 families. In 1800 the total stood at 169 exclusively Irish peers.[118] As a percentage of population, the Irish peerage was considerably larger than the English.[119]

A number of English magnates held large blocks of land in Ireland. Some of them played little role in the country's affairs. Even the Earls Fitzwilliam, who were responsible landowners and sympathetic to the plight of Catholics in Ireland, possessed only a small residence in County Wicklow and visited for a few weeks every other year or two. However, the image of a largely absentee elite is false. Many of the peers who did not take their places in the Dublin parliament were either legally debarred from doing so or held no land in Ireland. About two-thirds of the eighteenth-century Irish nobility were generally resident at their seats or in Dublin. Less than 20% of rentals were sent to permanent absentees.[120]

Identifying a date of social origin for settler families can also be tricky. For instance, the Abercorns arrived in Ireland already in possession of a peerage, while other families were from gentry backgrounds. But the mere fact that they crossed the sea to make a new start suggests that in many cases the position of the planters, adventurers and undertakers at home in England or Scotland was modest. Success once in Ireland usually had little to do with gentle birth. Generally, I have counted the date of social origin of the newly arrived families as the moment of their appearance in Ireland, unless they failed to acquire landed estates soon after they came. Only those with titles or who were sons of families of well-established stature in England, Scotland and Wales, with social origins pre-dating their new beginnings across the Channel, were so counted. It has also been difficult to categorize a few families whose interests straddled the Irish sea with a finally balanced stance, such as the Agar-Ellises, Brodricks and Percevals. Most families, however, fell clearly into one group or the other.

Keeping the reservations mentioned above in mind, let us turn to the data on the parliamentary elite. In total, 426 Irish families had three or more MPs or peers or were closely associated with such families between the Middle Ages and the twentieth century, and 352 elected at least one MP or peer between 1660 and 1945.[121] In the 1660s about three-fifths of all Irish MPs were from elite families. This proportion rose in 1692 to 71% and ranged between 79 and 90% between 1715 and 1835.[122] As the nineteenth century progressed elite MPs declined to two-thirds of the Irish delegation at Westminster in 1850, 45% in 1875, and only one in ten by 1900.

As with the Scottish elite, Irish families often elected few or no MPs before 1660.[123] This means that the proportion of parliamentary families with large numbers of MPs and peers was lower than for England and Wales. But because the Irish continued to possess their own parliament for nearly a century after the Scottish one ceased to meet, more seats were available to them than to their Caledonian counterparts. Thus a higher proportion of Irish families elected six or more MPs.

A greater number of historic Irish families are not included in this study than is the case for Wales, Scotland and England. The wealth of Gaelic families was wiped out, or their chiefs went into exile before 1660, though many descendants continued to live in Ireland, sometimes near or on the original patrimony of the family. About twenty families, for whom records exist, elected three or more MPs before the Restoration and none afterwards. These include Catholic burgesses such as the Archers and Rothes of Kilkenny, the Arthures of Limerick and the Sherlocks of Waterford. Usually, these families lost their property in the mid-seventeenth century. The last Rothe went abroad and was killed in French service in 1709. There were 'Old English' families too, such as the Sarsfields, who may have been Anglo-Norman in origin and rose as merchants and lawyers to a viscountcy in 1627. They too lost everything between 1653 and 1689. The number of such families is incalculable from the remaining parliamentary records, and twenty must be an underestimate.

Some old families survived but with relatively small estates and little access to parliament even though they might have borne ancient designations such as The O'Grady or The McGillycuddy of the Reeks. The Martins of Ballynahinch managed to hold on to 170,000 acres in Connemara, but they did not enter the Commons until Richard 'Humanity Dick' Martin (MP 1776–1827) was raised a Protestant. There was time for only one more MP before indebtedness and the Famine led to the sale of the estates. Some of the old peerage such as the Earls of Louth (1280), the Barons Kingsale (1310) and the Viscounts Gormanston (1370) elected few or no MPs but survived into modern times. The Earls of Howth and the Marquesses of Antrim, on the other hand, remained comparatively rich. The two MPs elected by each family under-represents their prestige. Some more recent peerage families also failed to elect many MPs or to achieve much representation in the British House of Lords. This list is a short one, however, amounting to only a half dozen or so families.[124] After 1660 few substantial landowners among the Protestant Ascendancy were not active in parliament.

Table 4.3 Examples of members of the Irish parliamentary elite and family relationships

BRUEN

Henry Bruen MP Jamestown 1783–90; County Carlow 1790–95		**Head**
Henry Bruen MP County Carlow 1812–31, 1835–37, 1840–52		**Head**
Francis Bruen MP Carlow 1835–37, 1839		**Younger Son**
Henry Bruen MP County Carlow 1857–80		**Head**

Although they came to Ireland in the mid-seventeenth century, the Bruens did not purchase estates in Carlow until the 1770s. Their house in Wexford was burned down in 1914 and they sold Oak Park, Carlow in 1957.

MONCK

Charles Monck MP Strabane 1634; Coleraine 1639	**Head**
Charles Monck MP Newcastle 1711–13, 1715–25; Innistiogue 1713–14	**Head**
George Monck MP Philipstown 1703–13	**Eldest Son**
Henry Monck MP Duleek 1755–60, 1761–68	**Head**
George Monck MP Coleraine 1763–68	**Grandson**
Thomas Monck MP Old Leighlin 1768–72	**Younger Son**
Charles Monck, 1st Viscount Monck MP Gorey 1790–97; IHLds 1797–1800	**Head**
William Monck MP Coleraine 1795–97; Gorey 1797–99	**Brother**
Charles Monck, 4th Viscount Monck MP Portsmouth 1852–57; HLds 1866–94	**Head**
Henry Monck, 5th Viscount Monck HLds 1894–1927	**Head**
Henry Monck, 6th Viscount Monck HLds 1927–45	**Head**

The Moncks were old Devon gentry distantly related to the Duke of Albemarle. An early seventeenth-century official purchased estates in Ireland. They briefly became Earls of Rathdown (1822–48). A UK peerage was conferred in 1866. Charleville was abandoned in 1921 and subsequently sold.

TAYLOUR

Sir Thomas Taylour, 1st Baronet MP Kells 1692–93, 1695–99; Belturbet 1703–13; Kells 1713–36	**Head**
Sir Thomas Taylour, 2nd Baronet MP Kells 1713–57	**Head**

James Taylour MP Kells 1737–97	**Younger Son**
Thomas Taylour, 1st Earl Bective MP Kells 1747–60; IHLds 1761–95	**Head**
Thomas Taylour, 1st Marquess of Headfort MP Kells 1776–90; Longford 1790–94; County Meath 1794–95; IHLds 1795–1800; Rep. Peer 1801–29	**Head**
Hercules Taylour MP Kells 1781–90	**Younger Son**
Robert Taylour MP Kells 1791–1800	**Younger Son**
Clotworthy Taylour, 1st Baron Langford MP Trim 1791–95; County Meath 1795–1800	**Younger Son**
Thomas Taylour, 2nd Marquess of Headfort MP County Meath 1812–29; HLds 1831–70	**Head**
Thomas Taylour MP County Dublin 1841–83	**Grandson**
Thomas Taylour, 3rd Marquess of Headfort MP Westmorland 1854–70; HLds 1870–94	**Head**
Thomas Taylour, Earl Bective MP Westmorland 1871–85; Kendal Div. Westmorland 1885–92	**Eldest Son**
Geoffrey Taylour, 4th Marquess of Headfort HLds 1899–1943	**Head**
Terence Taylour, 5th Marquess of Headfort HLds 1943–45	**Head**

The Taylours arrived in Ireland in the mid-seventeenth century and rose quickly through government service. They achieved a UK barony in 1831. In the nineteenth century they succeeded to the fortune and estates of the English ironmaster William Thompson. Clotworthy Taylour married the Rowley heiress, receiving a peerage in his own right, and his descendants are counted under that family. The house at Headfort, Meath, was converted into a boys' school after the Second World War, although the family retained a residence there.

The Irish 'five or fewer' MP/peer category was more of a mixture of types and wealth than in any other part of the British Isles. Families included in this group ranged from the very wealthy Marquesses of Clanricarde and the less well-endowed Earls of Castle Stewart to more recent peers such as the Mullins Barons Ventry and the Hare Earls of Listowel. Some very rich but late entrants included the Guinness Earls of Iveagh and the Mulholland Barons Dunleath. Other types include Gaelic princes such as the O'Conor Dons, old gentry like the Graces, military settlers such as the Saundersons, merchant families who eventually rose to gentry status, such as the Christmases of Waterford, legal eagles like the Fitzgibbon Earls of Clare, and the industrialist Harlands of Belfast. Big, untitled gentry with small representation in the Commons were much rarer in Ireland than in Scotland.

Anybody who was anybody tended to get a title and permanent representation in parliament at least until 1800. Thus the 'six-plus' MP category was dominated by peerage families, although there were some important gentry such as the Herberts of Muckross and the Wynnes of Hazelwood. Among the nobles were old Catholic families such as the Plunketts and aggressively Protestant new settlers such as the Earls of Bessborough and Cavan.

Like some Scottish families a few Irish dynasties did not have a large presence in the Commons after the Union but continued to play a regular role in political life as representative peers.[125] No further elections were held beyond 1922, and unlike the Scottish peerage, who were admitted to the upper house *en masse* in 1967, Irish lords without British titles floated in constitutional limbo.

More Irish elite families, as a proportion of the total number of entries, are to be found in Bateman than is true for England (65 to 55%). Because many of the settlers were of comparatively recent origin, fewer had become extinct by the 1870s than was the case among the English elite. Not many Irish families were rich on a Percian or Grosvenorian scale, and only three dynasties of ducal rank emerged: Ormonde, Leinster and Abercorn. More peers subsisted on meagre financial resources than in England. A few, such as the Aylmers and Lysaghts, fell into real distress during the eighteenth century. Much indebtedness existed long before the Famine, and large sales of land began with the Encumbered Estates Act of 1848.

Forty-six Irish families qualify as grandees during the eighteenth and nineteenth centuries using the criteria applied for great English dynasties in Chapter Two. Though fewer 'clans' existed than in England, branches of Boyles, Butlers, Gores, Hamiltons and Plunketts did proliferate.[126] As with the Scottish grandees, some important Irish families are excluded from the list because of the foreshortened nature of the parliaments abolished at the Union. The incomplete lists of returns before 1692 and the changes in landholding in the seventeenth century mean that some families who were undoubtedly of importance in Ascendancy Ireland did not have long lists of MPs or many years of service in either the Commons or the Lords. The Irish elite was also under-represented in categories such as holders of cabinet offices, from which Irish families were largely excluded until the nineteenth century, and the Order of Saint Patrick was established long after the Garter and the Thistle. If one applies the adjusted criteria used for the Scottish grandees, an additional eight families can be added to the Irish group raising the total number to fifty-four.[127]

Even after this adjustment, an argument can be made that a dozen or so other families ought to be included such as the Earls of Mayo, Desart, Granard, Ranfurly and Belvidere, and the Viscounts Doneraile and Templetown. In most cases they are disqualified by incomes that fell below £20,000.[128] Some of the old Catholic dynasties were knocked out both by moderate or even modest incomes and the sectarian laws which prevented their attendance in parliament for long periods. The grandee list of Ireland is the least satisfactory of the four included in this study because of fragmentary records, diverse levels of status and prestige, changes brought about by the Union, and the smaller scale of the Irish economy. The Conollys of Castletown do not appear on the list, yet the founder was said to have been the richest man in Ireland in the eighteenth century.[129]

Most of the grandees were of English origin, although they arrived in Ireland anywhere from the twelfth to mid-seventeenth century. Nine had Scottish backgrounds and only two were of Gaelic lineage. The Guinness claim of descent from the Magennises of Down is unlikely, but they were also native Irish. Twenty-two families had medieval origins, six Tudor, twenty-three seventeenth century and only three after 1700. Sixteen of the English families either had elected an MP or been raised to noble rank before coming to Ireland and five of the Scottish arrivals were cadets of noble families. Over half (52%) of the grandees were connected with the political elite before 1600.

Irish grandees were proportionately much less likely than English families to hold important offices of state, although the Boyles, Butlers and Ponsonbys gained high positions in the seventeenth and eighteenth centuries. In the nineteenth century a few served as viceroys of India, but after the Union the leading ministers with Irish connections such as Castlereagh, Lansdowne, Palmerston, Perceval and Wellington lived mostly or wholly in England.

Between 1692 and 1800, 18% of all Irish parliamentary seats were held by MPs from the fifty-four grandee families, a considerably lower rate than in England, Wales and Scotland, where the proportion ran anywhere from five to twelve points higher. Part of this disparity was due to the most powerful families choosing to elect some of their members for English seats and English families such as the Cavendishes and Petty-Fitzmaurices filling up Irish seats. This leads to an undercount of the Irish grandee presence in parliament. None the less, more middling gentry families had the opportunity to gain a place in the Dublin Commons, while there were 300 seats available, than was the case in the much leaner Scottish pool of places or in England where the amount of competition was much greater. After the Union the percentage of grandee MPs sitting for Irish seats rose to 22, slightly higher than for Wales but a bit lower than England and Scotland. Important grandee families began to disappear entirely from the Commons in greater numbers earlier in Ireland than elsewhere. The 2nd Marquess of Ormonde, the last Butler of the main line to be elected an MP, left the Commons in 1832, long before the family faded from social prominence. Only two ducal Fitzgeralds sat after the First Reform Act. When grandees did keep up the electoral tradition of the family it was sometimes for a non-Irish seat, in contrast to the other national elites who sat mainly for native constituencies. Of the five Beresfords who sat after 1832 three were elected in England.

As in Scotland the constriction in the number of seats in the Commons available after the Union created an artificial decline in the number of elite families, although the increased difficulty in obtaining a post-1800 seat helped to winnow the top elite from the rest. Between 1660 and 1800 there was a fair amount of turnover among gentry families with parliamentary pretensions.[130] Most of the disappearances can be attributed to biological extinction or financial decline. Unlike in England and Wales during the eighteenth century big estates tended to shrink in size and the number of lesser gentry grew in number, although few wealthy and influential families disappeared entirely from the elite.[131]

Twenty-five families with five or fewer MPs elected their last MP between 1760 and 1779, twenty-eight disappeared during the next two decades and thirty-eight between 1801 and 1819. Among 'six-plus' families, five became politically extinct between 1760 and 1779, and fifteen during the next two decades, but thirty-two disappeared in the years immediately after the Union. More families of all types ended their parliamentary histories in the decade before the Union (sixty-three) than in any other similar interval between 1660 and 1920.[132] Thirty-six families elected their last MP in 1800. This figure was twice as high as for any other decade except for the thirty-two who departed in 1830–39 immediately after the First Reform Act, the thirty-eight in the 1850s when reform and the financial impact of the Famine struck, and the thirty-two in the 1880s when further reform and the land war finished off some of the most potent dynasties.

Gentry and nobles who ended their tenure as parliamentary families in the twenty-five years before the Union included many who continued to hold sizeable estates in the late nineteenth century. Twenty-eight peerage families produced their last MP between 1783 and 1800 compared to six in the next eighteen years. A few other prominent families elected only one MP for an Irish seat after 1800. The Union of 1707 had little effect on 'six-plus' Scottish families, but many Irish ones ceased being parliamentary after 1800. In part this was because the Irish enjoyed proportionally fewer seats in the British House of Commons than the Welsh, Scottish or English which restricted the opportunities for election largely to the top elite.[133] None the less, most of the important families survived the compression of 1801. That situation changed in 1832. Many rich and influential noble families ceased to elect MPs from the time of the Reform Act or in the years immediately following. Of course, this may have been due to factors other than reform including the success of the Catholic Association and encumbered estates.

Just as the electoral disappearance of the great families was focused in a brief period, the entrance of new families came in more concentrated spurts than in England or Scotland. If one uses date of achieving gentry status as opposed to date of first MP, it is possible to construct a long-term image of entry into the elite, but it must be kept in mind that families under consideration composed the eighteenth- and nineteenth-century patriciate only. Three-quarters of the 'six-plus' families were either Gaelic, Old English, Tudor or early Stuart arrivals.[134] Few families of important standing emerged out of the Cromwellian planter category. The Ponsonbys were virtually unique among grandees in their Civil War origins, although many 'New Protestant' families of Tudor and early Stuart origins became much richer by purchasing expropriated land during the aftermath of the Civil Wars of the mid- and late-seventeenth century.[135] The top elite was closed by 1660. In 1800, before the Union, only 26% of the elite MPs who made up nine out of ten of the Commons membership were not from pre-1660 origins, and this stayed much the same ten years after the abolition of the Dublin parliament among the Irish delegation in Westminster (27%).[136]

These findings suggest that Tipperary, where Thomas Power found that a majority of the families providing MPs for the county were of Cromwellian origins, must have been atypical. Francis James's study of the Irish peerage showed that the 'controlling group' in the mid-eighteenth-century House of Lords came from pre-Cromwellian families, which is more in line with the findings of this study for the parliamentary elite in both Houses. James also found that about one-quarter of the peers who attended the Lords in 1692–1727 were of Gaelic or Old English origins. The statistics for the governing class as defined in this study were similar.[137]

The ruling class that emerged from the crisis of the mid-seventeenth century had deeper roots in Ireland than is often supposed. Most historians portray the Irish elite far differently than its counterparts in England, Wales and Scotland. It is frequently said that Irish society was less exclusive, except in religion, than other parts of the British Isles in the eighteenth and nineteenth centuries. The sectarian divisions may actually have encouraged an egalitarian spirit, religious brotherhood replacing breeding in each denominational camp as a source of solidarity.[138] Chaos also created unusual opportunities to rise as did large-scale forfeiture of land in 1653–65 and the 1690s. The Protestants who emerged as winners formed a thin layer atop Irish society, so that those with a stake in preserving the new system did not examine very closely claims to gentility of landowners who were vital to maintaining civil order. Ireland was also a home for remittance men, and it was more common in Ireland than elsewhere to find even quite distinguished families descended from the wrong side of noble blankets.

The most celebrated examples of Irish social mobility are William Conolly of Castletown and Richard Boyle, 1st Earl of Cork. The former was of Irish Catholic ancestry, the son of a publican. He began his career in 1685 and by 1722 was building one of the largest and finest country houses in Ireland; he controlled eight parliamentary boroughs and left £300,000 at his death. Lord Cork is said to have arrived in Ireland in 1588 with £27 in his pocket and by 1640 allegedly had become the richest landowner in the British Isles with an earl's coronet on his head.[139] These men were economic Napoleons, enormously skilled in exploiting the confused land markets of their day. Circumstances unique to Ireland lent themselves to fantastic rises in a single lifetime.

Less well-known fortunes were also created in spectacularly short periods. The Fosters came to Ireland as mowers of hay in the 1660s. By 1715 they had gained control of a parliamentary borough and went on to high office and a peerage. The 1st Viscount Avonmore started as an usher in a boarding school. Luke Gardiner, ancestor of the Earls of Blessington, was the grandson of a footman. Sir James Shaen's (baronet 1663) grandfather was supposed to have been a blacksmith. Lord Clonmell, whose brother was a provincial tallow chandler, became Lord Chief Justice.[140] Almost half of all the families with their first MP post-1500 in this study whose origins I was unable to uncover can be found among the Irish parliamentary elite.[141] Also, more Irish families came from unsavoury pasts, even after discounting the cruel expropriation of estates. Among the founders of parliamentary dynasties in this study who were notable for skulduggery or outright criminality in the achievement of high status, half came from the Irish elite.

But it would be incorrect to assume that in Ireland distinctions about birth were not drawn or that older families did not disdain new ones. The more established dynasties often denigrated recent arrivals. Gaelic and Old English families took enormous pride in their ancestry. The celebrated Countess of Fingall began her memoirs noting that her father was a Galway Burke: 'To anyone acquainted with Irish history, that says everything that need be said about our family.' Genealogies were also discussed by Ascendancy families, one member observed, 'with the eagerness of hounds on a hot scent'.[142] As in England, Irish society had genuinely ancient families and many gradations of wealth and status. New and old money were intermixed by marriage. Snobbery flourished. It is a mistake to believe that the Irish Ascendancy was monolithic in origins or social attitudes.

Much of the native or Gaelic aristocracy had been decimated by war and confiscation, but it would have changed greatly over the centuries even if the English had failed to arrive. It suffered a less catastrophic fate than that meted out to Saxon landowners by the Normans. The native kings lost most of their authority and much of their land, but some survived down to modern times in prosperity and with authority. The O'Neills, who claimed descent from Niall the Great (AD 379–405), are one of the oldest traceable families in Europe. They still own a large estate, possess a peerage and held the premiership of Northern Ireland in the 1960s. However, only they, the Kavanaghs and the O'Briens (who probably do descend from Brian Boru, High King in the early eleventh century, and reigned as Kings of Thomond until the sixteenth century) managed to cling to the magnate level. The Quins, Earls of Dunraven, claimed to date back to a third-century King of Munster, but unlike the O'Neills, if such an ancestry existed, it was long forgotten.[143] O'Conor Don, the descendant of the last High King, survived with a mere £2,030 in income in the later nineteenth century. The Crown restored a surprising number of Roman Catholic Irish peers to their estates and titles in 1660 and more outlawries were reversed in 1697. None the less, many families were destroyed by the wars or became permanent exiles.[144] Other survivors at a modest level included The O'Ferral Bouy, The O'Long, The MacCarthy Mor, The O'Morchoe and The Fox. Several native chieftains continued to be accorded demi-royal rank by old Catholic families in modern times, such as the Donnelans and The MacDermot, Prince of Coolavin. Daniel O'Connell, whose ancestry was probably quite old but not of high rank, was spurred to leadership by a fierce pride that was not just nationalistic but rooted in 'ancient' descent.[145] The Norse ancestry of the Plunketts may have some substance and they were at Dunsany by the twelfth century. The MacDonnells of the glens descended from the Lords of the Isles and were masters of over 300,000 acres in the seventeenth century, and still live at Glenarm as Earls of Antrim.[146]

The lineages of the great Anglo-Norman families of Ireland are also lengthy. The Ormonde office of Chief Butler of Ireland (created *c.* 1185), from which the family takes its name, is the most ancient hereditary dignity still extant in the male line in the British Isles. The Butlers were already a family of high rank when they came to Ireland with Prince John in 1185 and were seated at Kilkenny Castle from 1391 to 1935. A cadet branch held Cahir Castle for even longer. The Talbots were at Malahide Castle from 1185 until 1973. The dates of origins of the older Irish peerages are hard to pinpoint precisely.[147] The Fitzmaurices were summoned as barons in 1295, the DeCourcy Barony of Kingsale dates from 1320, and the Butlers were earls by 1328. Many such families 'went native' quite early, intermarrying with and inheriting the estates and outlook of the Gaelic chiefs. Many of these 'Old English' families also remained Catholic after the Reformation, and to distinguish in modern times between them and the Celtic lords is meaningless. Men such as the MacWilliam Burke were Irish chiefs in every sense of the word. Some of them acquired romantic titles such as the White Knight and the Knight of Kerry.

The Old English did not all arrive with 'Strongbow' in 1172. The Barrys came over with Henry II and achieved a barony in 1261. The Wellesleys (Wesleys) were said to have been in Ireland since 1226, and the Brownes of Oranmore and Browne appeared in 1316. The Fitzwilliams of Merrion settled during the reign of King John but were of only local importance until two brothers returned to England in the mid-sixteenth century to make their fortunes, and one became an MP.[148]

One of the mysteries of Irish history is the remarkable survival rate of the old families through the bloody chapters of such a violent past. Writs of summons to the Great Council of Ireland in 1375 were sent to a Burgh, Fitzgerald, Plunkett, Taafe and

Talbot, families that survived until recent times. The Barnewalls, Brownes, Prestons and others circumvented the penal laws via trusts and friendships. Those that conformed in religion and married into the Protestant elite did best. Altogether, slightly over 10% of the parliamentary elite were Anglo-Norman in origin.

Another 10 or 11% were founded by the next wave of arrivals during the Tudor period. Many of these were officials, military officers, undertakers and adventurers who have no real counterparts in early modern English history. It is not really appropriate to equate many of these swashbuckling characters with bureaucrats or lawyers elsewhere or during other periods. A settler could be a knightly warrior, an unscrupulous asset-stripper, a patriotic official, a pirate, a farmer or a combination of the above.[149] Those who stayed were not so much founding a fortune on government service as gaining wealth by speculation in or theft of real estate. Some of these families came from quite distinguished lineage in England, and held on to estates they already owned across the seas. In other cases settler wealth was derived from sources other than expropriation or official service. Some new arrivals came over with humble ancestry or as younger sons of minor families and made little or no immediate progress, rising later through agriculture, law or commerce.[150]

Attaining enough status to gain election to the English parliament before leaving for Ireland often eased the way to a passage across the Channel. A number of English parliamentary elite families founded cadet lines in Ireland.[151] Distinguished Scottish and Welsh families did the same. Sir Oliver Lambart was MP for Southampton in 1597, which gave him the *entrée* to gain important military posts and estates in Ireland. Gerard Lowther, a scion of a great English parliamentary family and MP for Cumberland in 1601, was able to win an Irish judgeship and built up an estate in Tyrone and Fermanagh. The Stopfords rose as noble servants, possessed land in Lancashire and elected an MP for Liverpool in 1558 before going to Ireland in Cromwellian service and rising to an Irish earldom.[152]

'New Protestant' arrivals can be roughly divided into military and official categories. For example, Edward Denny, already MP for Westmorland in 1593 and uncle of Lord Denny, went to Ireland in 1587 with an army command and founded a cadet line of an English peerage family with the initial grant of 6,000 acres near Tralee. The Needhams' fortunes were founded by an English judge in the mid-fifteenth century. They elected four MPs between 1442 and 1648 and retained important English estates, but one member of the family was an Elizabethan military commander in Ireland. His progeny produced nine Irish MPs between 1727 and 1874. One of the greatest families to rise through the campaigns against Hugh O'Neill at the end of Elizabeth's reign were the Marquesses of Downshire. Moyses Hill received his first grant of land in 1592 for military service. However, it was successive generations of the family who parlayed this small holding into a vast estate through marriage and opportune purchases during the seventeenth century.[153] A few Cromwellian officers, like the first Ponsonby, also managed to gain large estates. Several other families received Irish grants for military service under William III and Queen Anne such as the Prendergasts, later Viscounts Gort.

Englishmen enjoying senior civil appointments did better than soldiers, no doubt because they had the greatest opportunity for aggrandizement, and because they were often already rich and thus well positioned to exploit bargains when they came along. The Skeffingtons, St Legers and Chichesters, all well connected in England, came to Ireland as Lords Deputy. The Browne Earls of Kenmare arrived in the form of a pay official for the army under Elizabeth I, another position where both corruption and legitimate activities offered great scope for advancement. The first King (Earls of Kingston) held various offices under Elizabeth and James I and married the heiress of another official. The founder of the Irish May family crossed the Channel as an official in the 1690s, but he was the grandson of a Master of the Rolls and MP in England under James I. Only about 7% of the Irish elite can be tied directly to office as a principal means of their rise. Of this group, over half (55%) arrived under the Tudors and only 31% during the seventeenth century. Just three families succeeded in finding a place in the parliamentary elite through official careers in the eighteenth century.

Nearly one-quarter (24%) of all Irish elite families fell into the non-official adventurer category in origins. They were a diverse group not only in the methods by which they gained estates but also in their country and date of origin (mainly post-Elizabethans). The first Saunderson of Castle Saunderson became an undertaker in Ireland in 1618. His son was granted much larger amounts of land for military service in 1654, and further estates were purchased in 1666. The Molesworths had an ancient English pedigree, went to Ireland with Cromwell and received modest estates. It was as merchants in Dublin in the later seventeenth century, however, that they acquired great wealth and a viscountcy. A classic, if unusually complex, example of the problem of categorization in Ireland is provided by the Brownes of Westport. In 1585 John Browne acquired the family's first land. His great-grandson, Colonel John Browne, was a successful lawyer and married the daughter of the 3rd Viscount Bourke, the head of a distinguished Old English family who had acquired the Westport estate through descent from a marriage into the Gaelic O'Malley clan. The Brownes were Catholics and remained loyal to James II. They were obliged to sell 111,000 acres between 1698 and 1708 to pay off fines and debts incurred by their political resistance. An early eighteenth-century head of the family was worth only £700 p.a. but, fortunately, was raised as a Protestant. He married a daughter of the Earl of Arran, and was able to build the new Westport House, which is still the family residence. His son married a great West Indian heiress, who restored the family to riches. Eventually they became Marquesses of Sligo.[154]

Families founded via the professions are more clearly identifiable. Unlike elsewhere in the British Isles, the Church was a significant factor in launching a number of important dynasties, and even when clerical status was not decisive, having a bishop in the family could smooth the path to wealth. Ecclesiastical careers produced almost one in twenty of the parliamentary elite. Irish bishoprics, though not as lavishly remunerated as most English sees, could produce good incomes and wonderful opportunities for purchase of confiscated estates at low prices. The peculiar nature of the Church of Ireland also favoured profiting from pluralism and patronage. The high point of ecclesiastical entry into the elite was the seventeenth century when well over half made their fortunes.[155]

Only one or two physicians founded parliamentary families in Ireland, which was not so much due to Irish lack of interest in health as the absence of royal doctors. The St Georges, a family of Elizabethan heralds, moved across to Ireland in the early seventeenth century and were assisted in their rise by appointment as Kings of Arms.

As elsewhere, it was law that produced most of the professional families in Ireland who entered the elite. One in five (19%) Irish MPs under George II were lawyers, which was a higher proportion than in the Commons in England.[156] However, only 8% of all Irish elite families had primarily legal backgrounds, more than the 4% in Scotland but less than the 10% in England. It was perhaps more common in Ireland than across the Channel for even substantial landowners to be county MPs and practising lawyers. A number of businessmen, officials and land speculators were members of the bar. William Conolly, for instance, trained as a lawyer. However, I have tried to reserve this category for those who were primarily legal practitioners, although I have counted men such as James Verner who was an attorney, land agent and local official. Great fortunes could be made in legal practice. The father of the first Earl of Clare made £100,000 at the Irish bar.[157]

A few legal families rose under the Tudors or earlier. The first Preston of Gormanston was Justice of the King's Bench in Ireland in 1326. The Meade Earls of Clanwilliam and the Netterville viscounts were mid-sixteenth-century legal families. More arose in the seventeenth century, such as the Coxes, Levinges and Holmeses, but the great era of fortune-making, in contrast to the Church, was the eighteenth century when nearly half (44%) of the 'law' families rose into the elite. A number of comparatively humble men or their immediate heirs acquired large estates or rose to peerages through fortunes made by lawyers. The rate dropped off in the nineteenth century, but Lords O'Hagan and Ashbourne established parliamentary families in that century.

Altogether one-quarter (24%) of Irish families arose directly from professional careers and government service, higher than the 19% for England, 15 for Wales and 8 for Scotland. Ireland required more management than England or Scotland and if one adds the Ascendancy families who were launched by military officers and local officials, the proportion of the parliamentary elite deriving their origins from these categories was significantly greater than anywhere else in the British Isles.

Few of the new entrants were from commercial backgrounds. Only 19% of the total elite clearly had their origins in business, twice as high a rate as Scotland but almost half that in England. Part of this disparity is due to the more modest scale of the Irish economy. Dublin merchants could not compete in wealth with the great London bankers and overseas traders. It is fair to say that the Ascendancy was largely a landed class. Men with business backgrounds were not usually found in the Irish Commons and rarely appeared in the House of Lords.[158] However, this statement must be hedged by the caveat that founders of 'New Protestant' families, in government posts, as undertakers and in the professions, were usually men with entrepreneurial characters and the Irish elite produced many who were active in commercial ventures. But lack of scope to make big fortunes in a primarily agricultural country held back business families. The aristocracy could be welcoming, if estates were purchased and landed styles of life adopted.[159] Moreover, regions that enjoyed commercial opportunities did produce elite families.[160]

Finance was the most 'respectable' commercial activity and produced some important landed families. The Hoares were bankers in Cork in the seventeenth and eighteenth centuries; the Bagwell bankers acquired the estates of indebted landlords. The Dawsons were Dublin financiers and became Earls of Dartrey. The LaTouche clan of Huguenot bankers arrived in 1688 and were country gentlemen and Dublin businessmen simultaneously.

Thomas Maunsell made a large fortune in the East India Company service during the eighteenth century, though he came from a family of already established settlers. The 1st Earl Macartney rose in government service and made a fortune as President of Fort St George in India, but he had already inherited an established estate based on business, marriage and the law. Only two genuinely new families were founded by nabobs: the Gregorys of Coole and the Alexander Earls of Caledon, although the Stewarts of Mount Stewart were also assisted in their ascent by an East Indian fortune.

Important merchant families were concentrated mainly in the seventeenth century, when half of all business fortunes that achieved elite status were made, in contrast to the 17% in both the sixteenth and eighteenth centuries. In the early seventeenth century the Frenches, prosperous Catholic merchants in Galway, began to invest in land, buying out impoverished Gaelic proprietors and founding a parliamentary family. The Christmases (five MPs between 1695 and 1835) started as Bristol merchants and moved to Waterford in the 1660s. They married into the aristocracy and built a country seat in 1743. The father of the 1st Baron Cloncurry was in the wool trade in mid-eighteenth-century Dublin. Nathaniel Sneyd, a wine merchant, sat for County Cavan in 1801–26.[161]

Brewing produced two successful families. The Leeson Earls of Milltown created one of the most beautiful houses in Ireland at Russborough. The Guinnesses began their rise in the eighteenth century but took longer to achieve a peerage. They stayed connected with the company and eventually became spectacularly rich with large estates on both sides of the Irish Sea.

Ireland was even less industrial than it was mercantile. Lack of natural resources, shortage of capital and restrictive legislation imposed by the English hindered development. Sir Charles Coote had a large iron foundry in the mid-eighteenth century, and the LaTouches originally began in manufacturing before moving to banking. The 1st Earl of Cork was an ironmaster among his many interests.[162] The only significant parliamentary manufacturing fortunes were made in the north by the Stewarts of Mount Stewart and the Mulholland Barons Dunleath in the Belfast linen industry. The Harlands, whose gantries still dominate the Belfast skyline, made their millions as shipbuilders but never became an important landed family.

Country houses with defensive features were still being built in Ireland in the 1860s – and with good reason. A gulf of language, religion and culture led to misunderstanding, resentment and fear. Even after two centuries of occupation many members of the landed class regarded themselves, as David Thomson in his evocative portrait of Woodbrook called them, 'a garrison in a hostile land'. The Anglo-Irish felt an atavistic loyalty to the English Crown, but they also grew to resent the doubts their brethren across the water felt about the security of the Protestant grip on the land.[163] Their reliance on the military might of a London government that showed progressive signs of weakness on the question of subordinating Catholics caused unease. At the same time the elite became Irish enough in their feelings and orientation to seem alien to the English. They even began to intermarry with the Old English and Gaelic elites.[164] The 'Ascendancy', a designation coined in the eighteenth century, was composed of Gaelic, Old English, New English, Scottish undertaker and Huguenot stock.[165] Irish patriots such as Henry Grattan, Wolfe Tone, Lord Edward Fitzgerald, Isaac Butt, Charles Parnell, Lady Gregory, Roger Casement and Constance Markievicz were Ascendancy bred.

None the less, both historians and contemporary observers have judged the class a failed aristocracy that did too little to justify its privileged position.[166] Nineteenth-century Whig grandees in England, such as the 3rd Earl Spencer, called Irish sectarian privileges 'a disgrace to a civilized country', while the 5th Earl Fitzwilliam labelled the Ascendancy a 'tyrannical oligarchy'. By the end of the century even the noble leadership of the Tory Party in England regarded the Irish elite with contempt.[167] The governing class of England and Scotland left the Ascendancy to die, hammering home some of the spikes that did the deed, beginning with Catholic Emancipation and culminating in Wyndham's Act of 1903. Though not all the landowners of England favoured this course, in the end most were willing to abandon the elite in Ireland to prevent the breakdown of law and order. The Irish landlords were unable to save themselves.

As we have seen already, the reduction by two-thirds of the number of Irish parliamentary seats at the Union knocked out the lower tiers of the Ascendancy from parliamentary participation. In theory this should have meant that the remaining families who could gain seats would be the strongest and fittest survivors. However, granting Catholics the right to vote in 1793 began to weaken landlord power, although this was minimal at first owing to the use of intimidation and residual deferential feelings. The battle for Catholic emancipation during the 1820s strengthened the influence of the Catholic clergy, although the 'wings' attached to the Act drastically reduced the size of the electorate. Ironically, beginning in the 1820s there were revolts in Protestant strongholds against aristocratic patrons because some of them were considered too 'soft' on Catholics. This was quickly followed by the First Reform Act, which enfranchised more voters. Though the overall number of those qualified to vote was still down, more people actually participated in the 1832 election than in 1826. Corruption continued in the boroughs but landlord control was greatly diminished. The counties remained largely in elite hands, although less and less friendly to landlord interests as time progressed. Almost a third (30%) of Irish MPs returned in 1832 were close male relatives of peers and baronets.[168] Ulster remained an 'impregnable redoubt' of landlord power unshaken even by the end of the 1860s, while in the south some of the repealers of the Catholic party were pedigreed landlords.[169]

However, funds provided by the Catholic Association began to make it possible for men without independent means to stand for parliament. Between 1830 and 1835 the Irish governing class took a deeper plunge than the other elites in the British Isles in loss of parliamentary seats, declining 27 points from (83 to 56%) of all Irish MPs.[170] There was something of a recovery, however, and in 1850 elite families were back to filling two-thirds of the seats.[171] (See Figures 4.1 and 4.2.) Then decline set in again.[172]

The fall from controlling more than 80% of the seats in the early nineteenth century to less than 10% by 1905 is the story of a landed elite confronting a series of crises related to rising national feeling among the Catholic community, a breakdown in the relationship between landlords and tenants, and increasing assaults on their economic and psychological security caused by indebtedness, population growth, the Famine and the Land Acts. Not all of these factors, however, affected every elite family.

Perhaps one-quarter of all productive land in Ireland changed hands in the decade or so after the Famine. Much of the property of Martin of Ballynahinch, Viscount Gort, the Earl of Milltown and the Marquess of Donegall was sold. The Earl of Bantry disposed of 67,000 acres in 1851. The Duke of Devonshire began to sell estates in

Ireland in 1859 in order to shore up troubled finances at home in England. However, some landlords who survived the mid-century crisis purchased acreage from their bankrupt brethren, actually extending and strengthening their estates. By holding down rents during the 1850s and 1860s political influence could be purchased and some peers consolidated their electoral positions. On the other hand, Irish families did not benefit from the mineral deposits, urban growth, and industrial expansion which enriched many English aristocrats during the nineteenth century. Keeping down rents meant less capital was available for investment in increased agricultural production.[173] Gradually the financial position worsened for everyone.

Theodore Hoppen sees a 're-emerging sense of political power' among the landed elite after the Famine, with more prosperity and optimism. He also argues that the Second Reform Act left the Irish electorate proportionally much smaller than in England and Scotland and thus easier to control.[174] It is true that elite influence still prevailed in some places, and businessmen and lawyers were purchasing landed estates and entering parliament after mid-century.[175] Landlords who had acted humanely during the Famine were still the beneficiaries of residual respect as late as the 1890s. Families such as the Bandons, De Freynes, Enniskillens, Fitzwilliams, Hertfords, Kilmoreys, Leinsters, Ranfurlys, Sligos and Waterfords continued to elect MPs after 1868 at least down to 1885.[176] Ulster aristocrats like the Archdales and Downshires went on into the twentieth century, while the O'Neills held an Antrim seat almost continuously from 1783 to 1959.

But the Second Reform Act did have an impact. The number of elite MPs dropped from 61% in 1865 to 56 in 1870 and was at 45% by 1875 – the first time the proportion had fallen under half of Irish MPs since Cromwell invaded Ireland. The 1872 Ballot Act was a hammer blow to landlord interest in a country where the threat of intimidation made open voting less than democratic. Gladstone's first Land Act of 1870 was modest but symbolically important. Alternative sources of patronage and power were developing in rural Ireland in the 1860s and 1870s, largely anti-aristocratic in temperament. The benevolently Whig 6th Earl Fitzwilliam was shouted down in public during the Wicklow election of 1874, which distressed even the Catholic clergy. That year saw the elite's hold on Irish seats drop another 12%. Lord Otho Fitzgerald's defeat by a Catholic lawyer was as powerful a sign of the political decline of landlord power in Ireland as the Earl of Dalkeith's electoral demise was to be six years later in Scotland. Even the Gaelic prince, O'Conor Don, was defeated by a journalist.[177]

Rural unrest had periodically disrupted the countryside through much of the century, but radicals turned from maiming cattle to killing landlords and their agents. In the 1798 rising Colonel Mansergh St George had been hacked to death with a scythe, which more than hints at the level of animosity lurking near the surface of

Ascendancy Ireland. Later in the century Mr and Mrs Uniacke were thrown over a staircase railing, Viscount Wolseley's house was burned down, Mr Johnson Daragh of Eagle Hill, Kildare, was shot in the stomach, and Sir Henry Manix was killed in his garden. The 2nd Earl of Norbury was murdered in 1839, Bryan Butler in 1841, Denis Mahon of Strokestown House in 1847, the 3rd Earl of Leitrim in 1878, the 5th Viscount Mountmorres in 1880 and Lord Frederick Cavendish in 1882. The 1880s witnessed a number of other attempts such as the attack on a Herbert of Muckross and the bungled assassination of Henry Smythe of Barbavilla that led to the death of his sister-in-law, the daughter of Viscount Monck. A Carden of Templemore was known as 'Woodcock' because he was shot at so often. Other Ascendancy figures were kidnapped or burned in effigy. Attacks continued into the 1920s.[178] Such activities were unimaginable in Scotland or England.

The agricultural crisis of the later 1870s, the activities of the Land League in the 1880s, the Third Reform Act and the sequence of ever more effective redistributive legislation which culminated in the Land Act of 1903 ended the Ascendancy's existence as an elite. Nowhere else in the United Kingdom was the collapse of the governing class so rapid or so complete. Even after the First Reform Act 118 Irish peers and their sons had sat in the British House of Commons; in 1886 a single Irish peer remained.[179] In 1915 only nine Irish MPs came from elite families and by 1920 this was down to three. Outside Ulster landlord influence disappeared after 1885, and even there landed MPs declined in number. Presbyterian tenants became more hostile to Anglican overlords, and peers such as the Duke of Abercorn and the Earl of Antrim scaled back their political expenditures.[180] While in Scotland there was a revival in the number of aristocratic candidates after the Second World War, only a few Irish families, such as the Ponsonbys and the Needhams, sustained Ascendancy representation, sitting for English constituencies.

In the south representation at the Westminster parliament ended in 1922. A number of aristocrats initially served in the new Irish Senate despite threats to their lives and property. The Earl of Granard became the President of the chamber. The Esmondes of Ballynastragh are the only old governing family which has consistently maintained its presence in the new legislature. They elected seven MPs between 1613 and 1918, followed by the 11th Baronet who was a Senator during the Free State, and the 14th, 15th, and 16th Baronets who served in the Dáil as TDs between 1937 and 1977.

Most estates belonging to the elite were disposed of, leaving the surviving families either landless or with no more than the demesnes immediately surrounding their country houses. Those symbols of Ascendancy rule were routinely put to the torch during the early 1920s. About two hundred houses were destroyed as a direct result of the civil disturbances, and four hundred more were demolished or abandoned by their owners. In addition hundreds were sold to institutions or converted for other uses. One estimate suggests that only about a dozen big houses are still operated as aristocratic establishments in the south, and there has been continuing attrition. Some, like Bantry House and Glin Castle, are supported by paying guests. The Duke of Devonshire has not visited Lismore for years due to concerns about security, and Earl Mountbatten's continued use of his Sligo castle (which descended from Lord Palmerston) ended disastrously. Among Ireland's hundred richest families today, only the Guinnesses are a titled and/or parliamentary family.[181]

Perhaps fifty Ascendancy families maintain some sort of landed existence in the north. The Abercorns at Baron's Court still live in grandeur. Of the eight major houses in County Antrim in 1996, five are owned by the descendants of the original builders and all are in private hands.[182] In the 1920s and 1930s a few grandees such as the 3rd Duke of Abercorn played prominent political roles in the province. More recently Sir Basil Brooke, Terence O'Neill and James Chichester-Clark were leading figures in the Stormont government and more such men served as MPs and Senators. The Brookes attained two viscountcies in six years between 1946 and 1952. The Northern Irish governing class continued to produce military figures of the first rank including Alan Brooke and the son of Lord Caledon, Earl Alexander of Tunis.

Since the war the Ascendancy has had little visibility in the Westminster parliament aside from thoroughly Anglicized figures such as the Earl of Longford. The 5th Duke of Abercorn served as an MP in 1964–70, as did two O'Neills in 1915–52 and 1952–59, and the 5th Duke of Westminster, though an Englishman, sat for Fermanagh and Tyrone in 1955–64. A few families, such as the Bessboroughs, used their profits from land sales to purchase an English estate, but most got too little money to do so after mortgages were paid off or invested in the stock market. The old elite has little prestige in Ireland, even though the Irish government in the 1940s set up a registry for the Gaelic clan chiefs that is still maintained. Only private intervention saved Castletown House from possible demolition, and many fine smaller houses such as Bowen's Court have been destroyed. Even the spoor of the governing class is erased.

A Merged Elite?

In recent years increasing attention has been paid to writing British history as a story of multi-national interaction within what has come to be called the Atlantic archipelago. In part this development owes its ancestry to an article written by John Pocock in 1975.[183] It has won popularity perhaps because Marxist history is not so interesting as it used to be, and perhaps the uncertainties surrounding the future composition of the United Kingdom has added attraction to the approach. 'Englo'-centrism has been a bad habit of historians for centuries, and this new trend has offered refreshing insights.[184]

Much of the focus has been on the process of state formation in the early modern and modern periods as the English attempted to construct a British kingdom in the archipelago, and other countries more or less embraced or resisted this challenge to their individual identities. Obviously, the political elites were intimately involved in the process of forging a united nation. An early form of integration can be discerned in first a Welsh and then a Scottish family succeeding to the English throne. The British Isles had developed a largely anglophone elite by 1700, and it is argued that by the early 1800s this group was integrated into an 'authentically British' unit linked by education, intermarriage, common investment patterns, cross-border estates, a London-based social life and the Westminster House of Lords. This perception, argued powerfully by Linda Colley, is now propagated in textbooks, and we speak of the 'British' aristocracy. David Cannadine has called the supra-national elite a 'remade', 'reformed', 'new', and 'truly British territorial class'. Scottish and Irish aristocrats saw that their future lay in serving the British state and empire, which they helped to reinvigorate after the loss of the North American colonies.[185]

Undoubtedly, historical forces encouraged the integration of elites. The monarchy in the sixteenth and seventeenth centuries pursued a policy of creating an imperial and homogenous aristocracy. James I encouraged the Scottish nobility to establish themselves 'as cultural amphibians living partly in England and partly in Scotland'. An Anglo-Scottish nobility emerged by the 1630s with English wives, English-educated sons and English estates, and these practices continued among the higher nobility throughout the century and beyond.[186] James I's amphibious policy was extended by Charles I to Ireland where magnates also acquired English titles and wives. Considerable intermarriage took place and English education became more common among the grandees of Wales during the same period.[187] A number of Welsh, Scottish and English families established cadet lines in Ireland in the sixteenth and seventeenth centuries, and over time intermarriage produced Irish, Scottish and English grandee families with large holdings in two counties.

Words of warning about exaggerating the rapidity of the homogenization of the elites have been sounded. Diversity remained strong, at least through the first half of the eighteenth century.[188] The existence of separate parliaments, of course, was a powerful centrifugal force, not only politically, but also in keeping Edinburgh and Dublin as social centres for elite culture. The super-state builders liquidated these institutions and the physical transference of the legislative process to London clearly had an effect. That did not automatically create a merged aristocracy. Highland chiefs were still going to the Tower to be beheaded in 1747, and Lord Bute's unpleasant reception as Prime Minister by his English peers belied interest in integration of elites. Strong regional differences remained within the governing class even inside England as well as between the four nations.

It is a little noticed fact that the Scottish patriciate never embraced fox-hunting, a cultural and life-shaping passion among the English and Irish elites. A comprehensive study of baronets in all four countries in 1611–1880 found substantial variations in wealth, life expectancy, rates of duelling, proportions of bachelors and spinsters, significance placed on kinship, success in marrying heiresses, social origins and proportion of the elite with baronetcies. Although there was a narrowing of differences over time, Stuart Halliday believes that 'the most significant conclusion' of his study was the geographical variations among baronets.[189] My study has produced similar findings. The distinct histories of the four parliamentary elites indicate fundamental points of separation that were never fully bridged. The Welsh elite was small even when taking into account the size of the principality. The gap in wealth and social standing between the families able to sustain a parliamentary presence was much greater than elsewhere, despite the comparatively modest resources of the top families. Peerages were extremely rare in Wales, while in Scotland and Ireland most of the richer families gained titles. Proportionally more Irish landowners were nobles than in England. On the other hand, it is much harder to identify a list of grandees, pre-eminent in wealth, status and power, in Ireland than it is in England. The prominent role played over many centuries by a handful of great Scottish landed families is a unique national characteristic.

The proportion of Welsh and Scottish elite MPs with medieval origins was very high. The latter group was the most ancient and exclusive elite in the British Isles. A greater proportion of the Irish Ascendancy was pre-Cromwellian in origins than is often supposed, but they and the English elite were much more fluid and open to new entrants. Office and the professions were a major source of recruitment in England and Ireland, while comparatively few men rose by those means in Scotland and Wales. The rate of penetration into landed society by businessmen was rapid in England after 1660, but this route to entry was largely closed in the three other nations.

During the nineteenth century, when the integration of the elites is said to have become the dominant trend, the aristocracies experienced dramatically different fates as legislators. The plunge in parliamentary representation for landed families in Ireland after 1832 was steeper than elsewhere. Even top families foundered. They and the Welsh met fierce assaults from their own countrymen and lacked the vertical sense of solidarity that sustained remnants of landed leadership in Scotland and England even into the twentieth century. The much greater influx of nineteenth-century industrialists and financiers into the English elite injected a distinctive element that was absent elsewhere. In Scotland the increasingly vigorous sense of national identity, survival of giant estates and the self-confidence of the hereditary elite helped to restore the prominence of the landed class after the crofter crisis dissipated.[190] The contempt that even senior Tory peers felt for the Irish Ascendancy late in the nineteenth century and the sense of betrayal experienced by the latter suggests how deep divisions within the elite could still go. The Scottish and Irish peers maintained separate organizing committees in the Lords until the early 1900s.[191]

One of the most interesting discoveries I made while researching this study was how easy it was to divide most families into separate national elites. Although there were a few problem cases, the number of genuine straddlers was very low: no more than a couple of dozen out of over 2,800 families.[192] Well into the nineteenth century 'home' was still firmly planted in nations with unique problems and cultures inside the United Kingdom but yet distinctive. Shared imperial interests did not produce identical aristocracies.

Chapter 5
The Coming of Parliamentary Reform

One of the most distinguished students of nineteenth-century history has argued forcefully that what changed least in the years between 1815 and 1865 was the position of the traditional governing class. Norman Gash believes that the landed families who sent MPs to Westminster in 1865 would have been familiar to George III in 1765.[1] There is truth in this, but of all the families in England and Wales with at least one MP in 1765 only one-third elected an MP a century or more later. By way of contrast, half of the families with an MP in 1665 were still represented in the Commons in 1765 or later.[2] The hereditary element that was so prominent in the seventeenth and eighteenth centuries was fading faster than Gash's statement implies. It is to the disappearance of the governing families that this final chapter is devoted.

Considerable controversy surrounds the rate and nature of aristocratic decline in the nineteenth century. Some Whig leaders saw the Reform Bill as primarily a restructuring of the constitution to consolidate and secure aristocratic authority. The head of the reform administration, Earl Grey, took this view. 'I am indeed convinced,' he reassured a fellow peer in 1831, 'that the more the bill is considered, the less it will be found to prejudice the real interests of the aristocracy.'[3] It seems reasonable to believe that the Great Reform Act was the best bargain the governing class could make for itself in an attempt to prolong sovereignty for at least another generation. A sincere reformer erected a column on his estate in July 1832 to celebrate the passage of the Bill, but by 1838 his mood had darkened. He inscribed on the back: 'Alas to this Day, a HumBug.'[4] Perhaps reports of the death of aristocratic England were and still are being much exaggerated.

Professional historians of great experience and discernment have echoed Norman Gash's judgement cited above. George Kitson Clark noted in his magisterial overview of Victorian society: 'the most important single political fact in Britain in the middle of the century was the power of the old proprietary classes entrenched in the territorial structure of the countryside.'[5] A recent biographer of Lord Grey believes that 1832 opened 'a new era of aristocratic revival' and 'refreshed and revived that supremacy'.[6] W.D. Rubinstein goes so far as to argue that the middle classes probably lost ground after 1832 and that the years between the First and Third Reform Acts 'saw the apogee of the landed aristocracy as a governing class'.[7] Andrew Adonis boldly asserts: 'The persistence of the landed aristocracy as the principal economic, social and political elite in Britain until the First World War is now taken for granted by historians.' Although some scholars acknowledge that there were significant changes, those that do so believe that the grip of the aristocracy on power was pried loose one finger at a time, and they tend to stress continuity.[8]

Some contemporaries and later commentators, however, have argued that the decisive turning-point did take place in 1832.[9] For the Duke of Wellington, the Great Reform Act was a tragedy. He believed that the Bill 'must increase beyond measure the democratic power of the State – that it must constitute in the House of Commons a fierce democracy'.[10] The Tory *Quarterly Review* likened the Act to a 'devouring conflagration', while its liberal rival, the *Westminster Review*, believed: 'The passing of the Reform Bill was our taking of the Bastille; it was the first act of our great political change.' In 1864 the *Economist* asserted that without the 1832 Act 'England would be governed by Peers' sons and by men with £20,000 a year'.[11] Historians earlier in the twentieth century, such as Sir James Butler and H.W. Carless Davis, believed the Reform Act took 'us suddenly into another air' and 'made the House of Commons the effective instrument of the popular will'.[12] More recently it has been argued that 'the Reform Act could scarcely have caused a more drastic alteration in England's political fabric'.[13] Jonathan Clark sees the bitter resistance to the Bill as a realistic response to legislation that would shatter the electoral basis of the eighteenth-century Establishment. He points to the rapid disintegration of the cultural hegemony of the aristocracy and gentry in the wake of reform.[14]

To some degree, as with other issues discussed earlier in this book, the disagreements among the experts rest on differing definitions and terminology. One historian may see a decline of 25% in landed representation as a dramatic shift, while another points to the fact that the peerage still controlled over half of all MPs at such and such a date. Some include all baronets as part of the landed class or assume anyone listed in Walford's directory of 'county families' should be counted as gentry, even though a Victorian baronet might be nothing more than a clever dentist and Walford's was awash in business and professional families who owned little more than a villa with a large garden.[15] One interpretation may turn on the number of newly enfranchised voters, while another points to the actual frequency of votes cast.[16] Victorian England was an immensely complex society, changing rapidly. The more we uncover about Lancashire, Leeds, Lincolnshire and London the more unique regional and structural experiences appear. The ability to elect members of families to parliament, however, was still a sensitive indicator of status during the Victorian period. Never was the reputation of the institution higher. Housed in resplendent neo-Gothic grandeur, Members of Parliament were more likely than ever to be raised to a peerage and enjoy access to the most elevated social circles. Historians frequently turn to the composition of the Commons to take the temperature of an elite that was beginning to feel queasy. S.F. Woolley's influential 1938 article on the social backgrounds of MPs in the post-reform parliament, which argues that little change took place, still commanded the field in the 1990s.[17]

To what extent was the post-1833 Commons, more than ever the dominant chamber in parliament after the débâcle of May 1832, really 'landed' or, more importantly, derived from the same sort of families that had composed most of its membership for the past three centuries? This chapter examines the extent to which the elite began to retreat or be driven from the electoral stage at the national level and whether the 'persistence of the old regime' posited by some historians has substance.

Forces For and Against Change

Unquestionably, many factors favoured the continuation of landed domination in the Commons. Until the 1880s the elite remained genuinely divided about political issues of great importance, including religion, foreign policy and assumptions about the role of the State in society. The differences were wide enough to give voice to most of the significant social and economic interests in Victorian Britain. Much of England remained predominantly rural. The early reform acts left large boroughs and urban areas significantly under-represented. New peers, even when they came from non-landed backgrounds, quickly took on the colouring of the old elite. Middle-class challengers for Commons seats flowed in at a modest rate. In the mid-Victorian period men like the Dukes of Bedford, Sutherland and Westminster were still the richest people in the country, and until the agricultural depression towards the end of the century the peerage and greater gentry were more likely to have the time and income to campaign for office and live in London during the parliamentary season than any possible rivals. Some aristocratic leaders still had unthinking confidence in their fitness and right to rule. Other noblemen, although they may have had doubts about the future, gave virtuoso performances as speakers and politicians. Grey, Palmerston, Derby and Salisbury were impressive leaders even by modern standards. Ducal families continued to produce men of well above average ability who could convincingly lead the country, such as Russell, Hartington and the two Churchills. Both in the eighteenth and the mid-nineteenth centuries heavily urban constituencies in London and even manufacturing towns with wide franchises regularly returned titled aristocrats in preference to less well-bred candidates.[18]

Members of the landed elite continued to exercise a near monopoly on local offices through much of the period. Prominence in local constituency associations gave

wealthy families an important say in the selection of parliamentary candidates, even if
members of their own families no longer chose to or could win seats. Continued
corruption and bribery in many constituencies meant that if established parliamentary
families could no longer command voters, they could buy them. In some places
redrawn constituency boundaries and rescheduled franchises may have increased
territorial influence. A number of aristocratic and gentry families continued to be
active in boroughs and county elections. Some seats remained quasi-hereditary at least
until 1885.

But powerful undercurrents were concealed from view which doomed the
traditional elite. David Spring pointed out long ago that something was amiss with
aristocratic rule in Westminster. An 'illusion of stability' concealed serious
weakening at the centre.[19] Even in rural counties electoral politics became more
focused on national issues and more volatile in the 1810s and 1820s. The
disproportionate economic power of the landed elite began to fade. Although more
constituencies than ever seemed to be falling into the hands of the aristocracy,
control was increasingly difficult to sustain.[20] One study of the elite sees electoral
patronage peak as early as 1807, while other evidence suggests that the 1820s was
when the decline became obvious.[21] Some patrons such as the Marquess of Stafford
and the Dukes of Leeds and Northumberland simply abdicated borough influence
rather than face the increasing expense and inconvenience of continued
management.[22] After the devastating defeat of the Leveson Gowers in the
Staffordshire election of 1820, their agent James Loch, who was by no means a
reactionary, noted the changing political climate. 'The fact is the revolution is
begun, how and when it is to end God knows.'[23]

From at least 1832 onwards demographic changes and candidates from non-landed
backgrounds challenged aristocratic hegemony in both the boroughs and counties.
Increasingly professional management of estates to maximize income sapped the
roots of traditional loyalty.[24] Electoral reforms and the penetration of industrial
activity and urban population into rural constituencies ended political influence as it
had existed in the past.[25] Debate about democratization of the franchise awakened
interest in politics even among those who were not granted the vote. Organized
pressure groups, modern party institutions and national campaigns transformed the
electoral landscape.

After the passage of the First Reform Act eldest sons fled abroad to avoid the calls
of fathers still bent on asserting the family honour in the electoral lists.[26] A noble MP
told the Earl of Clarendon in 1836 that the aristocracy 'feel that they are already [in
terms of political power] less fortunate than their ancestors'. Soon after the passage of
the 1832 Act the Duke of Cleveland wrote to his son to discourage continuing an
electoral canvass: 'the time for such things is past. Family interests are no longer

worthy of cultivation.'[27] In some seemingly obedient boroughs the patron could now only nominate himself or his sons where once almost any name submitted was accepted, or the scion of a well-known family with property in a borough might gain a seat for reasons unconnected with his father's role in the constituency. In other places where once two seats had been available to a family, now only one could still be counted on.

The hurly-burly of popular, if still corrupt, elections became increasingly distasteful, while the additional burden of having to appear not only affable and genial but also subservient to the populace was too much to stomach for many elite candidates. While legislative activity became more businesslike, systematic and continuous, elections became more frequent and parliamentary sessions lengthier. To some eyes the status of MP seemed to diminish into little more than a cog in the government machinery.[28]

Within the upper chamber confidence was ebbing. Before the passage of the Third Reform Act Viscount Monck told his heir: 'It is very hard in argument to defend the House of Lords as a portion of our Constitutional arrangement. The best thing that could be said for it was that it worked well, but if it is found that this is not true, I fear its days are numbered.'[29] Attendance dipped seriously after 1841 and for the most part remained low throughout the rest of the century. More and more hostile propaganda was aimed at the peerage.[30] The governing elite backed down in 1832, and again and again thereafter in the face of assaults on the Game Laws, the Corn Laws and other legislation, knowing that to resist would cast them in the image of a mere lobby for class interest.[31]

The Reform Acts

The only way to escape judgements based on anecdotal evidence as to the degree to which membership of the Commons remained unchanged during the nineteenth century is to analyse statistically the social backgrounds of MPs. It has already been noted that the quality of some of the evidence collected even by respected cliometricians such as Aydelotte and social scientists like Guttsman is suspect owing to their undiscriminating use of baronetcies, knighthoods and other flawed measures of elite status.[32] More than ever before lines of social categorization were blurred during the nineteenth century. Increasing numbers of landed gentlemen had business interests. The proportion of MPs with professional careers of some sort rose substantially. Yet historians persist in the belief that the proportion of 'landed' MPs held steady.[33] The following pages examine two measures of aristocratic membership of the Commons. First we look at the proportion of the lower house that was related to the peerage and then to the whole parliamentary elite.

In an attempt to create both a uniform and realistic set of figures, I have counted the male relatives of nobles whose families had sat in the House of Lords as English, British or United Kingdom peers or Scottish and Irish representative peers for at least a quarter of the years between 1750 and 1914. This excludes Scottish and Irish titled families who were unable to exert the leverage necessary to gain access to the Lords either through appointment by the Crown or nomination by their fellow peers. It also removes most non-landed 'professional' peers (judges, generals, etc.) and pseudo-peers like Macaulay who were only elevated because it was known they had no male heirs (an early version of the life peerage). With very few exceptions the 454 families in this count were the richest and most influential members of the landed class during the half century before and the half century after the Reform Act of 1832.[34]

Table 5.1 shows that the number of noble MPs, as defined above, was rising at a significant rate after 1800. This was in part due to an increase in the size of the peerage, but also because the number of boroughs coming under the influence of titled patrons continued to grow. The fact that two out of five MPs were relatives in the male line of a peer in 1830 is quite remarkable, and the figure would be even higher if all peers and families that formerly had held a title were counted. One can also see, however, a dramatic decline in the number of noble MPs after 1832. The number of years of service by noble MPs also dropped almost by half after 1832, and because of the increasing size of the peerage post-1830 the representation of the House of Lords was much diluted. In ten years a 16% reduction occurred. The decline after that was more gradual. The figures confirm the changes effected by the First Reform Act.[35]

Of course, some historians have pointed to the fact that even before the Whig reforms substantial numbers of merchants and self-made men were entering the Commons.[36] One count categorizes nearly half the members of parliament in the Liverpool years as middle class or professional.[37] None the less, the assumption is widespread that for long after reform the character of the Commons remained essentially unchanged. An assiduous student of the modern political elite declared that before 1832 one-third of all MPs were aristocrats in the most restricted sense of the word and this proportion had not declined by 1865.[38] Another study found 76% of MPs landed in 1832 and still well over half (61%) from such backgrounds in 1865.[39] One of the most respected students of landed society believes three-quarters of MPs were landed in the 1840s, and another study posits that the same proportion of MPs were aristocrats either by connection with land or titles in the 1860s.[40] These and similar figures are regularly reiterated by authors of surveys of Victorian society.[41] Many similar examples could be cited. The data concerning the peerage in Table 5.1 suggests that such perceptions may be exaggerated. What about the whole of the parliamentary elite?

Table 5.1 Noble MPs in the House of Commons, 1801–1940*

Year	MPs	% of the Commons
1801**	184	27.9
1810	195	29.6
1820	249	37.8
1830	279	42.4
1840	175	26.5
1850	179	27.2
1860	166	25.2
1870	140	21.2
1880	141	21.6
1890	71	10.5
1900	70	10.4
1910	67	10.0
1920	22	3.2
1930	30	4.8
1940	33	5.3

* All peers and close relatives in the male line elected MPs while the family was titled.
** 1801 allows for the first election of Irish MPs to the imperial parliament.

If the reader looks back at Figures 2.1, 2.3, 4.1 and 4.2 and the tables in Appendices II and III, a clear pattern of serious decline of the traditional governing class in the Commons can be discerned. From the Restoration to 1832 parliamentary families supplied more than four out of five members of the Commons. Five years later the proportion of elite MPs had dropped 21 points to 60% during the first parliament elected after the passage of the Reform Bill. A recovery took place in the 1840s when the percentage rose as high as 69. This was, however, still 12 points down from 1830 and 17 below the mid-eighteenth-century level. The average proportion of elite MPs in the years between 1832 and 1867 was less than two-thirds of the Commons. Moreover, in 1850 only 57% of MPs came from already 'established' families. (See Table 2.1.) We can look at the electoral performance of old and important families by analysing the number of MPs from 'six-plus' dynasties after 1832. In 1830, 58% of the Commons came from such families. This figure dropped to 40% in 1835, and was never more than half again. It stood at 45 in the last parliament before the Second Reform Act.

More perhaps by accident than design the 1867 Act served as a 'Trojan horse' for constitutional, political and social transformation. The composition of the electorate became surprisingly broad and diverse in the 1870s and 1880s.[42] So too became the House of Commons. A dissenting minister was elected an MP in 1868, a self-educated ex-miner in 1874 and a journeyman stonemason in 1880. In 1874 a former working man defeated the son of the 18th Earl of Shrewsbury at Stafford, and the heirs of the Earl of Ellesmere, Marquess of Hertford and the Dukes of Wellington and Manchester failed to be returned. Families such as the Herveys, Lowthers, Montagus and Stanhopes, who had long been used to multiple representation in the Commons, were reduced to a single member per family. Norman Grosvenor, MP for Chester, retired in 1874 bringing to an end 159 years of his family's representation in the borough. Important men not only withdrew from electoral politics, but also failed to contribute to party funds after 1868.[43] Although most MPs were still wealthy, a majority were no longer members of the hereditary governing class.

Some historians do not agree that much was changed in 1867, and argue that the social backgrounds of MPs were essentially what they had been before.[44] Indeed, a few observers see the new Act as a boost for the influence of land. E.H. Green argues that after the 1880 election 'the House of Commons was still dominated by landed M.P.s'.[45] Even the third wave of reform in the mid-1880s left 40% of the adult male population without the franchise. One contemporary claimed in 1886: 'there are few noblemen today who are unable to secure the return of their eldest son to the House of Commons'.[46] Hillaire Belloc, writing a decade later, thought that in all essentials the territorial aristocracy, 'this ring of families', still controlled the country. Modern historians continue to refer to the manoeuvring at Westminster in these years as 'aristocratic politics'.[47]

A majority of analysts agree, however, that the 1880s witnessed what Harold Perkin has called a 'geological shift in the structure of politics'.[48] A. Tyrwhitt Drake, scion of an important parliamentary family, when urged by a friend in the 1880s to stand for election wrote: 'You know I have always been associated with gentlemen? . . . Then why in the world do you want to send me to the House of Commons.'[49]

Historians who suggest that it was only in the 1880s that things 'begin to slide' or that the 1885 election was 'the great turning-point' or that it was only in the last fifteen years of the century that 'the bottom dropped out' overestimate the importance of the third instalment of reform. It is true, however, that the rate of decline steepened again to the speed and angle achieved in the years immediately succeeding 1832. In 1890 only 37% of the Commons was composed of MPs from the parliamentary elite. In 1900 this was down to one-third, and in 1915 one-quarter.[50] If one deducts from this percentage new families who had no connection with land, such as the Lloyd Georges or the Hardies, the proportion is even lower – less than one in five.

Lingering Embers

Even before 1832, and more assuredly from that date forward, the social status related to becoming an MP began to decay. Increasingly, three factors made it impossible to use election to the Commons as the premier sign of rank other than a peerage. First, more and more constituencies were contested successfully by non-landed candidates, making seats unavailable to the traditional elite. Room no longer existed for every family that desired and could afford to elect a member to the Commons. Secondly, as the century progressed the landed elite began to solidify into a single ideological mass, which meant that only one political party could offer nominations to elite candidates. Eventually, this cut almost in half the number of places available in the Commons for members of the governing class. Furthermore the conservative principles to which more and more aristocrats and gentry adhered automatically guaranteed defeat in a larger proportion of constituencies as the franchise was extended, the secret ballot established, corruption diminished and constituency boundaries redrawn to reflect the economic and demographic realities of the later Victorian period. Thirdly, fewer and fewer members of elite families seemed interested in standing for parliament or felt a responsibility to enter national politics.[51] Even among the grandest families with powerful political traditions a point was reached when the number of family MPs was reduced not by defeat at the polls but by failure of candidates to show up at all.

To what degree failure to participate in elections marked a psychological and moral disintegration, or merely the recognition of reality and retreat to other venues of endeavour, such as county councils and the House of Lords, is not an easy question. The answer varied from family to family and individual to individual. A few great dynasties continued on with aplomb and filled seats in the Commons in phalanxes. The number of Cecils and Stanleys in politics, even after 1918, seemed limited only by the capacity of their respective breeding programmes.

The theme of resilience and even renewal in the governing class after the late Victorian agricultural depression and despite the setback of House of Lords Reform in 1911 is widespread in the historical literature.[52] Some important agricultural estates experienced little or no loss of income in the 1880s and 1890s. Many of the grandees, even if they suffered setbacks in farm rentals, were sustained and even grew richer owing to exploitation of mineral resources, development of urban property, purchases of land and other investments in America, Canada, South Africa and Australia and ever increasing consignment of their assets to the stock market. The massive land sales which took place were not all caused by financial hardship. When the profits were wisely invested elsewhere, which was often the object of the exercise, coupon clipping could sustain or strengthen the family's fortunes. Divestment of land should not be read, at least before 1918, as a sign that the estates system was in a state of irrevocable decay.[53] With good advice, diverse holdings, astute lawyers and a bit of luck in the dates of succession to the inheritance, really rich families could avoid many of the depredations of rising taxation. The greatest dynasties such as the Cavendishes, Cecils, Grosvenors, Howards, Percys, Spencers and Stanleys survived into the period when explosive growth in land prices and an inflated art market replaced them securely among the richest families in Britain and able to endow the continued maintenance of Alnwick, Althorp, Arundel, Chatsworth, Cranborne, Eaton, Hatfield, Knowsley and Syon with the sale of silver wine coolers, the odd codex and a painting here or there. Families less in the limelight, such as the Leghs and Newdigates, also continue to prosper and hold office. The hundreds of big houses in Britain, where family portraits still hang on the walls they were commissioned to fill, surrounded by parks and large agricultural estates is a phenomenon unknown anywhere else in the world.[54] When one takes into account biological extinctions, spendthrifts and other factors that have always produced turnover, the survival rate among the grandees is remarkably high. In 1979 some six million acres in England and Wales were held in blocks of at least 5,000 acres by some 1,200 private landowners. England and Scotland are the only European countries where large estates of this kind are widespread. About half the peers in the 1960s were still living primarily off their landed incomes. Only one-third were landless. One-half of a sample of families owning 1,000 or more acres in England in the 1880s still owned a landed estate a century later. In 1991 at least fourteen dukes owned over 10,000 acres, three of them over 100,000. Only three were landless.[55] Some estates have actually been expanded in size, while a number of great houses that had been unoccupied by their owners for decades have recently been reclaimed.[56] The continued prominence in politics of men such as Richard Needham, Tom Sackville, William Waldegrave and Viscount Cranborne, whose families were in parliament 500, 600 or 700 years ago, is unique to Britain and little short of incredible. None the less, by the mid-twentieth century the eclipse of the traditional elite in its role as a governing class was virtually complete.

On 7 September 1933 Sir Edward Grey, Viscount Grey of Fallodon, died. The Associated Press reported: 'Public life drew him, not because he had a taste for it, but because he was one of the Greys of Northumberland, a member of the great governing class of England.'[57] Among Sir Edward's generation of great landowners the day was past, however, when most men considered seeking a seat in the Commons their duty. His celebrated remark about the lamps going out all over Europe, made as he watched the remnants of the *ancien régime* race towards sunset in August 1914, was a benediction over an already dead tradition. The parliamentary fortress had been stormed, although tacit surrender made a peaceful conclusion possible.

Conclusion

A historian compiling a biographical dictionary of eighteenth-century Britain recently discovered to his surprise that 'the governing circle was smaller in numbers than it first appears'.[1] The more closely he examined the connections among MPs and ministers the more complicated and close-knit the elite revealed itself to be. The present study also demonstrates how small the governing class was, not just during the Georgian period but between the reigns of Elizabeth and Victoria. Little more than a thousand families at any given time formed an aristocracy of wealth and power in England while the governing classes of the three kingdoms and principality in the British Isles never amounted in total to much more than about 2,500.

For more than three centuries landed families dominated the House of Lords and the House of Commons. Parliament had been the perfect mechanism to embody and enhance their authority and status. The upper chamber provided both a guarantee that important families would have an automatic place in the legislature and offered a goal to which those on the make could aspire. The lower house ensured that the elite remained alert to interests other than their own. The electoral system, even when actual polls were rare, meant that those born blue-blooded had to compete for places and the door to the inner sanctum of the elite was kept open to the unpedigreed with energy, intelligence, and money.

The flexibility and adaptability of the English political elite helped to shape, and was shaped by, the institution through which it expressed its corporate authority. Legislative powers enabled the governing class to protect and expand its landholdings, religion and role as captains of the state. The structure of parliament obliged the elite to attend to the needs of their countrymen and to raise heirs who could look after themselves in a competitive system. This was a class that dominated a higher percentage of the nation's land in fewer hands than any other comparable European aristocracy. It was envied as a model which French, Russian, and other nobilities sought to emulate.[2] It presided over the birth of the first modern society. It ruled with commercial logic in aristocratic style. It curbed the power of the monarchy and inadvertently bequeathed liberal government and a language to a large portion of humanity.

The continuity and success of the English landed elite has long riveted the attention of historians. Recently, David Cannadine has once again focused our attention on the extraordinary 'unchangingness' of social patterns over the last three centuries in his study of class in Britain.[3] Yet repeated attempts to identify with precision the dynamics of the membership of the ruling class have failed. The case made here for the close congruence between the social, economic and political elite at the national level seated in parliament is incontrovertible for the years 1689–1832 and perhaps stretched from 1560–1885. Dividing the top layers of English society into the parliamentary elite and those not able to sustain repeated representation at Westminster offers a surer guide to classification than 'gentry versus aristocracy' or 'county families as opposed to squires' or similar divisions. The small size of the parliamentary elite, especially its inner core, those 164 English dynasties who provided such a large proportion of MPs, peers and officers of state, is striking. Identifying who they were is intrinsically interesting and important. Equally vital to our understanding of English government and society, however, is the evidence that the tiny, dense apex of the elite had fluid flanks. The turnover was frequent and made credible the assumption that social mobility was possible. Old families needed fresh infusions of money and blood. New men, century after century, were anxious for acceptance.

The symbiotic interaction of business and land within the precincts of parliament both enabled government to stay attuned effectively to the development of the economy and acted as a powerful emulsifier mixing new money and old. This study cannot offer proof that the English experience was different from developments in Spain, Germany or France. It is entirely possible that in the latter country, for example, there was more mobility into the nobility during the eighteenth or nineteenth century.[4] But no modern governing class was more successful over so long a period as the English elite, and its stability came from a social and political system which selected and sustained the families analysed in this book.

The Welsh, Scottish and Irish elites were less 'parliamentary'. The anatomies of those groups presented here are partial portraits. None the less, the evidence of unique patterns of recruitment and distinctive characteristics should make those who study the Atlantic archipelago wary of seeing the homogenization of a supra-national aristocracy for the whole of the British Isles. Even among grandee families in the nineteenth and twentieth centuries different cultures and even deep antagonism persisted as the rulers scrambled to benefit from the empire and avoid relegation and dispossession.

The 1832 Reform Act was attuned to individual national circumstances. Its impact was most significant in England. Many forces, including legislation, led to a profound transformation within the governing class during the Victorian period. The aristocracy gradually gave way to a less well-defined 'establishment' in which various forms of wealth and status were more mixed than before. The elite had always been moderately plutocratic, but the presence of the old and mighty grandees added a hereditary dimension of patrician exclusivity. The formative role of parliament in the social structure was damaged by the reform acts, and as barriers which had made entry into the top elite difficult disappeared members of the traditional governing class lost their sense of purpose. The mould imposed on the governing class by the peculiar patterns of the parliamentary system vanished. In the twentieth century England developed a different kind of social and political structure. The House of Commons and the aristocracy remained but were no longer entwined.

Appendix I

Table 1.1 Proportion of fathers of non-elite* MPs from various social backgrounds, 1660–1820

Occupation	1660–90	1715–54	1754–90	1790–1820
Landed	46.5	30.0	14.8	17.2
Office	4.8	3.6	3.2	3.6
Professions	17.2	15.0	21.8	23.8
law	(9.6)	(9.6)	(7.3)	(7.7)
clergy	(4.8)	(5.4)	(7.3)	(8.8)
military	(0.4)	(1.0)	(4.5)	(4.2)
Business	25.3	35.9	39.0	45.2

Table 1.2 Proportion of non-elite* MPs from various social backgrounds, 1660–1820

Occupation	1660–90	1715–54	1754–90	1790–1820
Landed	34.9	25.6	19.4	15.8
Office	12.9	14.6	8.7	7.8
Professions	27.1	28.7	27.9	30.5
law	(21.2)	(19.7)	(19.4)	(19.8)
military	(4.1)	(7.9)	(8.5)	(9.9)
Business	26.0	29.7	42.9	45.7

Note: Totals do not add up to 100 because the parents of MPs who are unknown and those to whom the volumes of the *History of Parliament* did not clearly ascribe an occupation have not been listed.

* Non-elite refers to MPs from families who did not elect three MPs/peers or were members of associated families.

Appendix II

Table 2.1 'Newness' of English parliamentary families in 1650 and 1750

Years*	With MPs post-1650				With MPs post-1750			
	≤5	≥6	T	%	≤5	≥6	T	%
1–50	103	44	147	13.9	82	19	101	11.5
51–100	83	62	145	13.7	73	23	96	10.9
101–150	58	56	114	10.8	50	43	93	10.5
151–200	28	35	63	5.9	33	53	86	9.7
201+	<u>198</u>	<u>393</u>	<u>591</u>	<u>55.7</u>	<u>140</u>	<u>366</u>	<u>506</u>	<u>57.4</u>
	470	590	1060	100	378	544	882	100

* Years between first entry into the elite and 1650 or 1750.

Table 2.2 Date of entry into the gentry for English parliamentary families with one or more MPs 1640 or later

	≤ 5 MPs		≥ 6 MPs		Total	
	N	%	N	%	N	%
Pre 1485	227	49.2	428	72.2	655	62.1
1485–1603	170	36.9	132	22.2	302	28.7
1604–1640	<u>64</u>	<u>13.9</u>	<u>33</u>	<u>5.6</u>	<u>97</u>	<u>9.2</u>
	461	100	593	100	1054	100

Table 2.3 Parliamentary service and wealth of English peerage, baronet and commoner elite families with at least one MP, 1660–1945*

	Peerage	Baronets	Commoners
	515 (34.6%)	391 (26.3%)	581 (39.1%)
Total MPS 1295–1994	5,597 (51.8%)	2,328 (21.6%)	2,875 (26.6%)
Average number MPs per family	10.9	5.9	4.9
Years of Service, 1660–1945	49,596 (57.3%)	17,444 (20.1%)	19,582 (22.6%)
Average years per family	96.3	43.9	33.7
Income in Bateman	71.5%	14.2%	14.2%
Average income per family	£21,955	£5,741	£3,893

* Peerage families are defined as those with at least one peer in the House of Lords in 1660–1945 even if they also had a baronetcy. Baronet families are those with a baronetcy but no peerage. Of 849 surviving baronetcies in 1880 (including those held by peers) 43.7% were owners of 3,000 or more acres with an income of at least £3,000 p.a. (Halliday, 'Social Mobility', 206.) This was quite a low proportion compared to the peerage.

Appendix III

Table 3.1 **Total** number of MPs from elite families in the Westminster Parliament, 1660–1940

	≤ 5 MP Families	≥ 6 MP Families	Total	% of Commons
1660	109	287	396	77.8
1665	91	314	405	79.6
1670	101	312	413	81.1
1675	95	312	407	79.6
1680	111	312	423	82.5
1685	112	300	412	80.3
1690	115	327	442	86.2
1695	118	309	427	83.2
1700	116	300	416	81.1
1705	115	279	394	76.8
1710	129	331	460	82.4
1715	142	294	436	78.1
1720	129	315	444	79.6
1725	119	324	443	79.3
1730	114	327	441	79.0
1735	112	331	443	79.3
1740	119	347	466	83.5
1745	123	344	467	83.7
1750	127	345	472	84.6
1755	120	357	477	85.5
1760	116	353	469	84.0
1765	111	344	455	81.5
1770	123	344	467	83.7
1775	118	350	468	83.9
1780	112	355	467	83.7
1785	117	326	443	79.4

1790	126	320	446	79.9
1795	122	325	447	80.1
1800	129	305	434	77.8
1805	143	362	505	73.7
1810	146	371	517	78.6
1815	146	363	509	77.4
1820	159	376	535	81.3
1825	158	359	517	78.6
1830	150	381	531	80.7
1835	124	269	393	59.7
1840	141	295	436	66.3
1845	139	314	453	68.8
1850	142	293	435	66.1
1855	120	284	404	61.4
1860	130	295	425	64.6
1865	139	294	433	65.8
1870	139	255	394	60.4
1875	131	224	355	54.6
1880	137	228	365	56.1
1885	123	191	314	48.3
1890	106	143	249	37.2
1895	109	126	235	35.1
1900	95	126	221	33.0
1905	105	120	225	33.6
1910	79	98	177	26.4
1915	82	87	169	25.2
1920	58	51	109	15.4
1925	47	69	116	18.9
1930	37	57	94	15.3
1935	40	70	110	17.9
1940	37	55	92	15.0

Table 3.2 Number of MPs sitting for **English** seats from parliamentary elite families, 1660–1940

	≤ 5 MP Families	≥ 6 MP Families	Total	% of English seats
1660	103	270	373	77.4
1670	98	294	392	81.3
1680	105	295	400	82.3
1690	105	311	416	85.6
1700	110	282	392	80.6
1710	117	282	399	82.1
1720	112	272	384	79.0
1730	97	284	381	78.4
1740	104	298	402	82.7
1750	108	301	409	84.2
1760	99	310	409	84.2
1770	107	302	409	84.2
1780	96	308	404	83.1
1790	107	275	382	78.6
1800	110	260	370	76.1
1810	102	267	369	75.9
1820	117	266	383	78.8
1830	114	268	382	78.6
1835	83	193	276	58.9
1840	108	206	314	67.1
1845	105	222	327	69.9
1850	106	208	314	67.1
1855	82	210	292	62.4
1860	90	215	305	65.2
1865	95	213	308	65.8
1870	106	179	285	62.8
1875	102	160	262	57.7
1880	105	164	269	59.2
1885	93	154	247	54.4
1890	81	121	202	43.8
1895	80	111	191	41.4
1900	70	110	180	39.0
1905	81	106	187	40.6

1910	56	83	30.1
1915	66	75	141	30.6
1920	51	47	98	19.8
1925	39	59	98	19.9
1930	31	52	83	16.8
1935	34	57	91	18.5
1940	30	45	75	15.2

Table 3.3 Number of MPs sitting for **Welsh** seats from parliamentary families, 1660–1940

	≤ 5 MP Families	≥ 6 MP Families	Total	% of Welsh seats
1660	6	17	23	85.2
1670	3	18	21	77.8
1680	6	17	23	85.2
1690	10	16	26	96.3
1700	6	18	24	88.9
1710	4	20	24	88.9
1720	3	17	20	74.1
1730	3	17	20	74.1
1740	3	17	20	74.1
1750	6	17	23	85.2
1760	6	17	23	85.2
1770	2	19	21	77.8
1780	4	18	22	81.5
1790	4	18	22	81.5
1800	4	18	22	81.5
1810	4	21	25	92.6
1820	4	21	25	92.6
1830	2	23	25	92.6
1840	3	19	22	68.7
1850	3	19	22	68.7
1860	7	17	24	75.0
1870	5	15	20	60.6
1880	4	12	16	48.5
1890	2	8	10	29.4
1900	3	5	8	23.5
1910	4	1	5	14.7
1920	1	0	1	2.7
1930	3	0	3	8.3
1940	3	0	3	8.3

Table 3.4 Number of Commissioners/MPs sitting for **Scottish** seats from parliamentary families, 1662–1940

	≤ 5 MP Families	≥ 6 MP Families	Total	% of Scot. seats
1662	27	33	60	61.2
1665	29	20	49	57.0
1670	28	35	63	56.3
1678	27	32	59	50.9
1681	33	30	63	52.9
1686	21	38	59	49.2
1690	23	41	64	46.4
1695	32	48	80	57.1
1700	32	38	70	45.8
1706	44	70	114	75.5
1710	8	29	37	82.2
1720	14	26	40	88.9
1730	14	27	41	91.1
1740	12	32	44	97.8
1750	13	27	40	88.9
1760	11	26	37	82.2
1770	14	23	37	82.2
1780	12	29	41	91.1
1790	15	27	42	93.3
1800	15	27	42	93.3
1810	19	22	41	91.1
1820	17	23	40	88.9
1830	20	21	41	91.1
1835	16	20	36	67.9
1840	12	25	37	69.8
1845	12	23	35	66.0
1850	12	18	30	56.6
1855	11	21	32	60.4
1860	16	19	35	66.0
1865	14	21	35	66.0
1870	11	19	30	50.0
1875	8	21	29	48.3
1880	11	21	32	53.3

1885	11	14	25	41.7
1890	13	9	22	30.6
1895	15	9	24	33.3
1900	14	7	21	29.2
1905	15	7	22	30.6
1910	12	8	20	27.8
1915	7	7	14	19.4
1920	5	2	7	9.6
1925	6	8	14	19.2
1930	3	4	7	9.6
1935	3	11	14	19.2
1940	4	8	12	16.4

Table 3.5 Number of MPs sitting for **Irish** seats from parliamentary families, 1662–1920

	≤ 5 MP Families	≥ 6 MP Families	Total	% of Irish seats
1662	45	113	158	62.2
1665	39	107	146	57.5
1693	72	141	213	71.0
1696	70	155	225	75.0
1706	73	153	226	75.3
1710	72	150	222	74.0
1716	65	172	237	79.0
1720	72	172	244	81.3
1730	75	178	253	84.3
1740	69	194	263	87.7
1750	63	202	265	88.3
1760	53	218	271	90.3
1770	67	188	255	85.0
1780	70	185	255	85.0
1790	63	175	238	79.3
1799	69	173	242	80.7
1805	19	65	84	84.0
1810	21	61	82	82.0
1820	21	66	87	87.0
1830	14	69	83	83.0
1835	19	40	59	56.2
1840	18	45	63	60.0
1845	19	47	66	62.9
1850	21	48	69	65.7
1855	21	36	57	54.3
1860	17	44	61	58.1
1865	22	42	64	60.9
1870	17	42	59	56.2
1875	16	30	46	44.7
1880	17	31	48	44.9
1885	12	15	27	26.2
1890	10	5	15	14.6
1895	11	4	15	14.6

1900	8	4	12	11.6
1905	6	3	9	8.7
1910	7	4	11	10.7
1915	6	3	9	8.7
1920	1	2	3	2.9

Table 3.6 Average number of years of service per family in the House of Lords (at Westminster, Dublin or in the Scottish parliament), 1660–1945, by families in this study with peerages

Number of MPs	England	Wales	Scotland	Ireland
3–5	6.6	5.6	31.4	10.9
6–14	46.1	17.3	74.0	48.5
15+	173.8	34.4	202.1	208.3

Table 3.7 Percentage of elite families with at least one MP, 1660–1945, who were commoners, baronets and peers

	England	Wales	Scotland	Ireland
Peers	34.6	23.0	32.3	39.0
Baronets	26.3	33.8	26.0	18.4
Commoners	39.1	43.2	41.7	42.6

Table 3.8 Average number of MPs per family in elite families with at least one MP, 1660–1945

	England	Wales	Scotland	Ireland
Peers	10.9	10.2	8.7	9.8
Baronets	5.9	8.5	4.6	5.5
Commoners	4.9	4.2	3.2	4.7

Table 3.9 Percentage of income in Bateman within each country received by elite families who had at least one MP, 1660–1945

	England	Wales	Scotland	Ireland
Peers	71.5	56.4	71.8	74.2
Baronets	14.2	30.7	14.5	11.4
Commoners	<u>14.3</u>	<u>12.9</u>	<u>13.7</u>	<u>14.4</u>
	100	100	100	100

Table 3.10 Total size of the parliamentary elites, 1400–1939†

{The figures below record the number of families who achieved gentry status before
the end of each period and elected at least one MP after the beginning date*}

	Wales	Scotland	Ireland
1400–19	48	235	96
1420–39	50	242	97
1440–59	53	260	102
1460–79	53	265	104
1480–99	54	271	106
1500–19	55	273	111
1520–39	56	278	114
1540–59	60	281	142
1560–79	60	291	148
1580–99	65	298	185
1600–19	64	303	237
1620–39	68	305	262
1640–59	68	308	306
1660–79	67	301	333
1680–99	65	275	342
1700–19	60	253	350
1720–39	54	203	345
1740–59	51	199	335
1760–79	49	191	338
1780–99	43	183	317
1800–19	44	175	276
1820–39	39	155	207
1840–59	34	133	168
1860–79	29	112	117
1880–99	18	92	83
1900–19	10	67	45
1920–39	5	42	22

† Note: The fact that a family ceased to elect MPs does not mean that they ended their political activities
either in participating in elections or in the House of Lords, nor were they necessarily forced into a lower
social standing. The decline in numbers does, however, broadly reflect the diminished power of the
traditional governing class to assert its power and status effectively on a national scale.
* For data on the English elite see Table 2.5 in Chapter 2.

Table 3.11 Parliamentary elite families who ceased to elect members to the House of Commons (at Westminster, Dublin or Edinburgh), 1660–1939

	England†	Wales		Scotland		Ireland	
	%*	N	%*	N	%*	N	%*
1660–79	6.0	3	4.5	27	9.0	4	1.2
1680–99	9.3	5	7.7	23	8.4	4	1.2
1700–19	12.6	6	10.0	47	18.6	8	2.3
1720–39	7.9	5	9.3	6	2.9	14	4.1
1740–59	8.8	2	3.9	8	4.0	10	3.0
1760–79	12.0	6	12.2	11	5.8	30	8.9
1780–99	12.2	2	4.6	12	6.6	43	13.6
1800–19	11.1	5	11.4	20	11.4	70	25.4
1820–39	18.0	5	12.8	19	12.3	42	20.3
1840–59	18.5	5	14.7	19	14.3	54	32.1
1860–79	22.2	12	41.4	22	19.6	35	30.0
1880–99	32.2	8	44.4	25	27.2	38	45.8
1900–19	43.8	5	50.0	24	35.8	23	51.1
1920–39	43.2	4	80.0	13	30.9	8	36.4

† For fuller information on England, see Chapter II.
* Percentage of the total existing parliamentary elite.

Table 3.12 New entrants to the parliamentary elite,† 1400–1919

	England	Wales		Scotland		Ireland	
	%*	N	%*	N	%*	N	%*
1400–19	8.1	5	10.4	9	3.8	3	3.1
1420–39	5.8	2	4.0	13	5.4	1	1.0
1440–59	8.1	2	3.8	9	3.5	3	2.9
1460–79	2.8	0	0	9	3.4	1	1.0
1480–99	2.4	1	1.8	8	2.9	2	1.9
1500–19	3.4	1	1.8	3	1.1	4	3.6
1520–39	8.0	1	1.8	5	1.8	3	2.6
1540–59	14.1	4	6.7	4	1.4	19	13.4
1560–79	3.4	1	1.7	10	3.4	5	3.4
1580–99	5.8	5	7.7	10	3.4	29	15.7
1600–19	5.3	1	1.6	8	2.6	46	19.4
1620–39	4.5	4	5.9	6	2.0	29	11.1
1640–59	6.3	1	1.5	7	2.3	55	18.0
1660–79	3.8	0	0	6	2.0	31	9.3
1680–99	4.8	1	1.5	3	1.1	11	3.2
1700–19	4.2	0	0	3	1.2	11	3.1
1720–39	2.2	0	0	0	0	2	0.6
1740–59	5.1	2	3.9	3	1.5	2	0.6
1760–79	3.5	0	0	1	0.5	10	3.0
1780–99	4.3	0	0	5	2.7	6	1.9
1800–19	6.1	3	6.8	5	2.9	2	0.7
1820–39	3.3	0	0	4	2.6	1	0.5
1840–59	4.3	0	0	2	1.5	1	0.6
1860–79	2.8	0	0	3	2.7	2	1.7
1880–99	5.0	2	11.1	2	2.2	1	1.2
1900–19	3.2	0	0	1	1.4	0	0

† By date of first entry into the gentry and not date of first MP.

* Percentage of the existing elite.

Table 3.13 Percentage of MPs sitting for English and Welsh, Scottish and Irish constituencies who came from families with at least two previous MPs by the year indicated

	England & Wales	Scotland	Ireland
1661/1662	68.6	46.9	41.7
1699/1700	66.9	44.4	50.0
1725	67.3	84.4	65.0
1750	73.1	80.0	76.0
1775	72.1	71.1	74.7
1800	64.5	80.0	79.0
1825	63.2	68.8	75.0
1850	56.8	52.8	60.0
1875	43.7	45.0	40.8
1900	38.4	29.2	11.6
1925	16.6	13.7	23.1

Bibliographical Note

The research necessary to identify and analyse the MPs and peers in this study was based on *The Complete Peerage* and *The Complete Baronetage*, supplemented by genealogical compendiums such as various editions of *Burke's Peerage*, *Burke's Landed Gentry*, J.C. Sainty, *Peerage Creations 1649–1800* (1998), C.J. Parry, *Index of Baronetage Creations* (Canterbury, 1967), and works on extinct peerages, the Scottish peerage, etc. The published volumes of the *History of Parliament* were invaluable. These include: J.S. Roskell, L. Clark, and C. Rawcliffe, *1386–1421* (1992), J.C. Wedgwood, *1439–1509* (1936), S.T. Bindoff, *1509–1558* (1982), P.W. Hasler, *1558–1603* (1981), B.D. Henning, *1660–1690* (1983); R. Sedgwick, *1715–1754* (1970), L. Namier and J. Brooke, *1754–1790* (1964), R.G. Thorne, *1760–1820* (1986). I was allowed to consult the unpublished volumes for 1690–1715, then being edited by David Hayton at the History of Parliament Trust in London. In addition I also consulted M. Keeler, *The Long Parliament* (1954), G.P. Judd, *Members of Parliament 1734–1832* (1954 – see, Ransome, 'Some Recent Studies', 141), and M. Stenton and S. Lees, *Who's Who of British Members of Parliament 1832–1979* (4 vols, 1976–81) and various monographs, dissertations and reference works on individual parliaments and constituencies. I also used the official list of *Returns of Members of Parliament for Great Britain and Ireland* printed in 1878. The latter is a somewhat haphazard affair of varying quality (see E.L.C. Mullins, 'The Making of the "Return of Members"', *Bulletin of the IHR*, 58 (1985), 189–209, and Moir, *Addled Parliament*, 184–6).

For Ireland I was able to cross-check my data with the as yet unpublished biographies of MPs in 1692–1800 researched by Dr Edith Johnston-Liik. This compendium, assembled by a single scholar, is history on a heroic scale. Information about pre-eighteenth-century Irish parliaments and peerages can be sketchy. Transfer of property was confused and genealogical reference works are more likely to be misleading than those compiled for England or Scotland. It has sometimes been impossible accurately to connect ancient and modern families who may have had a continuous tenure and retained authority through heiresses. Many MPs had the same surname and tracking down which Hamilton or Power was related to which is difficult.

For Scotland the biographies of 3,000 burgh and shire commissioners (1357–1707) catalogued by the History of the Scottish Parliament are, unfortunately, often uninformative about social, economic and family backgrounds [M.D. Young, *The*

Parliaments of Scotland: Burgh and Shire Commissioners (2 vols, Edinburgh, 1992–3)]. There are many omissions, most seriously among the lists of lairds of the sixteenth century. The introduction and overview essay in volume 2 are not very useful. (See Goodare, 'Who Was the Scottish Parliament?', *PH*, 14 (1995), 174–5.) I also used the *Scottish Parliamentary Commissioners 1357–1707* – Data Base, ed. A.I. Macinnes and F. Watson, deposited at the Institute of Historical Research, University of London.

Inevitably in projects on the scale of the *History of Parliament* errors have found their way into print. Wedgwood's lack of training and experience led to many problems, and the volumes covering 1439–1509 are now being redone. Bindoff's volumes lack a proper introduction, and no standard method of presenting statistical data was ever established. Histories of the constituencies were only added under pressure from Kitson Clark and Plumb and often display a Namierian outlook in interpretation (see *TLS*, 2 May 1980, 485). A new corrected version of the volumes in print has been issued on CD-ROM (see – ihr.sas.ac.uk/hop/mm.html). Unfortunately, several of the editors paid little attention to family connections and social origins. In part this was due to the relatively short periodization of the editorial divisions, in part to the pressure on the editors to publish promptly, and in part to the assumption that sociological analysis was unhistorical or impossible (see J. Namier, *Lewis Namier, a Biography* [1971], 282–329; Namier and Brooke, *HP*, i, 99; Henning, *HP*, i, 16). The volumes of MP biographies edited by Stenton and Lees are also inaccurate or misleading in places, and contain confusing duplications between volumes. *Burke's Peerage* and related works must be treated with great caution. Much of the genealogical information was provided by the families themselves. A volume of corrections has recently been published for *The Complete Peerage* (vol. xiv, ed. P.W. Hammond, Stroud, 1998). John Bateman's, *The Great Landowners of Great Britain and Ireland* (ed. D. Spring, Leicester, 1971 [1883]) is indispensable.

I have corrected, supplemented and amplified the data available in the printed and manuscript biographies by consulting innumerable volumes of local and family history. Readers are referred to the collections in the Genealogical and Local History Room of the Library of Congress and the English History and Local History Rooms at the Institute of Historical Research, University of London. I have also made considerable use of the reference collections of the British Library, Cambridge University Library, the National Library of Ireland, and the National Library of Scotland.

Notes

All books cited were published in London unless otherwise noted.

Introduction

1. The term 'governing class' has been widely employed to describe the political elite from the Middle Ages to 1914. I use the term 'class' not in a Marxian sense, but in that employed by John Vincent: 'a group contending over the structure of political authority'. J.R. Vincent, *Pollbooks* (Cambridge, 1967), 32–3.
2. J.S. Morrill, 'The Northern Gentry', *NH*, 15 (1979), 66–7.
3. L. Stone and J.C.F. Stone, *An Open Elite? England 1540–1880* (Oxford, 1984).
4. J. Dewald, *The European Nobility, 1400–1800* (Cambridge, 1996), 55, 62, 81, 92; D. Lieven, *The Aristocracy in Europe, 1815–1914* (1992), 13, 23, 27, 72, 203, 246.
5. F.W. Maitland, *The Collected Papers*, ed. H.A.L. Fisher (3 vols, Cambridge, 1911), i, 470–1.
6. J. Cannon, *Aristocratic Century, the Peerage of Eighteenth-Century England* (Cambridge, 1984), 8–9; W.D. Rubinstein, *Men of Property: the Very Wealthy in Britain since the Industrial Revolution* (1981), 218–19; E. Royle, *Modern Britain* (1987), 80–1; A.D. Harvey, *Britain in the Early Nineteenth Century* (1978), 8; J.V. Beckett, *The Aristocracy in England 1660–1914* (Oxford, 1986), 79, 117–18.
7. F. O'Gorman, *Voters, Patrons, and Parties: the Unreformed Electoral System of Hanoverian England, 1734–1832* (Oxford, 1989), 120, 234.
8. L. Stone, *The Crisis of the Aristocracy, 1558–1641* (Oxford, 1979); Stone and Stone, *An Open Elite?*, 30.
9. J. Powis, *Aristocracy* (Oxford, 1984), 2, 43–62.
10. S. Clark, *State and Status: the Rise of the State and Aristocratic Power in Western Europe* (Montreal, 1995), 189.
11. L. Colley, *Britons: Forging the Nation, 1707–1832* (New Haven, 1992), 52.
12. N. Wilding and P. Laundy, *An Encyclopedia of Parliament*, 4th edn (1972), 784.
13. Dewald, *European Nobility*, 5; A.L. Brown, 'The House of Commons 1386–1421', *PER*, 14 (1994), 18; K. Sharpe, 'James I, Civil War, and Restoration, 1603–1660', *The House of Commons*, eds R. Smith and J.S. Moore (1996), 83–99.
14. H.J. Habakkuk, *Marriage, Debt, and the Estates System: English Landownership 1650–1950* (Oxford, 1994), 404–13, 569; L. Namier and J. Brooke, *The House of Commons 1774–1790* (3 vols, 1964), i, 103. By and large, election to parliament confirmed social rank rather than helped to raise a family. This was true over many centuries. See M. McKisack, *The Parliamentary Representation of the English Boroughs during the Middle Ages* (Oxford, 1932), 101; R.O. Knapp, 'The Making of a Landed Elite: Social Mobility in Lancashire Society' (PhD thesis, Lancaster University, 1970), 301; C.G.A. Clay, 'Henry Hoare', *Landowners, Capitalists and Entrepreneurs*, ed. F.M.L. Thompson (Oxford, 1994), 126; H.L. Malchow, *Gentlemen Capitalists* (Stanford, 1992), 357–8; Y. Cassis, 'Bankers in English Society in the Late Nineteenth Century', *EcHR*, 38 (1985), 227.

15. B.G. Blackwood, *The Lancashire Gentry and the Great Rebellion 1640–60* (Manchester, 1978), 97–8; H. Trevor-Roper, *The Gentry 1540–1640* (1953), 18; E. Chalus, '"That Epidemical Madness", Women and Electoral Politics in the Late Eighteenth Century', *Gender in Eighteenth-Century England*, eds H. Barker and E. Chalus (1997), 158–9.

16. D. Cannadine, *The Decline and Fall of the British Aristocracy* (New Haven, 1990), 18; M.A. Kishlansky, *Parliamentary Selection, Social and Political Choice in Early Modern England* (Cambridge, 1986), 15–16; C. Given-Wilson, *The English Nobility in the Late Middle Ages* (1987), x, 11; W.L. Guttsman, *British Political Elite* (New York, 1963), 17–18; P. Langford, *Public Life and the Propertied Englishmen 1689–1798* (Oxford, 1991), 429; S. Payling, *Political Society in Lancastrian England* (Oxford, 1991), 1; C. Carpenter, *Locality and Polity: a Study of Warwickshire Landed Society, 1401–1499* (Cambridge, 1992), 244.

17. H.A. Clemenson, *English Country Houses and Landed Estates* (1982), 96.

18. L. Namier, *Crossroads of Power* (1962), 3, 5; L. Colley, *Lewis Namier* (1989), 82–9. See also K.B. McFarlane, *The Nobility of Later Medieval England* (Oxford, 1973), 297.

19. For information about the relevant volumes, see the bibliography. More generally, see E.M. Johnston, 'Managing an Inheritance: Colonel J.C. Wedgwood, the History of Parliament and the Lost History of the Irish Parliament', *Proceedings of the Royal Irish Academy*, 89 (1989), 167–86, and V. Cromwell, 'Computerizing the History of Parliament', *Storia & Multimedia*, eds F. Bocchi and P. Denley (Bologna, 1994), 544–7.

20. J.S. Morrill, 'Reconstructing the History of Early Stuart Parliaments', *Archives*, 21 (1994), 67; G.B. Stow, 'review', *Albion*, 26 (1994), 122; J. Goodare, 'review', *SHR*, 74 (1995), 117–18.

21. G.R. Elton, 'Studying the History of Parliament', *BSM*, 2 (1971), 4–14.

22. A. Sandall, 'The History of Parliament', *The Table*, 54 (1986), 88–9; Colley, *Namier*, 89.

23. J.H. Plumb, *Growth of Political Stability in England 1675–1725* (Baltimore, 1969), 10. See also, L. Stone, 'Prosopography', *Daedalus*, 100 (1971), 47; G.E. Aylmer, *The State's Servants: the Civil Service of the English Republic 1649–1660* (1973), 169–70.

24. D. Bruton and D.H. Pennington, *Members of the Long Parliament* (1954), 17, discovered that John Hampden and Charles I were cousins.

25. *VCH Wilts.*, v, 77.

26. P. Jenkins, *The Making of a Ruling Class: the Glamorgan Gentry 1640–1790* (Cambridge, 1983), xxiv, 28, 202–4; D. Southgate, *The Passing of the Whigs 1832–1886* (1962); M.E.W. Helms, 'The Convention Parliament of 1660' (PhD thesis, Bryn Mawr College, 1963), 101, 104.

27. S. Tillyard, *Aristocrats* (New York, 1995), 51–5; E.A. Smith, *Lord Grey 1765–1845* (Oxford, 1990), 261; L.G. Mitchell, 'Foxite Politics and the Great Reform Bill', *EHR*, 108 (1993), 344; D. Cecil, *The Cecils of Hatfield House* (Boston, 1973), 224–5; D. Cannadine, *Aspects of Aristocracy* (New Haven, 1994), 131; Guttsman, *British Political Elite*, 216–24.

28. D. Cressy, 'Kinship and Kin Interaction in Early Modern England', *PP*, 113 (1986), 40, 44, 47, 49; S. Walker, 'Strategies of the Gentry', *TLS* (31 July 1992), 22; R.A. Houlbrooke, *The English Family 1450–1700* (1984), 15, 52; M. Slater, *Family Life in the Seventeenth Century* (1984), 27–8, 45–6, 52; J.J. Hurwich, 'Lineage and Kin in the Sixteenth-Century Aristocracy', *The First Modern Society*, eds A.L. Beier, D. Cannadine and J. Rosenheim (Cambridge, 1989), 59–60; J. Goody, *Development of Family and Marriage in Europe* (Cambridge, 1983), 11.

29. L. Namier, *England in the Age of the American Revolution*, 2nd edn (1961), 10.

30. J. Rosenheim, *The Emergence of a Ruling Order* (1998), 6.

31. For example, J.C. Wedgwood, *History of Parliament 1439–1509* (2 vols, 1936), i, 171; S.T. Bindoff, *The House of Commons 1509–1558* (3 vols, 1982), i, 695; ii, 523, 638; iii, 116, 464; P.W. Hasler, *The*

House of Commons 1558–1603 (3 vols, 1981), i, 517; ii, 297; iii, 216, 634; Chalus, 'That Epidemical Madness', 151–78; A. Foreman, 'A Politician's Politician, Georgina, Duchess of Devonshire and the Whig Party', *Gender in Eighteenth-Century England*, eds H. Barker and E. Chalus (1997), 179–204; K.D. Reynolds, *Aristocratic Women and Political Society in Victorian Britain* (Oxford, 1998), 1–4, 129–87.

32. E. Hughes, *North-Country Life in the Eighteenth Century* (Oxford, 1952), 3; C.G.A. Clay, *Chapters in the Agrarian History of England and Wales 1500–1750* (2 vols, 1990), ii, 279; M. Bence-Jones, *The Catholic Families* (1992), 32; Hasler, *HP*, iii, 632; J.A. Hilton, *Catholic Lancashire from the Reformation to Renewal 1559–1991* (Chichester, 1994), 16, 17–20, 35, 50.

33. A. Jackson, *Colonel Edward Saunderson: Land and Loyalty in Victorian Ireland* (Oxford, 1995), 226–7.

Chapter 1

1. P. Laslet, 'Masham of Otes: the Rise and Fall of an English Family', *History Today*, 3 (1953), 535–43.
2. O. Fairclough, *The Grand Old Mansion: the Holtes and Their Successors at Aston Hall 1618–1864* (Birmingham, 1984).
3. K.S.S. Train, *Twenty Nottinghamshire Families* (Nottingham, 1970), 31–2; Payling, *Political Society*, 47–9; J.S. Roskell, L. Clark, and C. Rawcliffe, *The House of Commons 1386–1421* (5 vols, Stroud, 1992), iv, 452–5.
4. As hereditary peers who were eligible to take their seats, representative peers elected for Ireland or Scotland, or eldest sons summoned to the upper house in their fathers' lifetimes. Peers were only counted if they reached the age of majority and were not disbarred from sitting in parliament owing to religion, insanity, bankruptcy or contested claims to the title. They were not counted if they were known to be in exile, imprisoned, attainted, suffered a debilitating illness or refused to take their seats. Representative peers were counted from the year of election to the end of the parliament in the case of Scotland or until death for Ireland. No peer created or succeeding after 1945 was counted.
5. Euro MPs are not included, although several parliamentary families have produced them. Neither MPs in James II's Irish parliament (see Chapter 4) nor members of Cromwell's upper house are counted. Relatives by marriage are not included with the exception of husbands who directly benefited from being the masters of their wives' estates. Blood relatives in the male line, if the relationship was remote and unconnected with the parliamentary experience of the individual concerned, were not counted. For example, Samuel Holland (MP 1870s and 1880s) and the Holland Viscounts Knutsford (cr. 1895 and MPs 1874–99) were not counted as part of the same family even though they descended from the same great-grandfather. They derived their wealth and distinction separately. (Malchow, *Gentlemen Capitalists*, 19, 54.) If a younger son of a parliamentary family established a cadet branch with its own set of MPs/peers, or through marriage to an heiress continued another parliamentary family, his descendants were counted independently from his own stem line. For example, the descendants of Lord Langford are not included with the Taylours in Table 4.3. Where pedigrees were probable but not proven, I used my best judgement. If a merged family sustained a line of MPs (often elected for a family seat), all the MPs were counted as members of one family. If the male line had previous MPs and the female line did not, or vice versa, again all MPs were counted as one family. If both lines had MPs previous to the marriage, I counted the MPs from the female line as a separate family. Occasionally, very complicated marriage situations developed in which heiresses succeeded each other or brothers married heiresses, etc. I have had to exercise judgement and make the best arrangement I could. The guiding factor was the size of the estate. 'Associated' families were ones

with fewer than three MPs whose estates passed via an heiress to a parliamentary family (about 10% of the total number of families but a smaller proportion of individual peers and MPs). They are treated as separate from the main line but are included in the study as members of the parliamentary elite. When estates were split among multiple heirs, I normally treated such events as the end of a family. I have not included families connected by peerages by writ that became abeyant for long periods and rampaged unencumbered by landed property through multiple bloodlines, except when they provided access to the House of Lords for a member of an already established parliamentary family. (See: *CP*, iv, appendix H.)

6. Three brothers without a parent or successor in parliament was virtually unknown.

7. For some medieval parliaments virtually no data has survived. Many of the medieval MPs who may have gone unrecorded for one parliament, however, are listed for others, and in the cases of prominent families other records sometimes exist to confirm membership. However, the lists between the mid-sixteenth century and 1914, which comprise the central years of this study, are generally available.

8. P. Coss, 'Knights, Esquires, and the Origins of Social Gradations in England', *TRHS*, 5 (1995), 177, and 'The Formation of the English Gentry', *PP*, 147 (1995), 43, 49, 51–3.

9. Roskell, *HP*, ii, 522. The poet was himself an MP for Kent in 1386.

10. Payling, *Political Society*, 111–12; N. Saul, *Knights and Esquires: the Gloucestershire Gentry in the Fourteenth Century* (Oxford, 1981), 119–22, 126, 157; Given-Wilson, *English Nobility*, 16–17; J.R. Maddicott, 'County Community and the Making of Public Opinion in Fourteenth-Century England', *TRHS*, 28 (1978), 33; *VCH Salop*, iii, 234; C.E. Moreton, *The Townshends and Their World* (Oxford, 1992), 60; N. Denholm-Young, *The County Gentry in the Fourteenth Century* (Oxford, 1969), 72; C. Richmond, 'Bigwigs', *TLS* (10 April 1994), 22; G.L. Harriss, 'Medieval Parliament', *PH*, 13 (1994), 206–26; E. Acheson, *A Gentry Community; Leicestershire in the Fifteenth Century* (Cambridge, 1992), 112, 123. Some exceptions to this rule continued to occur. In the Tudor period and even later an occasional merchant or son of a man of humble origin did get elected, but these cases were exceptional.

11. But see: L. Clark, 'Magnates and Their Affinities in the Parliaments of 1386–1421', *The McFarlane Legacy*, eds R.H. Britnell and A.J. Pollard (New York, 1995), 127–53.

12. T.E. Hartley, 'The Sheriff and County Elections', *The Parliaments of Elizabethan England*, eds D.M. Dean and N.L. Jones (Oxford, 1990), 169, 189; Bindoff, *HP*, i, 186, 538–9; Hasler, *HP*, i, 112, 158, 166, 174–5, 179, 180–1, 203–4, 207–10, 223, 229, 234, 238–41, 245, 251, 267, 281, 453; ii, 149, 294; iii, 125, 161, 187, 506, 551.

13. Bindoff, *HP*, i, 351, 364, 378, 393, 395, 448, 494, 572, 557, 641, 698; ii, 1, 44, 82, 84, 298, 306, 342, 353, 478, 508, 543, 546, 568; iii, 9, 16, 78, 101, 122, 145, 155, 169, 221, 298, 313, 323, 396, 460, 462, 503, 521, 525, 528; Hasler, *HP*, i, 350, 356, 380, 483, 490–1, 546; ii, 15, 36, 96, 98, 214, 233, 250, 255, 256, 273, 286, 294, 299–301, 339, 347, 349, 358, 400, 409, 434, 487–9, 494, 496, 508; iii, 7, 12, 35, 107, 112, 124, 234, 525, 536, 549, 567, 604, 668; A. Emery, *Greater Medieval Houses of England and Wales 1300–1500* (Cambridge, 1996), i, 275; Coss, 'Knights, Esquires', 155–78.

14. *VCH Wilts.*, v, 124, and Bindoff, *HP*, ii, 546; iii, 122, 145, 155, 323; J.R. Lander, *Government and Community: England 1450–1509* (Cambridge, MA, 1980), 60; Hasler, *HP*, ii, 233.

15. Bindoff, *HP*, i, 273; Hasler, *HP*, i, 40, 62, 207–10, 394, 639; iii, 31.

16. V.G. Kiernan, *The Duel in European History* (Oxford, 1988), 155; Hasler, *HP*, ii, 223, 294; iii, 118, 541.

17. In three years during the 1560s, for example, Sir William Petre spent more than a Welsh squire's annual income on election dinners. Hasler, *HP*, iii, 211.

18. Hasler, *HP*, i, 204; J.G. Jones, *Early Modern Wales* c. *1525–1640* (New York, 1994), 194.

19. E.A. Wasson, *Whig Renaissance: Lord Althorp and the Whig Party 1782–1845* (1987), 32; R. Foster, *Politics of County Power: Wellington and the Hampshire Gentlemen 1820–52* (New York, 1990), 133; B.D. Hayes, 'Politics in Norfolk 1750–1832' (PhD thesis, University of Cambridge, 1958), 19–20; Kishlansky, *Parliamentary Selection*, 139.

20. W.H. Whiteley, 'Social Composition of the House of Commons 1868–1885' (PhD thesis, Cornell University, 1960), 345.

21. Bindoff, *HP*, iii, 462, 525; Hasler, *HP*, i, 267; iii, 505, 577; R.G. Thorne, *The House of Commons 1790–1820* (5 vols, 1986), iii, 379.

22. J.I. Kermode, 'Obvious Observations on the Formation of Oligarchies in Late Medieval English Towns', 98, and R. Horrox, 'The Urban Gentry in the Fifteenth Century', *Towns and Townspeople in the Fifteenth Century*, ed. J.A.F. Thomson (Gloucester, 1988), 22–38.

23. Historians still disagree about the precise period when the trend became an 'invasion' of the boroughs by the landed gentry. J.S. Roskell, *Parliament and Politics in Late Medieval England* (3 vols, 1981–83), i, 160–4; P. Jalland, 'The "Revolution" in Northern Borough Representation', *NH*, 11 (1976), 29; McKisack, *Parliamentary Representation*, 60–1, 100–1; M.A.R. Graves, *The Tudor Parliaments: Crown, Lords, and Commons, 1485–1603* (1985), 73; Denholm-Young, *Country Gentry*, 53n.; Langford, *Public Life*, 192; Lander, *Government and Community*, 58.

24. Bindoff, *HP*, i, 400, 543, 619; ii, 380–1; iii, 155; Hasler, *HP*, i, 267, 381; ii, 376; iii, 305, 401, 505.

25. Bindoff, *HP*, i, 718, 722; ii, 484; Hasler, *HP*, i, 508–9; iii, 355. The 8th Lord Mountjoy, 4th Lord Eure, the *de jure* 5th Earl of Kent, 1st Lord Hervey, 12th Lord Dacre, 8th Lord Bergavenny, 2nd Lord Paget, the 2nd and 3rd Lords de la Warr, and a number of heirs to peerages including the Earldom of Bedford and the Marquessate of Dorset served as burgesses before succeeding to their titles. One also finds more and more men sitting for boroughs remote from their estates and outside their home counties. For instance the 11th Lord Cobham, later the leading peer of Kent, sat for Hedon in Yorkshire in 1593. The 1st Earl of Devonshire, who lived in Derbyshire, sat for a borough in Cornwall.

26. E. Porritt, *The Unreformed House of Commons: Parliamentary Representation before 1832* (2 vols, New York, 1963 [1903]), i, 6–7, 153; D.M. Dean, 'Parliament and Locality', *The Parliaments of Elizabethan England*, eds D.M. Dean and N.J. Jones (Oxford, 1990), 143; D. MacCulloch, *Suffolk and the Tudors* (Oxford, 1986), 46; Bindoff, *HP*, i, 213, 356, 359, 604; iii, 3, 17, 90, 232, 567; Hasler, *HP*, ii, 244, 405; iii, 58, 371.

27. G.L. Harriss, 'The Dimensions of Politics', *The McFarlane Legacy*, eds R.H. Britnell and A.J. Pollard (New York, 1995), 13; Roskell, *Parliament and Politics*, i, 155–64, and *HP*, i, 43, 53, 172–5; P. Williams, *The Later Tudors: England 1547–1603* (Oxford, 1995), 137; J.E. Neale, *Elizabeth I and Her Parliaments 1559–81* (1969), 21, and *The Elizabethan House of Commons* (Harmondsworth, 1963), 141; Hasler, *HP*, i, 58.

28. *VCH Wilts.*, v, 112, 114, 119, and Bindoff, *HP*, i, 213, 356, 359, 604, 705; ii, 82; iii, 3, 17, 90, 232, 567; Hasler, *HP*, ii, 244, 405; iii, 58, 371; A. Aspinall, *Parliament through Seven Centuries: Reading and Its MPs* (1962), 45.

29. Nothing illustrates the change more dramatically than the number of men who ranked high enough to gain election for a county yet who also sat for a borough seat. As the data below show, in the early fifteenth century virtually no cross-over between shire knights and burgesses existed. Under Elizabeth I over half the knights also sat for a borough before or after their county election. The dividing line between knights of the shire and burgesses became increasingly vague:

	1386–1421	1439–1509	1509–1559	1559–1603
Counties only	94.3%	83.9%	64.6%	46.8%
Counties & Boroughs	5.7%	16.1%	35.4%	53.2%

30. However, Elizabeth I did incarcerate several critics and Charles I famously entered the chamber in order to arrest MPs.

31. Bindoff, *HP*, i, 369, 637; ii, 475; Hasler, *HP*, ii, 276–8.

32. The Queen created only two genuinely new titles in a reign of over forty years and was stingy with knighthoods as well. Hasler, *HP*, i, 23; Stone, *Crisis of the Aristocracy*, 97.

33. The debate about the constitutional place of the Commons in the century preceding the Civil War is still lively. There seems little doubt, however, that Graves is right to say Elizabeth's concerted attempts to limit the authority of parliament went against the historical trend. See M.A.R. Graves, *Thomas Norton: The Parliament Man* (Oxford, 1994), 5–12, 341, 353.

34. Bindoff, *HP*, i, 495, 685; iii, 30, 490–1; Hasler, *HP*, i, 41, 376, 423, 487, 539; ii, 473; iii, 55, 73, 340, 479, 598–601; W. Notestein, *The House of Commons 1604–1610* (New Haven, 1971), 4. Chronic absenteeism was as characteristic of sixteenth-century parliaments as it was of the eighteenth century. Moreover, in Elizabeth I's 44-year reign parliament met for a total of two-and-a-half years. But neither of these facts obviates the importance people placed on the institution or gaining election to it.

35. M.W. McCahill, *Order and Equipoise: the Peerage and the House of Lords 1783–1806* (1978), 212; Cannon, *Aristocratic Century*, 94–5, 123; H.J. Hanham, *The Nineteenth-Century Constitution* (Cambridge, 1969), 171–2; S. Panteli, 'House of Lords since 1830', *Contemporary Review*, 212 (1968), 211; D.R. Hainsworth, *Stewards, Lords and People: the Estate Steward and His World in Later Stuart England* (Cambridge, 1993), 145; A. Swatland, *The House of Lords in the Reign of Charles II* (Cambridge, 1993), 172; J.J. Sack, 'The House of Lords and Parliamentary Patronage in Great Britain, 1802–1832', *HJ*, 23 (1980), 913–37; C. Jones, 'The House of Lords and the Growth of Parliamentary Stability, 1702–1742', *Britain in the First Age of Party*, ed. C. Jones (1987), 108.

36. Kishlansky, *Parliamentary Selection*, 18–19.

37. R.A. Butt, *History of Parliament: the Middle Ages* (1989), 632; G.R. Elton, *Studies in Tudor and Stuart Politics and Government* (4 vols, Cambridge, 1974–92), ii, 42. Norman Ball suggests that the increase was largely due to the Crown's need for men to carry through a rapidly expanding volume of parliamentary business, but the numbers of new boroughs goes far beyond what was necessary in this regard – 'Representation in the English House of Commons, the New Boroughs 1485–1640', *PER*, 15 (1995), 117–24. Constituency entries and biographies in the *History of Parliament* make it clear that pressure from magnates was a major factor in creating the new boroughs, even in Cornwall.

38. Roskell, *HP*, i, 44–9; T.K. Rabb, 'Revisionism Revised: the Role of the Commons', *PP*, 92 (1992), 62–5; J.G.A. Pocock, 'The History of British Political Thought', *JBS*, 24 (1985), 292; D. Crouch, *The Image of Aristocracy in Britain, 1000–1300* (1992), 175.

39. Bindoff, *HP*, iii, 296.

40. For example, Bindoff, *HP*, i, 501, 523, 543, 561, 613, 708, 718; ii, 33, 59, 621; iii, 360; Hasler, *HP*, ii, 409, 420; iii, 382, 542, 597.

41. Bindoff, *HP*, i, 452; iii, 453; Hasler, *HP*, ii, 408ff; iii, 489ff.

42. For example, Bindoff, *HP*, ii, 30, 236; Hasler, *HP*, i, 507.

43. Bindoff, *HP*, i, 373, 384, 497; ii, 179–82, 497, 638; Hasler, *HP*, i, 59, 61–3, 485, 545, 580, 650–1; ii, 50–1, 471; iii, 505, 604.

44. *VCH Wilts.*, v, 122, 125.

45. G.R. Elton, 'Parliament', *The Reign of Elizabeth I*, ed. C. Haigh (1984), 80.

46. Rubinstein, *Men of Property*, 168.

47. Jones, *Early Modern Wales*, 46.

48. R. Sedgwick, *The House of Commons 1715–1754* (2 vols, 1970), i, 15; Bindoff, *HP*, i, 406; ii, 87, 94, 130; iii, 262, 595; Hasler, *HP*, ii, 125, 250, 465; B.D. Henning, *The House of Commons 1660–1690* (3 vols, 1983), iii, 517, 546.

49. Porritt, *UHC*, i, 283–91; Namier and Brooke, *HP*, i, 134; Sedgwick, *HP*, i, 15.

50. Hasler, *HP*, i, 41, 267, 384; iii, 527; W.A. Speck, *Tory and Whig: the Struggle in the Constituencies 1701–1715* (New York, 1970), 4; F. Heal and C. Holmes, *The Gentry in England and Wales, 1500–1700* (1994), 205.

51. B. Bradshawe and J.S. Morrill, *The British Problem* c. *1534–1707: State Formation in the Atlantic Archipelago* (1996), 133.

52. N. Ellenberger, 'The Transformation of London "Society" at the End of Victoria's Reign', *Albion*, 22 (1990), 635, 645–6.

53. Hasler, *HP*, i, 335, 433; C. Russell, *The Causes of the English Civil War* (Oxford, 1990), 141; P. Yorke, *The Royal Tribes of Wales* (Liverpool, 1887), 166.

54. W.M. Elofson, *The Rockingham Connection* (Montreal, 1996), 9; Colley, *Britons*, 50; A. Lambert, *Unquiet Souls: the Indian Summer of the British Aristocracy 1880–1918* (1985), 113; Hasler, *HP*, iii, 31, 70, 107; O. MacDonagh, *O'Connell* (1991), 273.

55. S.E. Lehmberg, *The Reformation Parliament 1529–1536* (Cambridge, 1970), 32.

56. Bindoff, *HP*, ii, 119, 536; Hasler, *HP*, iii, 93.

57. M. Keeler, *The Long Parliament, 1640–41* (Philadelphia, 1954), 27; Henning, *HP*, i, 13–15.

58. Namier and Brook, *HP*, i, 47–8; E. Richards, *The Leviathan of Wealth: the Sutherland Fortune in the Industrial Revolution* (1973), 29; M. Cragoe, *An Anglican Aristocracy: the Moral Economy of the Landed Estate in Carmarthenshire, 1832–1895* (Oxford, 1996), 130; Hainsworth, *Stewards*, 136–58.

59. Porritt, *UHC*, i, 154–5; Hasler, *HP*, ii, 487; Kishlansky, *Parliamentary Selection*, 20, 192, 194; C. Russell, *The Crisis of Parliaments: English History 1509–1660* (Oxford, 1971), 196–7; D. Hirst, *Representative of the People? Voters and Voting in England under the Early Stuarts* (Cambridge, 1975), 118; J.K. Gruenfelder, *Influence in Early Stuart Elections 1604–40* (Columbus, 1981), 19; B. Coward, *The Stanleys, Lords Stanley and Earls of Derby 1385–1672* (Manchester, 1983), 120.

60. Plumb, *Growth of Political Stability*, 93–101; Porritt, *UHC*, i, 77; P. Roebuck, *Yorkshire Baronets 1640–1760* (Oxford, 1980), 59; Henning, *HP*, i, 15, 694; ii, 102, 237; iii, 181, 313.

61. D. Eastwood, 'Contesting the Politics of Deference: the Rural Electorate, 1820–60', *Party, State, and Society: Electoral Behaviour in Britain since 1820*, eds J. Lawrence and M. Taylor (Aldershot, 1997), 36. For Irish expenses see Chapter 4. Thorne, *HP*, i, 39–58, 380, 438; iv, 432; R.A.C. Parker, *Coke of Norfolk* (Oxford, 1975), 131; R.G. Wilson, *Gentlemen Merchants: the Merchant Community in Leeds 1700–1830* (Manchester, 1971), 170. At least twenty MPs during the eighteenth century ruined themselves through elections. Sedgwick, *HP*, i, 154; Namier and Brooke, *HP*, i, 109; iii, 56, 380, 526. On the expenses of an earl's son, see Devon RO, Fortescue MSS 1262M/FC 89 1817. O'Gorman, *Voters*, 141–50; J.A. Phillips, *The Great Reform Bill in the Boroughs: English Electoral Behaviour, 1818–1841* (Oxford, 1992), 205, 212; Porritt, *UHC*, i, 76, 354–5; ii, 186.

62. W.B. Gwyn, *Democracy and the Cost of Politics in Britain* (1962), 101, and 21–128; K.T. Hoppen, 'Roads to Democracy: Electioneering and Corruption in Nineteenth-Century England and Ireland', *History*, 81 (1996), 559–60; G.H. Jennings, *An Anecdotal History of the British Parliament* (New York, 1881), 388–9; Whiteley, *SC*, 67.

63. M. Rush, *The Selection of Parliamentary Candidates* (1969), 29.

64. *Burke's Peerage* (1938) xxi–clxxxiv – assigns precedence to well over twenty thousand individuals.

65. R. Samuel, *TLS* (8 March 1996), 15.

66. F.G. James, *Lords of the Ascendancy: the Irish House of Lords and Its Members, 1600–1800* (Dublin, 1995), 95; T.P. Power, *Land, Politics and Society in Eighteenth-Century Tipperary* (Oxford, 1993), 112–13.

67. The proportion would be even lower if peers created when they were too young to have been legally elected to the Commons, peers created during the Interregnum when in exile and unable to be elected MPs first, and Irish peers who subsequently sat as English MPs before being promoted to a British peerage were excluded. During the period 1700–1850 such an adjusted percentage of new peers who had not been MPs was virtually zero. In the late nineteenth century some poets, painters, civil servants, philanthropists and industrialists began to be awarded peerages, but even then no more than 15% of the new peers gained a title without serving in the Commons.

68. British Library, Additional MSS. 51555 f. 146 Grey to Lord Holland 2 June 1831 (copy); Namier and Brooke, *HP*, i, 99; Thorne, *HP*, iv, 703.

69. *VCH Salop*, iii, 236.

70. McKisack, *Parliamentary Representation*, 114; A. Fletcher, *A County Community in Peace and War: Sussex 1600–1660* (New York, 1975), 231–2; S.E. Lehmberg, *The Later Parliaments of Henry VIII 1536–1547* (Cambridge, 1977), 4; Bindoff, *HP*, i, 236; Hasler, *HP*, i, 62; Neale, *Elizabethan House of Commons*, 185–203; Greuenfelder, *Influence in Early Stuart Elections*, 4–91, 168; T.L. Moir, *The Addled Parliament of 1614* (Oxford, 1958), 43–52.

71. Bindoff, *HP*, ii, 483; Hasler, *HP*, i, 207, 229, 240; iii, 395, 492; Heal and Holmes, *Gentry*, 175.

72. Hasler, *HP*, i, 240, 283; iii, 287; Jones, *Early Modern Wales*, 194; C. Silvester, *The Literary Companion to Parliament* (1996), xi; L. Namier, *The Structure of Politics at the Accession of George III*, 2nd edn (1970), 1; Gwyn, *Democracy*, 11.

73. R.K. Huch, *The Radical Lord Radnor* (Minneapolis, 1977), 76; V. Glendinning, *Anthony Trollope* (New York, 1993), 327.

74. J. Davies, 'Aristocratic Town-makers', *Patricians, Power and Politics in Nineteenth-Century Towns*, ed. D. Cannadine (New York, 1982), 47–8; D. Hawkins, ed., *The Grove Diaries* (Strawbridge, 1995), 249; Y. Cassis, *City Bankers, 1890–1914* (Cambridge, 1994), 267.

75. Bindoff, *HP*, ii, 148; Hasler, *HP*, i, 533, 629; ii, 244; iii, 626.

76. Hasler, *HP*, i, 11, 335; Henning, *HP*, i, 2; Sedgwick, *HP*, i, 137; Cannadine, *DFBA*, 185.

77. Clark, 'Magnates', 135.

78. *CP*, x, 664–5. Between 1439 and 1509 only twenty-five MPs became peers, ten by inheritance and fifteen by creation. Another twenty-seven close male relatives and a number of illegitimate offspring of peers also sat in the house, but no eldest son of a viscount or above was returned.

79. Porritt, *UHC*, i, 122–3; Bindoff, *HP*, iii, 230; Hasler, *HP*, iii, 308. The heir of the 1st Earl of Derby was MP for Lancashire in 1478, while his father sat in the upper house as Lord Strange. The uncle of the 1st Duke of Suffolk was MP for Norfolk in 1491–92, and he became the father of a subsequent duke. The 2nd Duke of Norfolk sat for Norfolk as Thomas Howard in 1478, but his father (MP 1449–56) was not created a peer until 1483.

80. Of the twelve commoners listed by William Cecil in 1588 as men of 'great possessions' able to sustain a peerage, ten sat as MPs. Hasler, *HP*, i, 23, lists only eight, but in the biographies Sir Henry Cromwell/Williams and Sir John Petre were also listed.

81. The 2nd Lord Marney in 1523, 2nd Lord Windsor and 3rd Lord Latimer in 1529, 2nd Lord Wharton in 1542, 10th Lord Cobham in 1547.

82. Neale, *Elizabethan House of Commons*, 289–90; Henning, *HP*, i, 8, 19; Mary Keeler, *Long Parliament*, 22, found 9.5% of MPs in the early 1640s were peers' sons. Henning, *HP*, i, 16, counted about 11% of MPs from peerage families in the later seventeenth century. Cannon, *Aristocratic*

Century, 112–14, found 27.1% a century later (my percentages). See Wasson, 'Crisis of the Aristocracy', 305–6, for nineteenth-century percentages and Table 5.1.

83. Henning, *HP*, i, 19; Swatland, *House of Lords*, 172. In the early nineteenth century over half the hereditary members of the House of Lords had been MPs. E.A. Smith, *The House of Lords in British Politics and Society 1815–1911* (1992), 63. If one discounts new peers who were soldiers, royalty, judges, the insane and peers who succeeded as minors, this proportion means that virtually all hereditary peers who were qualified by age served an apprenticeship in the Commons first.

84. I used A.F. Kinney, *Titled Elizabethans* (Hamden, 1973), as the source for Lords membership. The editor (p. 60) was in error in including the Ughtreds, who were not summoned after 1365. (*Burke's Dormant, Abeyant, Forfeited, and Extinct Peerages*, new edn [1996], 544.) But there was an Elizabethan Ughtred MP in any case.

85. Payling, *Political Society*, 10; Elton, *Studies*, ii, 42; Gruenfelder, *Influence*, 14; Hirst, *Representative of the People?*, 1–12; Kishlansky, *Parliamentary Selection*, 69, 73, 225; Fletcher, *County Community*, 231–2. There is a large literature on this topic for the eighteenth and nineteenth centuries. See citations in: O'Gorman, *Voters*, 53, 178, 259, 276–9, 310, 385–9 and passim; J.A. Philips and C. Wetherell, 'The Great Reform Act of 1832', *AHR*, 100 (1995), 80–97.

86. They did not include peers or younger brothers, uncles, sons, etc., in this count. *An Open Elite?*, 246. See also D. and E. Spring, 'Social Mobility and the English Landed Elite', *Canadian Journal of History*, 21 (1986), 349.

87. Hertfordshire 25.9%, Northamptonshire 45.9%, Northumberland 34%.

88. Stones, *An Open Elite?*, 246 and Table 7.7.

89. G. Tyack, *Warwickshire Country Houses* (Chichester, 1994); P. De Figueiredo and J. Treuherz, *Cheshire Country Houses* (Chichester, 1988); A. Oswald, *Country Houses of Dorset*, 2nd edn (Tiverton, 1994); N. Kingsley, *The Country Houses of Gloucestershire, 1500–1830* (2 vols, Cheltenham and Chichester, 1989–92); J. Heward and R. Taylor, *The Country Houses of Northamptonshire* (Swindon, 1996).

90. See E.A. Wasson, 'The House of Commons, 1660–1945', *EHR*, 106 (1991), 642.

91. J.T. Cliffe, *The World of the Country House in Seventeenth-Century England* (New Haven, 1999), 198–202.

92. The only significant exceptions were the Bishops of Durham in the Palatine and royalty such as Prince Rupert. J.C. Sainty, *Lists of Lieutenants of Counties 1585–1642 and 1660–1974* (1970, 1979, IHR).

93. C. Peters, *Lord Lieutenants and High Sheriffs of Oxfordshire* (Oxford, 1995).

94. *List of Sheriffs for England and Wales from the Earliest Times to AD 1831* (New York, 1963 [1898]). Note that some families may not appear on the list because they held sheriffdoms in two or more counties owing to the distribution of their property or because their estates passed to another important family who did not adopt their name.

95. Cornwall, Cumberland, Denbighshire, Essex, Hampshire, Herefordshire, Lancashire, Norfolk, Northamptonshire, Oxfordshire, Staffordshire, Worcestershire and Yorkshire.

96. *Baily's Hunting Directory, 1995–96* (Cambridge, 1995); G. Fergusson, *The Green Collars* (1993), 357.

97. M. Wolffe, *Gentry Leaders in Peace and War: the Gentry Governors of Devon in the Early Seventeenth Century* (Exeter, 1997), 19, 29–31 (74 out of 98 excluding clergy).

98. Hawkins, *Grove Diaries*, 21–7, 215–26.

99. Cragoe, *Anglican Aristocracy*, 13.

100. J.J. Cartwright, 'List of Persons in Yorkshire Who Paid the Tax on Male Servants in 1780', *Yorkshire Archaeological Journal*, 14 (1898), 65–80; J. Chartres, 'English Landed Society', *Land and Society in Britain, 1700–1914*, eds N. Harte and R. Quinalt (Manchester, 1996), 34–56.

101. R.J. Olney, *Rural Society and County Government in Nineteenth-Century Lincolnshire* (Lincoln, 1979), 32–3; J. Gerard, *Country House Life: Family and Servants, 1815–1914* (Oxford, 1994), 144ff.

102. In some of these cases employees were probably taxed at other residences outside the county.

103. Namier and Brooke, *HP*, iii, 310. Altogether men living off official or professional incomes composed nearly 40% of all non-elite MPs between 1660 and 1820. See Appendix I.

104. Roskell, *HP*, iv, 841–4; Hasler, *HP*, iii, 13, 414, 469, 565, 590; Henning, *HP*, i, 539; ii, 21, 373–4; iii, 93–4, 351–2, 649–51, 688–9, 741–2, 742–3; Sedgwick, *HP*, ii, 395, 476; Namier and Brooke, *HP*, ii, 254, 317–18; Thorne, *HP*, iii, 63–4, 204–5, 360; iv, 112, 290; *CB*, ii, 47–8; iv, 152; v, 195–6, 327; Earl of Bessborough and C. Aslet, *Enchanted Forest* (1984), 64–70; *DNB*, xix, 352.

105. Henning, *HP*, iii, 59, 379–80, 724, 735–6; *CB*, ii, 442; *Burke's Visitations of Seats*, 2nd edn (1854) i, 209.

106. Sedgwick, *HP*, ii, 416, 522; Namier and Brooke, *HP*, ii, 262; Thorne, *HP*, iii, 51, 63; iv, 258–9, 289–90.

107. Sedgwick, *HP*, ii, 68, 553.

108. History of Parliament, unpublished volumes 1690–1715, ed. D. Hayton, see E. Dummer; Henning, *HP*, i, 678–9; ii, 335; iii, 162, 230–2, 240–1, 321–2, 355–6, 514–17; Sedgwick, *HP*, ii, 306; Thorne, *HP*, iii, 288–9; iv, 14–16, 330–1; v, 367; Bindoff, *HP*, ii, 138; Hasler, *HP*, i, 520–1; ii, 123, 308; *CB*, ii, 64, 110, 174, 358–9; iii, 46; v, 225–6.

109. Namier and Brooke, *HP*, ii, 116; iii, 522; Thorne, *HP*, iv, 125, 642; v, 497; Sedgwick, *HP*, ii, 378.

110. Namier and Brooke, *HP*, ii, 326–7, 409–10, 668; Thorne, *HP*, iv, 126.

111. Henning, *HP*, i, 649; Sedgwick, *HP*, i, 485; ii, 490, 531; Namier and Brooke, *HP*, ii, 81, 166–7; iii, 21, 93, 170, 516, 568; Thorne, *HP*, iii, 435, 441; iv, 540–2, 651, 715; v, 15, 476, 579, 603. Sometimes they ended as tramps or suicides. Namier and Brooke, *HP*, iii, 443; Thorne, *HP*, iii, 433; iv, 642.

112. Henning, *HP*, i, 607; Sedgwick, *HP*, i, 542; ii, 386, 519; Thorne, *HP*, v, 258.

113. Namier and Brooke, *HP*, ii, 282, 592, 661–2; Thorne, *HP*, iii, 136, 184, 209–10, 493; iv, 147, 312, 592, 614, 713; v, 215, 228, 336, 358, 425, 443, 490.

114. Thorne, *HP*, iii, 223, 289, 314–18, 657; iv, 312, 375, 732, 781–3, 893; v, 17.

115. See Appendix I.

116. Henning, *HP*, iii, 321; Sedgwick, *HP*, i, 487; ii, 246; Thorne, *HP*, iii, 231–2; *CB*, ii, 110–11, 134–5, 174; v, 327–9.

117. J. Cornforth, 'Brockhall, Northamptonshire', *CL*, 136 (1964), 1430; J. Johnson, *The Gloucestershire Gentry* (Gloucester, 1989), 20–1; Kingsley, *Country Houses of Gloucestershire*, ii, 291–2.

118. Henning, *HP*, i, 732–3; ii, 509, 513, 655–6, 669; iii, 70; *CB*, iii, 80–2, 92–3; iv, 264; Thorne, *HP*, iii, 604–5.

Chapter 2

1. Heal and Holmes, *The Gentry*, 10.
2. Foster, *Politics of County Power*, 7–9, 152.
3. Virtually every standard source gives a different number. Counts of country houses are also all over the map and quite unhelpful owing to multiple ownerships.
4. F.M.L. Thompson, *The Rise of Respectable Society: a Social History of Victorian Britain 1830–1900* (1988), 63, 154.
5. D. Castronovo, *The English Gentleman* (New York, 1987), 10.
6. Clemenson, *English Country Houses*, 20.

7. 1,978. Nine of them were exclusively peerage families. Most families were relatively easy to categorize, although a few teetered on the knife-edge of being English/Irish or Scottish/Irish or Welsh/English, etc. See Chapter 4.

8. For example, 170 MPs from the English parliamentary elite sat in the Irish House of Commons between 1660 and 1800 and 69 sat for Irish seats after the Union. Between 1660 and 1945, 97 sat for Welsh constituencies. Three sat in the Scots parliament in 1660–1707 and 46 for Scottish constituencies in 1708–1945. Between 1660 and 1945, 245 predominantly Scottish, Welsh and Irish families had at least one MP elected for an English seat.

9. 1,487. They produced 6,727 MPs and 2,837 peers. More than 8,500 individuals compiled 150,000 years of parliamentary service. See Table 2.2. Years of service were calculated based on the first full year of service and each subsequent full or partial year in sequence. If an MP left the House and returned, the count for the second term began with the first full year. MPs whose election was successfully challenged within six months were not counted. In 'The House of Commons', *EHR* (1991), 635–51, I identified a smaller number. This discrepancy is largely due to adding families who had only one or two MPs in the 1660–1945 period, but who had additional MPs before 1660.

10. See also Appendix III, Table 3.13.

11. Some of the 'five or fewer' group were medieval burgesses. A few boroughs continued to return local families in the seventeenth and even eighteenth centuries, such as the Walkers of Exeter (MPs 1640–87) and the Webbs of Taunton (1705–80). The latter family, however, was very unusual. In the twentieth century a few political families arose who had no connection with the old elite, such as the Hendersons, Foots and Lloyd Georges.

12. E.P. Shirley, *The Noble and Gentle Men in England* (1866), 102. The Earls of Craven are the most notable other case, but they lacked the Nevilles' distinguished lineage.

13. Some multiple line families, such as the Bullers, Carews and Corbets, accumulated huge numbers of MPs but no single branch reached grandee status.

14. See Appendix II, Table 2.3.

15. C. Seebohm, *The Country House* (1989), 61; J.P. Cooper, *Land, Men and Beliefs: Studies in Early-Modern History*, eds G.E. Aylmer and J.S. Morrill (1983), 20; Stone, *Crisis of the Aristocracy*, 51–2; W.L. Burn, *Age of Equipoise* (1968), 313–14; Colley, *Britons*, 154; J.L. Sanford and M.Townsend, *The Great Governing Families of England* (2 vols, Edinburgh, 1865), i, 2; Beckett, *Aristocracy*, 88; F.M.L. Thompson, *English Landed Society in the Nineteenth Century* (1963), 28–9; W.S. Churchill, *A Roving Commission* (New York, 1930), 89; C.G.A. Clay, *Economic Expansion and Social Change: England 1500–1700* (2 vols, Cambridge, 1984), i, 155–6; P. Horn, *High Society: the English Social Elite, 1880–1914* (Stroud, 1992), 8.

16. In cases of unlisted mineral or urban property or families extinct before the New Domesday survey, I have used other sources to establish whether families were magnates in terms of income. I counted all income in Great Britain and Ireland.

17. The grandees not mentioned in the text were: Agar-Ellis, Alington-Sturt, Anson, Ashburnham, Ashley-Cooper, Baring, Bathurst, Beauclerk, Bertie, Boscawen, Bridgeman, Brodrick, Bromley-Davenport, Brudenell-Bruce, Byng, Cadogan, Capel, Cavendish-Bentinck, Cecil, Chomondeley, Clive, Somers-Cocks, Coke, Compton, Cornwallis, Courtenay, Coventry, Cowper, Offley-Crewe, Curzon, Cust-Brownlow, Dashwood, Digby, Dillon-Lee, Tyrwhitt-Drake, Duncombe, Dundas, Edgcumbe, Grey-Egerton, Egerton-Tatton, Eliot, Ernle-Erle-Drax, Fane, Finch, Finch-Hatton, Fitzroy, Foley, Forester, Fortescue, Fox-Strangways, Godolphin, Graham, Greville, Grey-Bennet, Grey-Booth, Grimston, Harley, Heathcote-Bertie, Herbert (Powis), Herbert (Pembroke), Herbert (Carnarvon), Hervey, Hobart, Howard (Norfolk), Howard (Carlisle), Howard (Suffolk), Howe, Knatchbull,

Lambton, Lascelles, Legge, Lennox, Leveson Gower, Long (Vts), Lovelace-King, Lumley-Saunderson, Lygon, Lyttelton, Maynard, Molyneux, Monckton, Monson, Montagu (Manchester), Montagu (Sandwich), Mordaunt, Neville (Abergavenny), Hicks-Noel, North, Osborne, Paget, Peel, Pelham (Chichester), Pelham-Anderson, Pelham-Clinton, Perceval, Percy, Petty-Fitzmaurice, Pierrepont, Pitt, Pleydell-Bouverie, Portman-Berkeley, Poulett, Powlett-Orde, Proby, Rawdon-Hastings, Robartes-Hunt, Robinson, Ryder, Sackville, St John (Earls), St John (Vts), St John-Mildmay, Savage-Nassau, Seymour-Conway, Shirley-Ferrers, Smith (Carrington), Somerset, Sondes, Spencer-Churchill, Stanhope (Chesterfield), Stanhope (Harrington), Stuart-Wortley, Sidney, Talbot, Tollemache, Trelawney, Tufton, Vane, Vane-Tempest-Stewart, Verney-Willoughby, Vernon-Venables, Child-Villiers, Villiers (Clarendon), Waldegrave, Walpole, Ward, Wellesley, Wentworth-Fitzwilliam, West, Wharton, Willoughby (Middleton), Windsor (Plymouth), Wodehouse, Wyndham (Egremont), Yorke.

18. A tier of great gentry who came close to qualifying but failed to establish themselves for any length of time in the Lords and tended to focus on county affairs includes the Carews, Corbets, Fownes Luttrells, Harveys, Hoghtons, Lucys, Knightleys, Musgraves, Myddeltons and Newdigates. This group, however, was small in number.

19. Hainsworth, *Stewards*, 15–16.

20. Shirley, Legh, Lowther, Manners, Molyneux, Hastings and Bagot. Roskell, *HP*, ii, 108; iv, 364; Wedgwood, *HP*, 557; Acheson, *Gentry Community*, 95, 234; Hasler, *HP*, iii, 60.

21. Shirley, *Noble and Gentle Men*, 253.

22. A. Adonis, 'The Political Role of the British Peerage in the Third Reform Act System *c.* 1885–1914' (D.Phil. thesis, University of Oxford, 1988), 165.

23. I include Lords Lieutenant of Ireland, often a cabinet post requiring active not merely honorific duties. The great offices counted before Walpole were First Lord of the Treasury, Lord Privy Seal, the Secretaries of the Northern and Southern Departments, Lord President of the Council and Lord Chancellor.

24. A. Aspinall, 'Extracts from Lord Hatherton's Diary', *PA*, 17 (1964), 263.

25. Namier, *England in the Age of the American Revolution*, 181.

26. Roskell, *HP*, iv, 735–9, 752–3; Hasler, *HP*, iii, 564, 567.

27. McFarlane, *Nobility*, 144ff; Cooper, *Land, Men and Beliefs*, 2–3; H. Miller, *Henry VIII and the English Nobility* (Oxford, 1986), 35; R.R. Davies, *Lordship and Society in the March of Wales 1282–1400* (Oxford, 1978), 48.

28. Cannon, *Aristocratic Century*, 14–15.

29. Given-Wilson, *English Nobility*, 59.

30. No disappearances took place in 1630–39 because parliament was not summoned. Gaps between sessions varied before 1689, when annual meetings began, which had an affect on failure rates. Some peerage families continued in existence with a seat in the House of Lords, long after they elected their last MP. This was particularly true after the reforms in the suffrage during the nineteenth century. As peers they continued to participate in politics and retained high status. Before 1832, however, loss of interest or ability to participate in the Commons was usually a sign of serious dysfunction as an aristocratic family.

31. Blackwood, *Lancashire Gentry*, 162.

32. For an excellent summary of the literature on the 'demographic crisis' see Stones, *An Open Elite?*, 100–9, and T.H. Hollingsworth, 'Demography of the British Peerage', *Population Studies*, supp. 17 (1964), 1–108.

33. Heal and Holmes, *Gentry*, 240–2, believe this retreat post-1688 was among the greater gentry, but my numbers suggest it was more common among the middling families.

34. History of Parliament, unpublished volumes 1690–1715, ed. D. Hayton; *Burke's, Visitations of Seats* (1854), i, 209.

35. Measurements are impossible to compare precisely because they are based on conflicting criteria. J.S. Morrill, *Cheshire 1630–1660: County Government and Society During the English Revolution* (Oxford, 1974), 3–4; A. Everitt, 'Social Mobility in Early Modern England', *PP*, 33 (1966), 63–5; C. Holmes, *Seventeenth-Century Lincolnshire* (Lincoln, 1980), 66.

36. Beckett, *Aristocracy*, 96, 98; G.E. Mingay, *The Gentry: the Rise and Fall of a Ruling Class* (1976), 17.

37. For more detailed data, see Appendix II, Tables 2.1 and 2.2.

38. Carpenter, *Locality and Polity*, 90; A. Hughes, *Politics, Society and Civil War in Warwickshire, 1620–1660* (Cambridge, 1987), 27.

39. McFarlane, *Nobility*, 8–9; Denholm-Young, *Country Gentry*, 4–5; M. Jones, *Gentry and Lesser Nobility in Late Medieval Europe* (New York, 1986), 9; Payling, *Political Society*, 31; M. Bennett, 'Careerism in Late Medieval England', *People, Politics and Community in the Late Middle Ages*, eds J. Rosenthal and C. Richmond (New York, 1987), 19–39.

40. P. Coss, *Lordship, Knighthood and Locality: a Study in English Society, c. 1180–c. 1280* (Cambridge, 1991), 131; A. Smith, '"The Greatest Man of that Age": the Acquisition of Sir John Fastolf's East Anglian Estates', *Rulers and Ruled in Late Medieval England*, eds R.E. Archer and S. Walker (1995), 149–50; R.V. Turner, *Men Raised from Dust: Administrative Service and Upward Mobility in Angevin England* (Philadelphia, 1988), 139–40; Habakkuk, *MDE*, 365–79; J.V. Beckett, 'The Pattern of Landownership in England and Wales, 1660–1880', *EcHR*, 37 (1984), 10, 13; B.A. Holdernesse, 'The English Land Market in the Eighteenth Century', *EcHR*, 27 (1974), 562, 573 n.1.

41. It is true that more parliaments met earlier, thirty-one in the years 1400–40 for example. The number of names missing on lists of MPs is high for some of the early Tudor parliaments, but this should not unduly affect the data on rates of entry since many MPs were elected on more than one occasion. Moreover the data on entry based on date of first MP and that based on other signs of entry into the gentry such as purchase of an estate or selection as sheriff show similar patterns.

42. Kishlansky, *Parliamentary Selection*, ix–x.

43. B. English, *The Great Landowners of East Yorkshire 1530–1910* (New York, 1990), 51; Stones, *An Open Elite?*, 182; Clay, *Economic Expansion*, i, 143; R.B. Smith, *Land and Politics in the England of Henry VIII: the West Riding of Yorkshire – 1530–46* (Oxford, 1970), 213.

44. Hughes, *Politics, Society and Civil War*, 28–9.

45. J. Guy, *Tudor England* (Oxford, 1990), 48; G. Holmes, *The Making of a Great Power: Late Stuart and Early Georgian Britain 1660–1722* (1986), 70; Stones, *An Open Elite?*, 182, 258; Heal and Holmes, *Gentry*, 381; M. James, *Family, Lineage and Civil Society: a Study of Society, Politics and Mentality in the Durham Region 1500–1640* (Oxford, 1974), 70–1; W. Notestein, *The English People on the Eve of Colonization 1603–30* (New York, 1962), 48–9.

46. M. Airs, *Tudor and Jacobean Country House: a Building History* (Stroud, 1995), 3; Kingsley, *Country Houses of Gloucestershire*, i, 2–6.

47. Mingay, *The Gentry*, 4.

48. Stones, *An Open Elite?*, 183, 258–9.

49. Heal and Holmes, *Gentry*, 11; Blackwood, *Lancashire Gentry*, 5, 164; A. Everitt, *The Community of Kent and the Great Rebellion 1640–60* (Leicester, 1966), 33–4; J.T. Cliffe, *The Yorkshire Gentry from the Reformation to the Civil War* (1969), 15–16; English, *Great Landowners*, 21–6; Roebuck, *Yorkshire Baronets*, 22–4.

50. Brunton and Pennington, *Members of the Long Parliament*, 18.

51. Clay, *Chapters from the Agrarian History*, 275.

52. G.E. Mingay, *English Landed Society in the Eighteenth Century* (1963), 26–8, 50; Harvey, *Britain*, 8; R. Porter, *English Society in the Eighteenth Century* (Harmondsworth, 1982), 67; J.C.D. Clark, *English Society 1688–1832* (Cambridge, 1985), 7; D.W. Howell, *Patriarchs and Parasites: the Gentry of South-West Wales in the Eighteenth Century* (Cardiff, 1986), 24; Cannon, *Aristocratic Century*, 33; Stones, *An Open Elite?*, 246.

53. Habakkuk, *MDE*, 606; Langford, *Public Life*, 41; L. Colley, *In Defiance of Oligarchy: the Tory Party 1714–60* (Cambridge, 1982), 8; Beckett, 'Pattern of Landownership', 14; Holdernesse, 'English Land Market', 562.

54. M.W. Barley, 'The Buildings of the Countryside 1500–1750', *Chapters from the Agrarian History of England and Wales 1500–1750*, ed. J. Thirsk (Cambridge, 1990), 91; Stones, *An Open Elite?*, 301–2, 384; Kingsley, *Country Houses of Gloucestershire*, ii, 8; Habakkuk, *MDE*, 535, 619–20.

55. I.R. Christie, *British 'Non-Elite' MPs* (Oxford, 1995), 66–7, 206.

56. J. Franklin, *The Gentleman's Country House and Its Plan 1835–1914* (1981), 1.

57. Families are counted as members of the elite from date of entry into the gentry until date of the last MP.

Chapter 3

1. *DNB*, iii, 567.

2. Cannon, *Aristocratic Century*, 22.

3. L. Rich, *Inherit the Land* (1987), 17; *DNB*, xix, 845; D. Johnston and D. Shawe-Taylor, *The Newcastles of Clumber* (Nottingham, 1992); Hasler, *HP*, iii, 156–7.

4. It should be noted that not all historians accept the distinction between 'genteel' professional careers and other forms of wealth accumulation. Stones, *An Open Elite?*, 225–8; W. Prest, *The Professions in Early Modern England* (1987), 20; Bennet, 'Careerism', 32.

5. *VCH Berkshire* (1924), iv, 472; M. Craven and M. Stanley, *The Derbyshire Country House* (Derby, 1991), 113–15.

6. C. Aslet, 'Stansted Park, Sussex', *CL*, 171 (1982), 346.

7. Coss, *Lordship*.

8. Payling, *Political Society*.

9. Knapp, 'Making of a Landed Elite', 1–25.

10. Johnson, *Gloucestershire Gentry*, 258–60.

11. Coss, *Lordship*, 46, 189; Bindoff, *HP*, iii, 478; Hasler, *HP*, iii, 525; A. Wagner, *English Genealogy* (Oxford, 1960), 46–8.

12. Roskell, *HP*, iii, 277; Hasler, *HP*, iii, 524; Henning, *HP*, ii, 208.

13. R. Fleming, *Kings and Lords in Conquest England* (Oxford, 1991).

14. F.M. Stenton, 'English Families and the Norman Conquest', *TRHS*, 26 (1944), 2–3, 5–6, 10; Bence-Jones, *Catholic Families*, 34; Blackwood, *Lancashire Gentry*, 21.

15. Modern scholarship has also confirmed their genuine descent from Charlemagne: R. McKitterick, 'A Frankish Aristocratic Family of the 10th Century', *The Sudeleys* (1987), 21–33; Johnson, *Gloucestershire Gentry*, 10; Roskell, *HP*, iv, 638.

16. Henning, *HP*, ii, 471, and *CP*, ii, 406; C. Hussey, 'Crowecombe, Court, Somerset', *CL*, 73 (1933), 414; 'Glyndebourne, Sussex', *CL*, 85 (1939), 554–8; A. Oswald, 'Okeover Hall, Staffordshire', *CL*, 134 (1964), 172. See also: Roskell, *HP*, iii, 277; J. Lees-Milne 'Severne End', *CL*, 158 (24 July 1975), 194ff; Wagner, *English Genealogy*, 34–6.

17. Wagner, *English Genealogy*, 54; Roskell, *HP*, iv, 364, and Carpenter, *Locality and Polity*, 149; C. Rawcliffe, *The Staffords, Earls of Stafford and Dukes of Buckingham* (Cambridge, 1978); I.J. Sanders, *English Baronies: a Study of Their Origin and Descent 1086–1327* (Oxford, 1960), 103; English, *Great Landowners*, 11; *CP*, x, 435–7.

18. A sample would include: Acland, Basset, Bedingfield, Chomondeley, Clifford, Compton, Courtenay, Edgcumbe, Fawkes, Fiennes, Gorges, Grey, Grosvenor, Guise, Hanmer, Hastings, Heneage, Hervey, Hoghton, Howard, Lambton, Legh, Leighton, Leycester, Littleton, Lucy, Lumley, Luttrell, Molesworth, Musgrave, Oglander, Poulett, Radcliffe, Rous, Stanhope, Stourton, Talbot, Tremayne, Tuchet, Vachell, Vernon, Vyvyan, Waldegrave, Ward, Wentworth, Wilbraham, Wolryche, Wolseley, Wrottesley and dozens of others.

19. Coward, *The Stanleys*, x.

20. H.M. Thomas, *Vassells, Heiresses, Crusaders and Thugs: the Gentry of Angevin Yorkshire 1154–1216* (Philadelphia, 1993), 59; Davies, *Lordship and Society*, 416.

21. Carpenter, *Locality and Polity*, 135–6 and 73–4; Cliffe, *Yorkshire Gentry*, 18–19; James, *Family*, 40; M. Campbell, *The English Yeomen under Elizabeth and the Early Stuarts* (New York, 1942), 38–63.

22. Henning, *HP*, ii, 668; Cliffe, *Yorkshire Gentry*, 96–7.

23. Sedgwick, *HP*, ii, 539; Bindoff, *HP*, ii, 259; M. Girouard, 'Shadwell Park, Norfolk', *CL*, 136 (1964), 19; Namier and Brooke, *HP*, iii, 640–1; Hasler, *HP*, iii, 625.

24. If the father of the first MP/peer was clearly qualified by wealth and had purchased an estate to establish himself as a member of the landed elite, but for some reason did not enter parliament, his was the social origin ascribed to the family. This system was adopted for the analysis found in Tables 3.1, 3.2 and 3.5 so that I could compare data on parliamentary families with other studies of social mobility such as those made by the Stones and Ian Christie, who allowed for a 'near purchaser' or 'transition' generation in ascribing categories for social origins. In some cases the 25-year limit encompassed a grandparent, uncle or other relative who had established the family's wealth and then passed it on to the first MP. Stones, *An Open Elite?*, 224; and Christie, *BNE*, 22, 27, 29, 34–6. See also A. Gillette, 'The New Aristocrats: a Study of Bourgeois Gentrification in Eighteenth- and Nineteenth-Century England' (PhD thesis, State University of New York, Binghamton, 1992), chapters 6, 7, 8, 10. Thus, even when the money used to acquire a landed estate was made in business or the law, if more than one generation intervened between the 'founder' of the family and the first MP the social category assigned to the family in this study was 'landed' unless subsequent holders of the estate continued to be active in the family firm. This system undercounts the number of elite families who arose from non-landed origins. However, long gaps between achieving landed status and entry into parliament were mostly confined to the medieval and Tudor period. From the seventeenth century onwards, purchase of an estate and entry into parliament tended to follow quickly upon each other.

25. Mingay, *The Gentry*, 48; Stone, *Crisis of the Aristocracy*, 190.

26. See Appendix III, Table 3.1.

27. M. Tomline, *Ham House* (1986), 90–3; *CP*, iv, 562.

28. C.R. Young, *The Making of the Neville Family in England 1166–1400* (Woodbridge, Suffolk, 1996); Turner, *Men Raised from Dust*, 8, 11, and passim; Richmond, 'Bigwigs', 22; Carpenter, *Locality and Polity*, 90; McFarlane, *Nobility*, 284.

29. Roskell, *HP*, iii, 314–15; T.B. Pugh, 'Magnates, Knights, and Gentry', *Fifteenth-century England 1399–1509*, eds S.B. Chrimes et al. (New York, 1972), 92; Hasler, *HP*, iii, 102.

30. Bindoff, *HP*, ii, 187; Hasler, *HP*, iii, 406.

31. M.L. Robertson, 'Profit and Purpose in the Development of Thomas Cromwell's Landed Estates', *JBS*, 29 (1990), 318; Miller, *Henry VIII and the English Nobility*, 22, 34; W.T. MacCaffery, 'England: the Crown

and the New Aristocracy, 1540–1600', *PP*, 30 (1965), 53–5; M. Howard, *The Early Tudor Country House, Architecture and Politics 1490–1550* (1987), 36; Stones, *An Open Elite?*, 257 and Table 6.2.

32. Roskell, *HP*, iv, 258.

33. Cecil, *Cecils of Hatfield*, 57–61; Bindoff, *HP*, i, 602–6.

34. Stone notes, however, that after 1640 office-holders as purchasers of large country houses virtually disappear. Stones, *An Open Elite?*, 198; G.E. Aylmer, *The King's Servants: the Civil Service of Charles I*, rev. edn (1974), 78ff and 325–6; Habakkuk, *MDE*, 414–16.

35. J. Brewer, *The Sinews of Power: War, Money, and the English State, 1688–1783* (Cambridge, MA, 1990), 206; P.J. Jupp, *Lord Grenville, 1759–1834* (Oxford, 1985), v.

36. Brewer, *Sinews of Power*, 254–6.

37. Namier and Brooke, *HP*, i, 107.

38. W. Prest, *The Rise of the Barristers, 1590–1640* (Oxford, 1991), 2–3; G. Holmes, *Politics, Religion and Society in England 1679–1742* (1986), 319–21, 331–2; Prest, *Professions*, 5–8; P. Corfield, *Power and the Professions in Britain 1700–1850* (1995), 20, 24, 27–36, and passim.

39. Henning, *HP*, i, 10; Sedgwick, *HP*, i, 3, 141–5.

40. Stones, *An Open Elite?*, 197; Rubinstein, *Men of Property*, 71.

41. Cannon, *Aristocratic Century*, 22; I. Roy, 'The Profession of Arms', *The Professions in Early-Modern England*, ed. W. Prest (1987), 206; but see: Sedgwick, *HP*, ii, 298; Thorne, *HP*, iv, 220.

42. Horrox, 'Urban Gentry', 30; Wedgwood, *HP*, 781; Bindoff, *HP*, iii, 36–7, 579; Hasler, *HP*, i, 522, 526–7; ii, 481; iii, 33.

43. S. Halliday, 'Social Mobility and Demographic Change in the British Baronetage, 1611–1880', (PhD thesis, University of Sunderland, 1993), 162–3 and 211 n.28; Thorne, *HP*, iii, 775; Staffordshire RO, Hatherton MSS 26/8/69 diary 16 June 1832.

44. Stones, *An Open Elite?*, 229; Habakkuk, *MDE*, 418–19.

45. Roskell, *HP*, i, 168–71; Neale, *Elizabethan House of Commons*, 289–90; Hasler, *HF*, i, 20; Moir, *Addled Parliament*, 57; Henning, *HP*, i, 8; D. Lemmings, *Gentlemen and Barristers: the Inns of Court and the English Bar 1680–1730* (Oxford, 1990), 181–2; M. Ransome, 'Some Recent Studies of the Composition of the House of Commons', *University of Birmingham Historical Journal*, 6 (1958), 140; Sedgwick, *HP*, i, 145; Namier and Brooke, *HP*, i, 126; D. Duman, *The English and Colonial Bars in the Nineteenth Century* (1983), 169; Christie, *BNE*, 206.

46. Bindoff, *HP*, i, 471; Hasler, *HP*, ii, 91.

47. Prest, *Rise of the Barristers*, 118–22, 151–61, 166–78, 180–1, 253–4.

48. Holdernesse, 'English Land Market', 561, 566.

49. Hasler, *HP*, ii, 502; Henning, *HP*, ii, 783; Sedgwick, *HP*, ii, 231; Bindoff, *HP*, ii, 558.

50. Prest, *Rise of the Barristers*, 94–5, and *Professions in Early Modern England*, 9 and 88–91; Lemmings, *Gentlemen and Barristers*, 163; E.W. Ives, *The Common Lawyers of Pre-Reformation England* (Cambridge, 1983), 30–2; Knapp, 'Making of a Landed Elite', 98, 101; Duman, *English and Colonial Bars*, 16, 19; L. Stone, 'Spring Back', *Albion*, 17 (1985), 168 n.2; E. and D. Spring, 'A Rejoinder', *Albion*, 17 (1985), 394–5 n.1; G. Holmes, *TLS* (10 August 1990), 851; Christie, *BNE*, 30; M. Miles '"A Haven for the Privileged": Recruitment into the Profession of Attorney in England, 1709–1792', *SH*, 11 (1986), 197–210, but see Corfield, *Power and the Professions*, 228.

51. A. Simpson, *The Wealth of the Gentry, 1540–1660: East Anglian Studies* (Cambridge, 1961), 28–9, 52; T.G. Barnes, *Somerset 1625–1640: a County's Government During the 'Personal Rule'* (Cambridge, MA, 1961), 20; G. Jackson-Stops, *Wimpole Hall* (1981).

52. A.L. Rowse, *The Early Churchills* (New York, 1956), 2, 6, 315; J. Pearson, *Serpent and the Stag* (New York, 1983), 11; J.M. Robinson, *The Dukes of Norfolk* (Oxford, 1982), 1.

53. Coss, *Lordship*, 309; Elton, *The English*, 60; Denholm-Young, *Country Gentry*, 129–30; Carpenter, *Locality and Polity*, 135–6; Payling, *Political Society*, 31; Moreton, *Townshends*, 192; Ives, *Common Lawyers*, 389; M. Girouard, *Robert Smythson & the Elizabethan Country House* (New Haven, 1983), 5; Hasler, *HP*, i, 20; Heal and Holmes, *Gentry*, 133; Knapp, 'Making of a Landed Elite', 119; Habakkuk, *MDE*, 443.

54. Stones, *An Open Elite?*, Table 6.2.

55. Prest, *Rise of the Barristers*, 7–8.

56. The number of first MPs is artificially low in the 1630s because no parliaments met. Among lawyers achieving gentry status in the 1640s and 1650s and pretty much always thereafter the election of first MP took place at the same time as purchase of an estate.

57. Lemmings, *Gentlemen and Barristers*, 152, 155; Halliday, 'Social Mobility', 160, chart 155, and appendix 23; Stones, *An Open Elite?*, 197; G.M. Ditchfield, 'Lord Thurlow', *Lords of Parliament*, ed. R.W. Davis (Stanford, 1995), 66.

58. Corfield, *Power and the Professions*, 70–94.

59. E. Halévy, *England in 1815* (New York, 1968), 25.

60. Duman, *English and Colonial Bars*, 29, 154–5, 204; Rubinstein, *Men of Property*, 71.

61. M. Girouard, 'Blackmoor House, Hampshire', *CL*, 156 (1974), 554 and 556. The 1st Viscount Esher, a self-made man and senior judge 1868–97, estimated in the 1890s that he would be able to leave £130,000 to his son in addition to landed property. J. Lees-Milne, *The Enigmatic Edwardian* (1986), 77.

62. Holmes, *Making of a Great Power*, 74; Stones, *An Open Elite?*, Table 6.2.

63. Horrox, 'Urban Gentry', 22–5; Turner, *Men Raised from Dust*, 2, 92; Crouch, *Image of Aristocracy*, 25–6; S.L. Thrupp, *The Merchant Class of Medieval London* (Chicago, 1948), 120ff; M. Sayer, *English Nobility: the Gentry, the Heralds and the Continental Context* (Norwich, 1979), 10ff; Roskell, *HP*, i, 73–4; Bennett, 'Careerism', 21; Pugh, 'Magnates', 87; McFarlane, *Nobility*, 14.

64. Roskell, *HP*, i, 155–9, 161–5, 168–71, and *The Commons in the Parliament of 1422* (Manchester, 1954), 125; S.H. Rigby, *English Society in the Late Middle Ages: Class, Status and Gender* (1995), 194; Hasler, *HP*, i, 20; Moir, *Addled Parliament*, 57; Keeler, *Long Parliament*, 21; Henning, *HP*, i, 10; R. Grassby, *The Business Community of Seventeenth-Century England* (Cambridge, 1995), 42; Sedgwick, *HP*, i, 3, 141–53; Christie, *BNE*, 206.

65. Ives, *Common Lawyers*, 327–8; R. Grassby, 'Personal Wealth of the Business Community in Seventeenth-Century England', *EcHR*, 23 (1970), 227–8.

66. Hasler, *HP*, ii, 334.

67. The most important aldermanic studies include: R.G. Lang, 'Social Origins and Social Aspirations of Jacobean London Merchants', *EcHR*, 27 (1974), 28–9, 40, 45; N. Rogers, 'Money, Land, and Lineage: the Big Bourgeoisie of Hanoverian London', *SH*, 3/4 (1979), 438, 444–52; P. Earle, *The Making of the English Middle Class: Business, Society and Family Life in London, 1660–1730* (Berkeley, 1989), 152–7; Stones, *An Open Elite?*, 222, but see H. Horwitz, '"The Mess of the Middle Class" Revisited in the Case of the "Big Bourgeoisie" of Augustan London', *Continuity and Change*, 2 (1986), 264–84; R. Grassby, 'English Merchant Capitalism in the Late Seventeenth Century: the Composition of Fortunes', *PP*, 46 (1970), 92–3; D.T. Andrew, 'Aldermen and Big Bourgeoisie of London Reconsidered', *SH*, 5 (1980), 359–67; Habakkuk, *MDE*, 557–9, 571–3, 615–16; Wilson, *Gentlemen Merchants*, 19–20, 228, 230; Clay, 'Henry Hoare', 113. Lang, Rogers and others, discussing the London and provincial business communities, have all pointed to relatively low levels of mobility between business and the landed elite. C.W. Brooks, 'Review', *EHR*, 101 (1986), 178. But this is only if one is looking at the percentage of all businessmen.

68. D. Hancock, *Citizens of the World: London Merchants and the Integration of the British Atlantic Community, 1735–1785* (Cambridge, 1995), 273, n.71, 274; Habakkuk, *MDE*, 615–16.

69. History of Parliament, unpublished volumes 1690–1715, ed. D. Hayton, John Bromley MP 1705–7.

70. Namier and Brooke, *HP*, ii, 78; iii, 161.

71. Stones, *An Open Elite?*, 205; Beckett, *Aristocracy*, 91 n.1; D.W. Gutzke, 'The Social Status of Landed Brewers in Britain since 1840', *Histoire Sociale – Social History*, 17 (1984), 93–113.

72. Bindoff, *HP*, iii, 197, 328.

73. Eight banking families post-1830 compared to three in brewing. See for comparison Rubinstein, *Men of Property*, 86ff, and M. Lisle-Williams, 'Merchant Banking Dynasties in the English Class Structure: Ownership, Solidarity and Kinship in the City of London, 1850–1960', *British Journal of Sociology*, 35 (1984), 340–6.

74. Knapp, 'Making of a Landed Elite', 303.

75. N. Gash, *Politics in the Age of Peel* (New York, 1971 edn), 196–9; A. Howe, *The Cotton Masters 1830–1860* (Oxford, 1984), 91–5.

76. J.T. Cliffe, *The Puritan Gentry Besieged, 1650–1700* (1993), 74; Namier and Brooke, *HP*, iii, 493; *CP*, viii, 708.

77. Rubinstein, *Men of Property*, 61–8, 'The Structure of Wealth-holding in Britain, 1809–39: a Preliminary Anatomy', *HR*, 65 (1992), 76, 85, 88–9, 'Debate: "Gentlemanly Capitalism" and British Industry 1820–1914', *PP*, 132 (1991), 150–70, and *Capitalism, Culture, and Decline in Britain 1750–1990* (1994), 24, 145–7; M.J. Wiener, *English Culture and the Decline of the Industrial Spirit 1850–1980* (Cambridge, 1982), 128–9; Stone, 'Spring Back', 173; G. Ingham, *Capitalism Divided? The City and Industry in British Social Development* (New York, 1984), 15–39; Cassis, *City Bankers*, 3–4; M.J. Daunton, '"Gentlemanly Capitalism" and British Industry 1820–1914', *PP*, 122 (1989), 119–58; Clark, *English Society*, 4–7.

78. For problems with Rubinstein's data see: R. Pahl, 'New Rich, Old Rich, Stinking Rich?', *SH*, 15 (1990), 232; Springs, 'Social Mobility', 339–42; E. Spring, 'Businessmen and Landowners Re-engaged', *HR*, 72 (1999), 77–88; H. Perkin, *The Rise of Professional Society in England since 1880* (1989), 71–3, 257–8; Howe, *Cotton Masters*, 91–5. M.J. Daunton, 'Reply', *PP*, 122 (1989), 170–87; G. Ingham, 'British Capitalism: Empire, Merchants and Decline', *SH*, 20 (1995), 349–50.

79. Rubinstein, 'Debate: "Gentlemanly Capitalism"', 153.

80. Cannon, *Aristocratic Century*, 114.

81. Christie, *BNE*, 206 and passim.

82. Stones, *An Open Elite?*, 147, 217–18, 222, 403; Springs, 'English Landed Elite', 153–4.

83. Stones, *An Open Elite?*, 218, 221, 280, 402–5, 423.

84. J. Berlatsky, 'Lawrence Stone', *Recent Historians of Great Britain*, ed. W.L. Arnstein (Ames, Iowa, 1990), 95; A. Briggs, 'History as Communication', *Encounter*, 64 (1985), 53; D. Cannadine, 'No Entrance', *New York Review of Books* (20 December 1984), 85; H. Perkin, 'An Open Elite', *JBS*, 24 (1985), 496–501; A.W. Purdue, 'An Open Elite?', *NH*, 22 (1986), 311–13; Springs, 'English Landed Elite', 151, and 'Social Mobility', 333–51; F.M.L. Thompson, *TLS* (7 September 1984), 990. For examples of the widening influence of the Stone thesis, see: P. Anderson, 'Figures of Descent', *New Left Review*, 161 (1987), 28, 33; D. Kynaston, *The City of London* (1994), i, 381; H.T. Dickinson, *The Politics of the People in Eighteenth-Century Britain* (1995), 4; S.J. Connolly, *Religion, Law, and Power: the Making of Protestant Ireland, 1660–1710* (Oxford, 1992), 64.

85. Stones, *An Open Elite?*, 194.

86. Springs, 'English Landed Elite', 152, 154–5; Perkin, 'An Open Elite', 499; English, *Great Landowners*, 55.

87. Stones, *An Open Elite?*, 257–8.

88. Stones, *An Open Elite?*, 163, 222; Springs, 'English Landed Elite', 153–4.

89. See footnote 24.

90. Stones, *An Open Elite?*, 208–10, 224, 276 table 7.3; Purdue, 'An Open Elite?', 311; F.M.L. Thompson, *TLS* (7 September 1984), 990.

91. Indeed, the Springs point out that Stone's own tables 5.4 and 6.2 show that lawyers, office-holders and businessmen 'sold out' at about the same rate and most sold because they had no heir. ('Social Mobility', 347, and 'English Landed Elite', 151–2, 154–6; Perkin, 'An Open Elite', 498–500.) See also Cannadine, 'No Entrance', 66.

92. English found a rate of 20% every fifty years and 40% per century in 1530–1910 among the top landowners of the East Riding (*Great Landowners*, 55). For my data on rates of turnover, see Chapter 2. For perceptions of a more open elite than Stone will allow, see: Cliffe, *Yorkshire Gentry*, 94–5; Purdue, 'An Open Elite?', 312–13; Halliday, 'Social Mobility', 168, 176, 269; Knapp, 'Making of a Landed Elite', 254, 303.

93. The smaller size of many Northumberland country houses seems to account for the particularly serious problems with the Stone sample in that county. Purdue, 'An Open Elite?', 312–13; F.M.L. Thompson, *TLS* (7 September 1984), 990. Stones, *An Open Elite?*, 8, 10–11, 63, 437–42, and L. Stone and J.F.C. Stone, 'Country Houses and Their Owners in Hertfordshire 1540–1879', *Dimensions of Quantitative Research in History*, eds W.O. Aydelotte, A.C. Bogue and R.W. Fogel (Princeton, 1972), 69–75.

94. C. Platt, *The Great Rebuilding of Tudor and Stuart England* (1994), 29–132; Airs, *Tudor and Jacobean Country House*, 3–22, 31, 66, 74, 95–8; Girouard, *Robert Smythson*, 4–6; Kingsley, *Gloucestershire Country Houses*, i, 4–7; Dewald, *European Nobility*, 91.

95. T. Murdock, ed., *Boughton House* (1992), 186–7.

96. For English's doubts about the Stone method of measuring wealth, see *Great Landowners*, 26, 36–7, 53, 242 n.69. Eileen Spring also pointed out the Stones' errors in using Bateman: *Law, Land, and Family: Aristocratic Inheritance in England 1300 to 1800* (Chapel Hill, 1993), 14.

97. Stone, 'Spring Back', 170, and *OE*, 224–5; Payling, *Political Society*, 105; MacCulloch, *Suffolk*, 9.

98. L. Weaver, 'Moor Park, Hertfordshire', *CL*, 31 (6 January 1912), 18.

99. Everitt, 'Social Mobility', 60; Beckett, 'Pattern of Landownership', 135.

100. Stones, *An Open Elite?*, 256, 276; Springs, 'English Landed Elite', 154 n.5.

101. W.D. Rubinstein, 'Businessmen into Landowners: the Question Revisited', *Landed Society in Britain 1700–1914*, eds N. Harte and R. Quinalt (Manchester, 1996), 92–3; Briggs, 'History as Communication', 53; Springs, 'English Landed Elite', 150.

102. Stone himself argues that commercial values permeated the elite beginning in the fourteenth century and overrode antagonism between landed and moneyed interests promoting stability, but both he and Wiener see the capitalism of the aristocracy as 'rentier' and not entrepreneurial. Stones, *An Open Elite?*, 28–9, 284; Wiener, *English Culture*, 8.

103. Horrox, 'Urban Gentry', 25, 27; Colley, *Britons*, 56; Langford, *Public Life*, 310, 313; Wilson, *Gentleman Merchants*, 220; Jenkins, *Making of a Ruling Class*, xviii; Earle, *Making of the English Middle Class*, 7, and 86; G.R. Searle, *Entrepreneurial Politics in Mid-Victorian Britain* (Oxford, 1993), 15–16; Dickinson, *Politics of the People*, 7–8; R.J. Morris, *Class, Sect, and Party: the Making of the British Middle Class, Leeds 1820–1850* (Manchester, 1990), 329; K. Wilson, *The Sense of the People in Politics, Culture and Imperialism in England 1715–1785* (Cambridge, 1995), passim; N.E. Koehn, *The Power of Commerce: Economy and Commerce in the First British Empire* (Ithaca, 1994), passim.

104. Elton, *Studies*, ii, 42, and 'Parliament', 18–19; Clarke, *State and Status*, 297.

105. On the importance of this concept see: R.H. Trainor, *Black Country Elites: the Exercise of Authority in an Industrialized Area 1830–1900* (Oxford, 1993), 79–80; K. Wrightson, *English Society 1580–1680* (1982), 22; Briggs 'History as Communication', 53–4; K. Wood and F. Wood, eds, *A Lancashire Gentleman* (Stroud, 1992), 32; Morris, *Class, Sect and Party*, 36.

106. *CP*, xii, 159–60; Ditchfield, 'Thurlow', 65–6.

107. Hasler, *HP*, iii, 278.

108. Duke of Argyll, *Autobiography and Memoirs* (2 vols, 1906), i, 279; Namier, *England in the Age of the American Revolution*, 6.

Chapter 4

1. R.R. Davies, *The Age of Conquest, Wales 1063–1415* (Oxford, 1987), 14, 57–8, 70–1, 117, 120, 125–6, 155, 224, 228; J.G. Jones, *Concepts of Order and Gentility in Wales 1540–1640* (Llandysul, 1992), 124–5.

2. Jones, *Early Modern Wales*, 3, 177; P. Williams, 'Tudor Gentry', *Wales through the Ages*, ed. A.J. Roderick (Llandybie, 1960), 33.

3. £21,121 contrasted to £5,930.

4. B.E. Howells, 'Society in Early Modern Wales', *The Satellite State in the 17th and 18th Centuries*, eds S. Dyrvik, K. Mykland and J. Oldervoll (Oslo, 1979), 85; R. Grant, *The Parliamentary History of Glamorgan 1542–1976* (Swansea, 1978), 28; G. Jones, *The Gentry and the Elizabethan State* (Swansea, 1977), 42–3; Jones, *Concepts of Order*, 177–8.

5. Sedgwick, *HP*, i, 20; G.H. Jenkins, *The Foundations of Modern Wales 1642–1780* (Oxford, 1993), 156.

6. G. Morgan, *A Welsh House and Its Family: the Vaughans of Trawsgoed* (Llandysul, 1997), 122; Thorne, *HP*, i, 4, 42, 63–4; Jenkins, *Foundations of Modern Wales*, 156–7, 160, 302, 305; Howell, *Patriarchs*, 133; Namier and Brooke, *HP*, i, 36, 38; Jenkins, *Making of a Ruling Class*, 183; W.R. Williams, *The Parliamentary History of the Principality of Wales 1541–1895* (Brecknock, 1895), iv.

7. See Appendix III, Table 3.3.

8. 96% in the 1690s, 93% in 1705 and 1810–30.

9. The later group, all magnates, formed 9% of all Welsh elite families.

10. P.D.G. Thomas, 'Eighteenth Century Politics', *Wales through the Ages*, ed. A.J. Roderick (Llandybie, 1960), 95; Jenkins, *Making of the Ruling Class*, xv–xvi, 16.

11. 'Glynde, Sussex', *CL*, 22 (1907), 348; Davies, *Age of Conquest*, 78; R. Haslam, 'Rug, Clwyd', *CL*, 174 (1983), 989; *DWB*, 570–1; Crouch, *Image of Aristocracy*, 10; Jenkins, *Foundations of Modern Wales*, 240–1; T. Nicholas, *Annals and Antiquities of the Counties and County Families of Wales* (2 vols, Baltimore, 1991 [1872]), i, 355–6.

12. On ancient descents see: P. Jenkins, *History of Modern Wales 1536–1990* (1992), 40; Wagner, *English Genealogy*, 14–15, 27–9; A. Powell, 'A Principality and Its Pedigrees', *TLS* (31 January 1992).

13. Thorne, *HP*, v, 596; Colley, *Britons*, 163; Bindoff, *HP*, iii, 63; Jenkins, *Making of a Ruling Class*, 28, 202–4, and *History of Modern Wales*, 6, 52, 65; Jenkins, *Foundations of Modern Wales*, 307–8.

14. Owning 60.7% of the land as opposed to 56.1% in England and 92.8% in Scotland. Cannadine, *DFBA*, 9.

15. Only 3.4% of land in the later nineteenth century was owned by peers compared to 41.2% in Scotland and 33.5 in England. Bindoff, *HP*, ii, 525; for incomes see: D.W. Howell, 'Landlords and Estate Management in Wales 1640–1750', 379, and T.J. Pierce, 'The Nobility and Gentry', 135–6, *Chapters*

from the Agrarian History of England and Wales 1500–1750, ed. C. Clay (Cambridge, 1990); G.D. Phillips, *The Diehards: Aristocratic Society and Politics in Edwardian England* (Cambridge, MA, 1979), 29.

16. P.R. Roberts, 'The Decline of the Welsh Squires in the Eighteenth Century', *National Library of Wales Journal*, 13 (1963–64), 157; Jenkins, *Foundations of Modern Wales*, 92–4, 261, 267–8; Thomas, 'Eighteenth Century Politics', 95.

17. Note Cragoe, *An Anglican Aristocracy*, 106.

18. Of course, non-Welsh families who inherited great estates in the principality functioned as magnates in the counties where they owned land, but they are listed under the heading of their native countries.

19. See Appendix III, Table 3.11.

20. Philip Jenkins, who counted families continued by an heiress as 'new', uncovered 'a violent caesura' in the history of the Glamorgan ruling class during the first half of the eighteenth century in which the old families were replaced by a 'new elite'. His distinction between new and old is anachronistic. P. Jenkins, 'Glamorgan Politics 1789–1868', *Glamorgan County History*, ed. P. Morgan (Cardiff, 1988), vi, 4, 198, 'Demographic Decline of the Gentry in the Eighteenth Century', *WHR*, 11 (1982), 31–49, and *Making of a Ruling Class*, xxi, 48; Howell, *Patriarchs*, 24.

21. Davies, *Age of Conquest*, 115; Howell, *Patriarchs*, 10, 'Landlords', 419–20, and 'Society in Early Modern Wales', 85, 88; Jenkins, *History of Modern Wales*, 49, 280–1, and *Making of a Ruling Class*, 35–6, 57, 277, 279.

22. Bindoff, *HP*, i, 539; Hasler, *HP*, iii, 43.

23. Three each in the sixteenth and seventeenth centuries, and one in the eighteenth. Not counting the Powys Barons Lilford and the Hanmers who deserted their native land for permanent residence in England.

24. For example, Henning, *HP*, iii, 547; *CB*, ii, 159.

25. Thorne, *HP*, iii, 675.

26. Nicholas, *Annals*, i, 94; Hasler, *HP*, iii, 622.

27. *DWB*, 570–1; Davies, *Age of Conquest*, 429; Jenkins, *History of Modern Wales*, 49; Sedgwick, *HP*, ii, 105; Whiteley, *SC*, 358; F. Jones, *Historic Houses of Pembrokeshire and Their Families* (Newport, 1996), 190–1.

28. Roberts, 'Decline of the Welsh Squires', 157; A.H. Dodd, 'The Landed Gentry after 1660', *Wales through the Ages*, ed. A.J. Roderick (Llandybie, 1960), 84.

29. Thorne, *HP*, iv, 440; Morgan, *A Welsh House*, 109, 147; H.M. Vaughan, *The South Wales Squires* (1926), 200; N. Canny, 'Irish, Scottish and Welsh Responses to Centralisation *c.* 1530–*c.* 1640', *Uniting the Kingdom? the Making of British History*, eds A. Grant and K.J. Stringer (1995), 161–2; C. Brady, 'Comparable Histories? Tudor Reform in Wales and Ireland', *Conquest and Union: Fashioning a British State, 1485–1725*, eds S.G. Ellis and S. Barber (1995), 66; Jenkins, *Foundations of Modern Wales*, 219; Jenkins, *Making of a Ruling Class*, 194, 205–6, 213; Howell, 'Landlords', 386.

30. Cragoe, *Anglican Aristocracy*, 3, 70, 103–10, 254. Not all members of the landed elite were hostile to Methodism. Jones, *Historic Houses of Pembrokeshire*, 124.

31. Colley, *Britons*, 347; D. Beales, 'The Electorate before and after 1832: the Right to Vote and the Opportunity', *PH*, 11 (1992), 147.

32. K.O. Morgan, *Wales in British Politics 1868–1922* (Cardiff, 1980), 347; Beales, 'The Electorate', 149; Jenkins, *History of Modern Wales*, 286–7, 325–9; H.J. Hanham, *Elections and Party Management: Politics in the Time of Disraeli and Gladstone*, 2nd edn (Hassocks, 1978), 14; Malchow, *Gentlemen Capitalists*, 35–7; T. Lloyd, *The General Election of 1880* (Oxford, 1968), 120.

33. Malchow, *Gentlemen Capitalists*, 41; Morgan, *Wales in British Politics*, 21–2; Cragoe, *Anglican Aristocracy*, 144–9.

34. Whiteley, *SC*, 335–6, 344, 355.

35. J. Davies, 'The End of Great Estates and the Rise of Freehold Farming in Wales', *WHR*, 7 (1974), 186, 188–92, 210; Cannadine, *Aspects of Aristocracy*, 53.

36. See also Vaughan, *South Wales Squires*, 58.

37. A.D. Rees, *Life in the Welsh Countryside* (Cardiff, 1951), 158–9.

38. A. Grant, 'The Development of the Scottish Peerage', *SHR*, 57 (1978), 1–13, 20; *CP*, xii/i, 92 n.c. Large parts of Scotland remained outside the control of or were only marginally associated with the Crown, and thus important leaders from the north and west long remained aloof from the institution of parliament.

39. J.R. Young, *The Scottish Parliament 1639–1661* (Edinburgh, 1996), 1, 46, 304, 324–6; J. Goodare, 'The Estates in the Scottish Parliament 1286–1707', *The Scots and Parliament*, ed. C. Jones (Edinburgh, 1996), 32, 58–72; A.V. Dicey and R.S. Rait, *Thoughts on the Union between England and Scotland* (Westport, 1971 [1920]), 62.

40. B.P. Levack, *The Formation of the British State: England, Scotland and the Union 1603–1707* (Oxford, 1987), 45; P.W.J. Riley, 'The Structure of Scottish Politics and the Union of 1707', *The Union of 1707: Its Impact on Scotland*, ed. T.I. Rae (Glasgow, 1974), 1–30; M. Lee, 'The Anglo-Scottish Union of 1707: the Debate Reopened', *BSM*, 9 (1979), 23–34; M. Goldie, 'Divergence and Union: Scotland and England 1660–1707', *The British Problem* c. *1534–1707: State Formation in the Atlantic Archipelago*, eds B. Bradshaw and J. Morrill (1996), 220–45; D. Hayton, 'Constitutional Experiments and Political Expediency 1689–1725', *Conquest and Union: Fashioning a British State, 1485–1725*, eds S.G. Ellis and S. Barber (1995), 277.

41. M. Brown, 'Scottish Identity in the Seventeenth Century', *British Consciousness and Identity, the Making of Britain, 1533–1707*, eds B. Bradshaw and P. Roberts (Cambridge, 1998), 239–40; Colley, *Britons*, 51; A.I. Macinnes and F.J. Watson, 'Biographical Data and Its Presentation: Scottish Parliamentary Commissioners 1375–1707', *Storia & Multimedia*, eds F. Bocchi and P. Denley (Bologna, 1994), 711; C.S. Terry, *The Scottish Parliament: Its Constitution and Procedure 1603–1707* (Glasgow, 1905), 94–102; E. Richards and M. Clough, *Cromartie: Highland Life 1650–1914* (Aberdeen, 1989), 27; I.D. Whyte, *Scotland before the Industrial Revolution: an Economic and Social History* c. *1050* – c. *1750* (1995), 158; A. Wightman, *Who Owns Scotland* (Edinburgh, 1996), 9.

42. Including a handful of Scots and Englishmen who sat for English constituencies such as the Earls of Ancrum and Kincardine and Lord Fairfax.

43. In 1600 eight commissioners had noble connections. This rose to twenty-three in 1661.

44. In the next two decades the sons of Lords Cardross, Cochrane, Duffus, the Viscount of Arbuthnot, and the Earls of Argyll, Findlater, Hyndford, Melville, Morton and Seafield all entered parliament sitting for towns. Sir James Ogilvie, a younger son of the 3rd Earl of Findlater, sat for Cullen 1689–95 and was created a viscount in his own right in 1698. His son succeeded as the 5th Earl. Sir Alexander Home (Kirkwall 1698–1702) succeeded his father as 2nd Earl of Marchmont. In 1701, thirty-four commissioners from shires and burghs had noble connections, and in 1707 fifty-three. Scottish Parliamentary Commissioners – mss. Database, eds A.I. Macinnes and F.J. Watson (IHR); J.S. Shaw, *The Management of Scottish Society 1707–1764: Power, Nobles, Lawyers, Edinburgh Agents, and English Influences* (Edinburgh, 1983), 3.

45. Young, *Scottish Parliament*, 327; Porritt, *UHC*, ii, 26, 39, 67.

46. See Appendix III, Table 3.4.

47. Henning, *HP*, i, 16–17. Nineteen Scottish lords, some Englishmen, sat as English MPs from 1620 to 1707, *CP*, v, 239 n.d.

48. A.S. Turberville, 'The Scottish and Irish Representative Peers 1783–1837', *Proceedings of the Leeds Philosophical and Literary Society*, 6 (1944), 22; Shaw, *Management of Scottish Society*, 4.

49. Whyte, *Scotland*, 107, 157–8.
50. Porritt, *UHC*, ii, 35–6, 47; Young, *Scottish Parliament*, 5, 197, 304, 332–7; Terry, *Scottish Parliament*, 2, 21, 49, 125–33; M. Lynch, *Scotland, a New History* (1992), 217; P.W.J. Riley, *King William and the Scottish Politicians* (Edinburgh, 1979), 43 n.8. It is very difficult to get accurate totals of the number of commissioners. Constituencies sometimes did not send their full complement. Calculations about numbers of members of the Scottish parliament can differ substantially. (See J.R. Young, 'Seventeenth-Century Scottish Parliamentary Rolls and Political Factionalism', *PH*, 16 [1997], 152–70.) I count 118 in 1661, but Young gives 120 as the figure. Bruce Lenman says there were 159 elective seats in 1706, but I count 151; Lenman, *Integration, Enlightenment, and Industrialization: Scotland 1746–1832* (1981), 15. I am grateful to Professor Lenman for clarifying points related to his count in correspondence with me. Neither of us has been able to resolve the problem, which is further evidence of the difficulty of getting the numbers right.
51. Riley, *King William*, 32.
52. M. Dyer, 'Burgh Districts and the Representation of Scotland 1707–1983', *PH*, 15 (1996), 288–9, 291. Sixty-five burghs were squashed into fourteen 'district' seats. Porritt, *UHC*, ii, 34; Thorne, *HP*, i, 77–8.
53. Even if one counts only MPs from families with at least two previous representatives in parliament, 45% of commissioners 1661–1707 and 77% of MPs 1707–1832 qualified as members of the elite.
54. There is no standard spelling for this title. (See *CP*, v, appendix H.) Perhaps due to the 'auld alliance,' marquis is more commonly found in Scotland and less so in England. Since the Scottish nobility was distinctive in a number of ways, I have chosen to use this variant for families north of the Tweed, and the more English style of marquess for all other such families. See J. Fergusson, *Sixteen Peers of Scotland* (Oxford, 1960), 25–6.
55. Sedgwick, *HP*, i, 20; Thorne, *HP*, i, 70–1; Namier and Brooke, *HP*, i, 38–40; Lynch, *Scotland*, 386; D. Hayton, 'Traces of Party Politics in Early Eighteenth-Century Scottish Elections', *The Scots and Parliament*, ed. C. Jones (Edinburgh, 1996), 83.
56. Thorne, *HP*, i, 76–8; M. Fry, *Patronage and Principle: a Political History of Modern Scotland* (Aberdeen, 1987), 8; Porritt, *UHC*, ii, 3.
57. A. Murdock, 'The People Above', *Politics and Administration in Mid-Eighteenth-Century Scotland* (Edinburgh, 1980), 28–103; M. Fry, *The Dundas Despotism* (Edinburgh, 1992) and *Patronage and Principle*, 7; J.M. Simpson, 'Who Steered the Gravy Train, 1707–1766?', *Scotland in the Age of Improvement* (Edinburgh, 1970), 54.
58. R.M. Sunter, *Patronage and Politics in Scotland, 1707–1832* (Edinburgh, 1986), 5, 233–4; Namier and Brooke, *HP*, i, 42–4; Thorne, *HP*, i, 42–78; D.J. Brown, '"Nothing but Strugalls and Coruption", the Commons' Elections for Scotland in 1774', *The Scots and Parliament*, ed. C. Jones (Edinburgh, 1996), 105, 119; Hayton, 'Traces of Party Politics', 79; W. Ferguson, 'Introduction', *The Scots and Parliament*, ed. C. Jones (Edinburgh, 1996), 8–9.
59. Sixty or so Scots sat for non-Scottish constituencies between 1760 and 1790, and 130 sat between 1790 and 1820. Colley, *Britons*, 49; Clark, *State and Status*, 102.
60. A few of these noblemen were not Scottish by origin or residence. Some were from English families raised to a Scottish peerage by the Stuarts, others were foreigners elevated by William III; the Abercorns lived in Ireland. J.M. Robinson, 'Pride in Genealogy', *CL*, 181 (1987), 82.
61. Harvey, *Britain*, 6; A. Bruce, 'Lairds and Blood Feuds – the Scottish Nobility to the Act of Union: 1707', *The House of Lords*, ed. R. Smith (1996), 87–8; G. Hamilton-Edwards, *In Search of Scottish Ancestry*, 2nd edn (Baltimore, 1984), 4.
62. Shaw, *Management of Scottish Society*, 5–6, 8, 12–13.

63. F.M.L. Thompson, 'Britain', *European Landed Elites in the Nineteenth Century*, ed. D. Spring (Baltimore, 1977), 43; Cannadine, *DFBA*, 9; Whyte, *Scotland*, 155; R.F. Callender, *The Pattern of Landownership in Scotland* (Finzean, 1987), 9–10, 60, 130; L.R. Timperley, 'The Pattern of Landholding in Eighteenth-Century Scotland', *The Making of the Scottish Countryside*, eds M.L. Parry and T.R. Slater (1980), 150.

64. If one removes from the count seventeen large landowners who, due to their Jacobite pasts or other reasons, did not elect at least three MPs, the average income of the non-parliamentary families in Scotland was only £5,254 compared to £17,043 for governing dynasties, a ratio similar to that prevailing in Wales.

65. 249 of these families had three or more MPs, four more elite families had no MPs but at least three peers, and the rest were families with fewer than three MPs but were closely associated with the parliamentary elite.

66. The elective peers serving 3,300 years or an average of 15.6 years per peer, which compares to 22.4 years per peer for GB and UK peerages held by Scots post-1781 or 22.0 years for English families with E, GB or UK peerages, so Scottish representative peers had shorter careers in the Lords. E.A. Smith, *House of Lords*, 73–4. A few English families did gain election as representative peers, such as the Lords Falkland and Irvine.

67. A. Grant, 'Crown and Nobility in Late Medieval Britain', *Scotland and England 1286–1815*, ed. R.A. Mason (Edinburgh, 1987), 47; Callender, *Pattern of Landownership*, 28, 39–41.

68. *CP*, viii, 104–6, 398–433, 827–54, and Fergusson, *Sixteen Peers*, 53–60.

69. R.A. Dodgshan, '"Pretense of Blude" and "Place of Their Duelling": the Nature of Scottish Clans, 1500–1745', *Scottish Society 1500–1800*, eds R.A. Houston and I.D. Whyte (Cambridge, 1989), 170–5; P. Gaskell, *Morvern Transformed, a Highland Parish in the Nineteenth Century* (Cambridge, 1968), 1, 159; T.M. Devine, *Clanship to Crofter's War: the Social Transformation of the Scottish Highlands* (Manchester, 1994), 10; E. Cregeen, 'Tradition and Change in the West Highlands of Scotland', *The Satellite State in the 17th and 18th Centuries*, eds S. Dyrvik, K. Mykland and J. Oldervoll (Oslo, 1979), 101–2; Richards and Clough, *Cromartie*, 96–101; K.M. Brown, 'The Nobility of Jacobean Scotland 1567–1625', *Scotland Revisited*, ed. J. Wormald (1991), 63, 71; L. Weaver, 'Ardkinglass, Argyllshire', *CL*, 29 (1911), 750–1. For other examples of clan chiefs helping in elections see: J. Stevenson, *Two Centuries of Life in Down 1600–1800* (Belfast, 1920), 30–1; M.D. Young, *Parliaments of Scotland: Burgh and Shire Commissioners* (2 vols, Edinburgh, 1992–93), ii, 527; History of Parliament, unpublished volumes 1690–1715, ed. D. Hayton, George Mackenzie MP 1710–13.

70. Namier and Brooke, *HP*, i, 172; Devine, *Clanship*, 6, 11; Cregeen, 'Tradition and Change', 108–15; Richards and Clough, *Cromartie*, 11–12, but see 98 for vestigial remains; A.I. Macinnes, 'Landownership, Land Use, and Elite Enterprise in Scottish Gaeldom: from Clanship to Clearance in Argyllshire, 1688–1858', *Scottish Elites*, ed. T.M. Devine (Edinburgh, 1994), 11–12.

71. The Airlie earldom was suppressed in 1717–1826 for Jacobite activity, but they were active in the Lords with four representative peers in the nineteenth and twentieth centuries.

72. For example, the Lords Blantyre, Saltoun and Somerville.

73. The 19th Chief did serve in the Scottish parliament in 1669 and 1686.

74. A.M. Mackintosh, *The Mackintoshes and Clan Chattan* (Edinburgh, 1903); Thorne, *HP*, iv, 489–90; J.L. Campbell, *Canna, the Story of a Hebridean Island* (Edinburgh, 1994), 149–50, 203ff.

75. Such as the Earls of Lauderdale, Leven and Melville, and Rothes.

76. Only a few aristocratic estates in all of Europe matched the Duke of Sutherland's 1,300,000 acres or the Duke of Argyll's 500 square mile dominion.

77. This number falls to only twenty-nine if one counts cadets as part of single clans. The Leveson-Gowers (Dukes of Sutherland) are counted as English. The Scottish grandees were: Abercromby, Bruce (Elgin), Campbell (Argyll), Campbell (Cawdor), Campbell (Breadalbane), Carnegie, Dalrymple, Douglas-Steuart (Dukes), Douglas (Morton), Douglas (Queensberry), Drummond, Erskine (Mar), Gordon (Dukes), Gordon (Aberdeen), Graham (Dukes), Grant (Seafield), Hamilton (Dukes), Hamilton-Baillie, Hay (Tweeddale), Hay (Kinnoull), Home, Hope, Innes-Kerr, Kieth-Falconer, Kennedy (Ailsa), Kerr (Lothian), Lindsay-Crawford, Bowes-Lyon, Maitland, Montagu-Douglas-Scott, Montgomerie (Eglinton), Murray (Dukes), Murray (Mansfield), Munro-Ferguson, Primrose, Ramsay-Maule, Stewart (Galloway), Stuart (Moray), Crichton-Stuart, Wemyss-Charteris.

78. Anstruther, Boyle (Glasgow), Dundas (Melville), Elliot, Fraser (Lovat), Johnston (Annandale), Murray (Elibank), Ogilvy (Airlie), Stirling-Maxwell. The Scots were discriminated against in the distribution of cabinet office in the eighteenth century and the system of lord lieutenants was established much later than in England.

79. Whyte, *Scotland*, 78, for the medieval estimate.

80. R.A. Dodgshan, *Land and Society in Early Scotland* (Oxford, 1981), 94; Wormald, 'Lords and Lairds in Fifteenth-century Scotland: Nobles and Gentry?', *Gentry and Lesser Nobility in Late Medieval Europe* (New York, 1986), 191; Lenman, *Integration*, 9; Lynch, *Scotland*, 247, 261; Whyte, *Scotland*, 78, 89, 156–7; T.R. Slater, 'Mansion and Policy', *The Making of the Scottish Countryside*, ed. M.L. Parry and T.R. Slater (1980), 225–6; Wightman, *Who Owns Scotland*, 9–10.

81. They were exceeded by the Welsh in the decades immediately after 1800 and in the later nineteenth century, sometimes running twice as high as among the English.

82. See Appendix III, Table 3.11.

83. A. Morrow, *Picnic in a Foreign Land* (1990), 56; L. Weaver, 'Castle Stewart and Craigston Castle', *CL*, 37 (1915), 115; P.L. Pielou, *The Leslies of Tarbert* (Dublin, 1935), 1–2; *Burke's Visitations of Seats*, 2nd ser. (1854) i, 166; C. Hussey, 'Logan House, Wigtownshire', *CL*, 116 (1954), 426; A.H. Millar, *The Historical Castles and Mansions of Scotland* (1892), 319; M. Bence-Jones and H. Montgomery-Massingberd, *The British Aristocracy* (1979), 144–5; R. Douglas, *The Baronage of Scotland* (Edinburgh, 1798), 332; D.P. Menzies, *The 'Red and White': Book of Menzies* (Glasgow, 1894), xv–xviii.

84. Thorne, *HP*, iii, 572; D. Sellar, 'Highland Family Origins – Pedigree Making and Pedigree Faking', *The Middle Ages in the Highlands*, ed. L. MacLean (Inverness, 1981), 103–16; Devine, *Clanship*, 7; K.J. Stringer, *Essays on the Nobility of Medieval Scotland* (Edinburgh, 1985), 167–8.

85. B.E. Crawford, 'William Sinclair, Earl of Orkney, and His Family', 232, and A. Grant, 'Extinction of Direct Male Lines Among Scottish Noble Families in the Fourteenth and Fifteenth Centuries', 213, *Essays on the Nobility of Medieval Scotland*, ed. K.J. Stringer (Edinburgh, 1985); L.G. Pine, *The Story of the Peerage* (1952), 71–2.

86. A. Rowan, 'Balbirnie House, Fife', *CL*, 151 (1972), 1670.

87. Nearly one in ten was a close male relative of a peer. Prest, *Rise of the Barristers*, 94–5; Lynch, *Scotland*, 255; Shaw, *Management of Scottish Society*, 21–2; A.J.G. Cummings, 'The Business Affairs of an Eighteenth-century Lowland Laird', *Scottish Elites*, ed. T.M. Devine (Edinburgh, 1994), 44.

88. Which might explain why the number of well-bred lawyers increased so dramatically. Colley, *Britons*, 127 and 396 n.52.

89. Namier, *England in the Age of the American Revolution*, 6.

90. Whyte, *Scotland*, 157; Timperley, 'Pattern of Landholding', 138–40.

91. Gaskell, *Morvern*; Macinnes, 'Landownership', 25; P. Harris, *Life in a Scottish Country House: the Story of A.J. Balfour and Whittinghame House* (Haddington, 1989), 15.

92. Young, *Parliaments of Scotland*, ii, 540–1; Lenman, *Integration*, 24, 53–4; Everitt, 'Social Mobility', 72; Timperley, 'Landholding', 151; Hancock, *Citizens of the World*.

93. W. Ferguson, 'Introduction', 10, and 'The Reform Act (Scotland) of 1832: Intention and Effect', *SHR*, 45 (1966), 113; Colley, *Britons*, 347; Gash, *Politics in the Age of Peel*, 35; J.I Brash, *Papers on Scottish Electoral Politics 1832–1854* (Edinburgh, 1974), x–xii, xxxviii and 'The New Scottish County Electors in 1832', *The Scots and Parliament*, ed. C. Jones (Edinburgh, 1996), 122–36; I.G.C. Hutchinson, *A Political History of Scotland 1832–1924* (Edinburgh, 1986), 1–3; Lloyd, *General Election of 1880*, 120, 124; Hanham, *Elections*, 13; M. Dyer, 'Burgh Districts', 293–4, and '"Mere Detail and Machinery", the Great Reform Act and the Effects of Redistribution on Scottish Representation, 1832–1868', *SHR*, 62 (1983), 30, 34.

94. Brash, *Papers on Scottish Electoral Politics*, ix, xxvii; Fry, *Patronage and Principle*, 7, 73; Whiteley, *SC*, 396; Gash, *Politics in the Age of Peel*, 38; Sack, 'House of Lords', 917, n.24; Hanham, *Elections*, 160.

95. Lynch, *Scotland*, 415–16; Whiteley, *SC*, 362–3, 369; K.T. Hoppen, 'Landlords, Society, and Electoral Politics in Mid-Nineteenth-Century Ireland', *PP*, 75 (1977), 82–91; Fry, *Patronage and Principle*, 80, 99–100; Ferguson, 'The Reform Act', 114; Gaskell, *Morvern*, 97–9; Hanham, *Elections*, 23–4.

96. H. Pelling, *Social Geography of British Elections 1885–1910* (New York, 1967), 372–3; Devine, *Clanship to Crofter's War*, viii, 67–8; I.G.C. Hutchinson, 'The Nobility and Politics in Scotland, c. 1880–1939', *Scottish Elites*, ed. T.M. Devine (Edinburgh, 1994), 104–12, 131–2; Macinnes, 'Landownership', 5–6; Richards and Clough, *Cromartie*, 340.

97. M. Thatcher, *The Downing Street Years* (1993), 291; F.M.L. Thompson, 'English Landed Society in the Nineteenth Century', *The Power of the Past: Essays for Eric Hobsbawm*, eds P. Thane, G. Crossick and R. Floud (Cambridge, 1984), 4–5; Hutchinson, 'Nobility and Politics', 144–6; Cannadine, *DFBA*, 161–2; R. Perrott, *Aristocrats* (New York, 1968), 77, 213–22; S. Winchester, *Their Noble Lordships: Class and Power in Modern Britain* (New York, 1982), 87; *Sunday Times* (14 April 1996), sec. 3, p. 6.

98. 340 over 5,000 acres in the Highlands compared to about 200 estates of the latter size in England and Wales combined. In 1995 an estimated two-and-a-half million acres were owned by titled families. Callender, *Patterns of Landownership*, 9–10, 80–1; S. Glover, 'The Old Rich: a Survey of the Landed Class', *Spectator* (1 January 1977), 16; Wightman, *Who Owns Scotland*, 142; J. McEwen, *Who Owns Scotland? a Study in Land Ownership* (Edinburgh, 1977); D. Sutherland, *The Landowners*, 2nd edn (1988), 17, 66.

99. D. McCrone and A. Morris, 'Lords and Heritages: the Transformation of the Great Lairds of Scotland', *Scottish Elites*, ed. T.M. Devine (Edinburgh, 1994), 182. Neither Wightman nor McEwen is entirely accurate. Estimates of aristocratic wealth are also often off track. *The Times* reported that the Marquis of Bute was worth £60 million in 1990. He left £144 million when he died three years later. Beresford, *Book of the British Rich*, 155; *Evening Standard* (3 July 1996). Beresford's work is getting more accurate. See, *Sunday Times* (6 April 1997) 'Rich List'. The Duke of Buccleuch's listing at £45 million, however, is unlikely to be correct. The Lovat estate imploded owing to poor management. See, A. Cramb, *Who Owns Scotland Now? the Use and Abuse of Private Land* (Edinburgh, 1996), 77–94, 117, 186–7.

100. G.O. Sayles, *The Irish Parliament in the Middle Ages*, 2nd edn (Philadelphia, 1964); B. Farrell, *The Irish Parliamentary Tradition* (Dublin, 1973), 1–90; J.G. Crawford, *Anglicizing the Government of Ireland: the Irish Privy Council and the Expansion of Tudor Rule, 1556–1578* (Dublin, 1993), 185, 402.

101. James, *Lords of the Ascendancy*, 16; A.J. Ward, *The Irish Constitutional Tradition: Responsible Government and Modern Ireland, 1782–1992* (Washington, 1994), 16–17; J. Smyth, '"Like

Amphibious Animals": Irish Protestants, Ancient Britons, 1691–1707', *HJ*, 36 (1993), 791, 796; S.G. Ellis, *Tudor Ireland, 1470–1603* (1985), 175–8.

102. James, *Lords of the Ascendancy*, 39; Porritt, *UHC*, ii, 415; A.P.W. Malcolmson, '"Parliamentary Traffic of the Country", *Penal Era and Golden Age*, eds T. Bartlett and D.W. Hayton (Belfast, 1979), 141; Thorne, *HP*, iii, 438; P. Galloway, *The Most Illustrious Order of St. Patrick 1783–1983* (Chichester, 1983), J. Bardon, *History of Ulster* (Belfast, 1992), 238; G.C. Bolton, *The Passing of the Irish Act of Union* (Oxford, 1966), 100–3, 205; E.M. Johnston, *Great Britain and Ireland 1760–1800, a Study in Political Administration* (Edinburgh, 1963), 4, 26.

103. Plumb, *Growth of Political Stability*, 182; T.C. Barnard, 'Scotland and Ireland in the Later Stewart Monarchy', *Conquest and Union: Fashioning a British State, 1485–1725*, eds S.G. Ellis and S. Barber (1995), 267; Bolton, *Passing the Irish Act of Union*, 34.

104. Thorne, *HP*, i, 77; Malcolmson, 'Parliamentary Traffic', 140–6; R.F. Foster, *Modern Ireland 1600–1972* (1988), 234–6.

105. T.W. Moody and W.E. Vaughan, *A New History of Ireland, Eighteenth-Century Ireland 1691–1800* (Oxford, 1986), 74; Johnston, *Great Britain and Ireland*, 119; Bolton, *Passing of the Irish Act of Union*, 31–2.

106. W. Allingham, *A Diary* (1985), 20; Johnston, *Great Britain and Ireland*, 175; A.P.W. Malcolmson, *John Foster: the Politics of the Anglo-Irish Ascendancy* (Oxford, 1978), 111; Hoppen, 'Landlords', 83–4; J.H. White, 'Landlord Influence at Elections in Ireland, 1760–1885', *EHR*, 80 (1965), 74–43; W.G. Jones, *The Wynnes of Sligo and Leitrim* (Manorhamilton, 1994), 30–1.

107. Tillyard, *Aristocrats*, 54.

108. Namier and Brooke, *HP*, i, 145.

109. Foster, *Modern Ireland*, 226, 231; Bolton, *Passing of the Irish Act of Union*, 35; F.G. James, 'Active Irish Peers in the Early Eighteenth Century', *JBS*, 18 (1979), 52; Johnston, *Great Britain and Ireland*, 215–16.

110. The Irish elite was the least well-endowed in the British Isles. Their average income was over £4,000 p.a. less than that of their English counterparts.

111. Over half (53%) of new Irish peers had Commons careers (including some who sat for English seats) between 1650 and 1699. This rose to 87% in 1700–1749 and 86% in 1750–1850. Between 1692 and 1727 thirty-seven of the ninety-nine peers attending the Lords had been Irish MPs. Later in the century the proportion rose to nearly two-thirds. James, *Lords of the Ascendancy*, 127–8; Johnston, *Great Britain and Ireland*, 216; Bolton, *Passing the Irish Act of Union*, 39; Thorne, *HP*, i, 106.

112. Porritt, *UHC*, ii, 194–8, 414; F.G. James, *Ireland in the Empire 1688–1770* (Cambridge, MA, 1973), 47; Malcolmson, 'Parliamentary Traffic', 149; W.H. Crawford, 'The Social Structure of Ulster in the Eighteenth Century', *Ireland and France: 17th – 20th Centuries*, eds L.M. Cullen and F. Furet (Paris, 1980), 118.

113. J. Kelly, 'That Damn'd Thing Called Honour', *Duelling in Ireland 1570–1860* (Cork, 1995), 49, 98–104, 139–47, 237, 264; C. Chenevix Trench, *Grace's Card: Irish Catholic Landlords 1690–1800* (Cork, 1997), 93.

114. The Dingle constituency was also the first known to be sold. Porritt, *UHC*, ii, 186, 357ff; D. Clarke, *Arthur Dobbs, Esquire 1689–1765* (Chapel Hill, 1957), 25; Malcolmson, 'Parliamentary Traffic', 154–5, 160; D.A. Cronin, *A Galway Gentleman in the Age of Improvement: Robert French of Monivea, 1716–79* (Dublin, 1995), 42; J.L. McCracken, 'From Swift to Grattan', *The Irish Parliamentary Tradition*, ed. B. Farrell, (Dublin, 1973), 140; Johnston, *Great Britain and Ireland*, 122, 129, 174–5; *DNB*, xviii, 1233; Thorne, *HP*, i, 101; iii, 338; Bolton, *Passing the Irish Act of Union*, 33, 38–9; W.A. Maguire, *The Downshire Estates in Ireland 1801–1845* (Oxford, 1972), 9–10, 18;

Malcolmson, *John Foster*, 331; W.E. Vaughan, *Landlords and Tenants in Mid-Victorian Ireland* (Oxford, 1994), 133; L.J. Proudfoot, *Urban Patronage and Social Authority: the Management of the Duke of Devonshire's Towns in Ireland, 1764–1891* (Washington, 1995), 305–6.

115. Englefield, 'The Irish Houses of Parliament in the Eighteenth Century', *PA*, 9 (1956), 57–64; Porritt, *UHC*, ii, 375–9.

116. H. Kearney, 'The Irish Parliament in the Early Seventeenth Century', *The Irish Parliamentary Tradition*, ed. B. Farrell (Dublin, 1973), 92; T.C. Barnard, 'Planters and Policies in Cromwellian Ireland', *PP*, 61 (1976), 32; Connolly, *Religion, Law, and Power*, 14–16; Moody and Vaughan, *New History of Ireland*, iv, 2, 34; P. Somerville-Large, *The Irish Country House: a Social History* (1995), 212; M. Bence-Jones, *Burke's Guide to County Houses – Ireland* (1978); T.K. Hoppen, *Elections, Politics, and Society in Ireland 1832–1885* (Oxford, 1984), 110; Proudfoot, *Urban Patronage*, 60.

117. Owners of estates over 1,000 acres held 78.4% of the land compared to 56.1 in England and 92.8 in Scotland.

118. 225 in all, counting those with British titles, making up one-third of all barons and above in the United Kingdom.

119. On the other hand, there were proportionately fewer baronetcies. Halliday, 'Social Mobility', 283–8.

120. Johnston, *Great Britain and Ireland*, 269; R.E. Burns, *Irish Parliamentary Politics in the Eighteenth Century* (2 vols, Washington, 1989), i, 18; James, *Lords of the Ascendancy*, 87, 209.

121. 1,761 MPs from Irish families sat between 1660 and 1800 and 542 between 1801 and 1922 with 32,380 years of service. 248 sat for English constituencies in 1660–1945, about the same number as English MPs from the Scottish elite. Only five of these MPs sat in the Scottish parliament. Seven sat for Welsh seats. A few sat both in Dublin and London simultaneously.

122. See Appendix III, Table 3.5.

123. Previous to which lists of returns are inadequate guides in any case.

124. Such as the Earls of Norbury and Bantry.

125. Such as the Earls of Rosse and Wicklow.

126. Some English grandee families were also prominent in Ireland, most notably the Cavendishes, Fitzwilliams (Earl), Petty-Fitzmaurices and Seymour Conways. The Wellesleys were initially Irish, but became English. The Abercorns, one of the few families to hold peerages in Scotland, England and Ireland, retained large estates in their original homeland, some of which they still own today. The Irish grandees were: Annesley, Beresford, Bernard, Bingham, Bligh, Boyle, Brabazon, Browne (Sligo), Burgh, Butler (Ormonde), Butler (Lanesborough), Caulfield, Chichester, Clements, Cole, Conyngham, Coote, Dawson-Damer, Fitzgerald (Leinster), Fortescue, French (De Freyne), Gore, Gore-Ormsby, Hamilton (Abercorn), Hamilton-Russell, Hamilton-Blackwood, Hill-Trevor, King, Loftus, Lowry-Corry, Maxwell, Moore, Needham, Nugent, O'Brien, O'Neill, Pakenham, Parsons, Ponsonby, Rowley, Skeffington-Foster, Southwell, Stopford, Taylour, Trench, Wingfield.

127. Alexander, Barry, Browne (Kenmare), Creighton, Dawson, Guinness, McDonnell, Vesey.

128. Some of these families may have been richer during the seventeenth or eighteenth centuries and their estates were later reduced by confiscation or sales through indebtedness.

129. Castletown eventually passed by marriage to a grandee family.

130. See Appendix III, Tables 3.11 and 3.12.

131. Power, *Land, Politics, and Society*, 7–8, 325; D.J. Dickson, 'Property and Social Structure in Eighteenth-century South Munster', *Ireland and France, 17th–20th Centuries*, eds L.M. Cullen and F. Furet (Paris, 1980), 130.

132. Dr Johnston-Liik suggests that the impact of the Place Bill of 1793, which allowed seats to be vacated, may have accelerated this trend. (Correspondence with the author.)

133. Clark, *State and Status*, 103.
134. One-quarter of all the families with six or more MPs arrived during the sixteenth century; 11% were Elizabethans; 20% came during the reigns of James I or Charles I (pre-1640); and 21% gained landed status during the Civil War or immediately afterwards. Few families established themselves after 1690.
135. K. McKenny, 'The Seventeenth-century Land Settlement in Ireland: Towards a Statistical Interpretation', *Ireland from Independence to Occupation 1641–1660*, ed. J.H. Ohlmeyer (Cambridge, 1995), 181–200; Barnard, 'Planters and Policies', 33 and passim; Dickson, 'Property and Social Structure', 129–30.
136. The proportion of elite MPs with pre-Tudor social origins was 25% in the mid-eighteenth century and rose to 38% in 1820. As the proportion of MPs coming from elite families declined (60% of Irish seats in 1870), 42% of them came from families prominent before 1500.
137. I found 24% of elite MPs sitting in 1693 Commons also had ancestors in parliament more than a century earlier and pre-Tudor social origins. In 1750, when 88% of MPs were members of 'three-plus' families, nearly half (46%) of the elite representatives came from families with an MP or peer who had sat in the Irish parliament more than a century earlier, before Cromwell's arrival. As late as 1820, when 87% of all Irish MPs were provided by the parliamentary elite, 38% of these MPs came from families who were landed before the Tudors came to the throne. This does not accord entirely with, Power, *Land, Politics, and Society*, 222; James, *Lords of the Ascendancy*, 11–12, 52, 99. However, most of the new arrivals were presumably part of the 12–13% of MPs unconnected with established parliamentary families or were founders of elite families.
138. J.C. Beckett, *The Anglo-Irish Tradition* (Ithaca, 1976), 65; Malcolmson, *John Foster*, 4–5; Connolly, *Religion, Law and Power*, 62–4, 71; James, *Lords of the Ascendancy*, 102–3.
139. Burns, *Irish Parliamentary Politics*, i, 31–3; J.F. Mills, *The Noble Dwellings of Ireland* (New York, 1987), 84–5; Moody and Vaughan, *New History of Ireland*, iv, 35; M. Girouard, 'Lismore Castle, County Waterford', *CL*, 136 (1936), 336; Stone, *Crisis of the Aristocracy*, 140.
140. Malcolmson, *John Foster*, 2–5; Connolly, *Religion, Law and Power*, 61, 64; *The Irish Builder*, 35 (1 July 1893), 150; M. Craig, *Dublin 1660–1860* (Dublin, 1952), 229.
141. Ireland 44.4%, England 37.5%, Scotland 16.6% and Wales 1.4%.
142. Connolly, *Religion, Law and Politics*, 65; *DNB*, xv, 419; Countess of Fingall, *Seventy Years Young* (Dublin, 1972 [1937]), 17; K. Everett, *Bricks and Flowers* (1949), 11, 20; M. Girouard, *Town and Country* (New Haven, 1992), 104; Chenevix Trench, *Grace's Card*, 230.
143. J. Cornforth, 'Adare Manor, Limerick', *CL*, 145 (1969), 1231.
144. James, *Lords of the Ascendancy*, 34–5, and 'Active Irish Peers', 55; Chenevix Trench, *Grace's Card*, 40–50; K.J. Harvey, *The Bellews of Mount Bellew* (Dublin, 1998). For a bleaker picture, see D.E. Jordan, *Land and Popular Politics in Ireland: County Mayo from the Plantation to the Land War* (Cambridge, 1994), 33–6.
145. Twenty recognized chiefs survive today; eight of them live in exile. Count d'Angerville, *The Royalty and Peerage and Nobility of Europe*, 96th edn (Monte Carlo, 1997), 193–4; MacDonagh, *O'Connell*, 4–5.
146. J.H. Ohlmeyer, *Civil War and Restoration in Three Stuart Kingdoms: the Career of Randal MacDonnell, Marquis of Antrim 1609–83* (Cambridge, 1993).
147. Lord Dunboyne, *Butler Family History*, 7th edn (Dublin, 1991), 6; Wagner, *English Genealogy*, 76–9. As in England, baronies in the thirteenth and fourteenth centuries were not hereditary but were held by tenure and by individual summons; the Lords Gormanston were summoned *c.* 1370 but the first hereditary peer was not created until 1478. *CP*, vi, 19; vii, 201; i, Appendix A.

148. J. Healy, *The Castles of Cork* (Dublin, 1988), 422; *Burke's Visitations of Seats* (1855), i, 82; E. Bourke, *Burke, Bourke, De Burgh* (Dublin, 1990), 4; Hasler, *HP*, ii, 129; *Burke's Extinct Peerage*, 214–15.

149. R.J. Hunter, 'Sir Ralph Bingley, *c.* 1570–1627: Ulster Planter', *Plantation to Partition*, ed. P. Roebuck (Belfast, 1981), 14–28; Bardon, *History of Ulster*, 129.

150. Jordan, *Land and Popular Politics*, 27–33; Power, *Land, Politics, and Society*, 68; M. O'Dowd, *Power, Politics, and Land: Early Modern Sligo 1568–1688* (Belfast, 1991), 94; T.G. Simms, *The Williamite Confiscation in Ireland 1690–1703* (1956), 154; M. Perceval Maxwell, *The Scottish Migration to Ulster in the Reign of James I* (1973), 170ff; T.H. Mullin, *Coleraine in Bygone Centuries* (Belfast, 1976), 156.

151. Among them: Burdett, Colclough, Cope, Eyre, Fortescue, Gorges, Greville, Molyneux, Slingsby, Southwell, Tichborne, Upton, Waller and Wingfield.

152. Crawford, 'Social Structure of Ulster', 118; J. Dickson, 'The Colvill Family of Ulster', *Ulster Journal of Archaeology*, 2nd ser., v, 139–45; Jenkins, *History of Modern Wales*, 52; Jones, *The Wynnes*, 7–12; Hasler, *HP*, ii, 432–43, 495; Bindoff, *HP*, iii, 386.

153. Hasler, *HP*, ii, 30; Maguire, *The Downshire Estates*, 1–6.

154. M. Girouard, 'Westport House, County Mayo', *CL*, 137 (1965), 1010–11.

155. 29% of the 'religious' families were Tudor in origins. 35% surfaced in the period 1605–33, 23% arose between 1660 and 1692. None did so in the eighteenth century, although the Agars were undoubtedly assisted further in their rise by an Archbishop of Dublin who died in 1809. The really juicy opportunities for cheap land purchase were long gone.

156. Connolly, *Religion, Law and Power*, 59.

157. Cronin, *Galway Gentleman*, 11–12, 14; History of the Irish Parliament, 1692–1800, unpublished biographies, ed. E.M. Johnston-Liik, Verner; Malcolmson, *John Foster*, 4–5.

158. Johnston, *Great Britain and Ireland*, 246; Connolly, *Religion, Law and Power*, 59; James, *Lords of the Ascendancy*, 128.

159. Proudfoot, *Urban Patronage*, 49; W.H. Crawford, 'Ulster Landowners and the Linen Industry', *Land and Industry*, eds J.T. Ward and R.G. Wilson (Newton Abbot, 1971), 117–44; Cronin, *Galway Gentleman*, 28–32; M. O'Callaghan, 'Franchise Reform, "First Past the Post" and the Strange Case of Unionist Ireland', *PH*, 16 (1997), 102.

160. Of the thirty-two large (which is a comparative word when contrasted to the scale of buildings in England) country houses in County Antrim still standing, two were erected by nabobs, one by a West Indian merchant, and eight by businessmen. C.E.B. Brett, *Buildings of County Antrim* (Belfast, 1996), 71–118.

161. Cronin, *Galway Gentleman*, 10–11; M. Girouard, 'Whitfield Court, County Waterford', *CL*, 142 (1967), 522ff.

162. Johnston, *Great Britain and Ireland*, 246; Bardon, *History of Ulster*, 189; Stone, *Crisis of the Aristocracy*, 140; Barnard, 'Planters and Policies', 34.

163. Somerville-Large, *Irish Country House*, 289; D. Thomson, *Woodbrook* (Harmondsworth, 1976), 71–2; Habakkuk, *MDE*, 483.

164. Kiernan, *The Duel*, 106–7; James, *Lords of the Ascendancy*, 11–12, 24; E. Batt, *The Moncks of Charleville House* (Dublin, 1979), 4–5.

165. Foster, *Modern Ireland*, 170–3; Malcolmson, *John Foster*, xvii–xviii. The term has been much misunderstood and misused. Connolly, *Religion, Law and Power*, 103–4; L.M. Cullen, 'Catholics under the Penal Laws', *Eighteenth-century Ireland*, 1 (1986), 28, 30; Smyth, 'Like Amphibious Animals', 786.

166. Vaughan, *Landlords and Tenants*, 221; Clark, *State and Status*, 214; A. de Tocqueville, *Journeys to England and Ireland*, ed. J.P. Mayer (New York, 1968), 127.

167. *Parl. Deb.*, lxxxi (4 June 1845), 31–7; E.A. Wasson, 'The Old Whigs: Bedford, Fitzwilliam, and Spencer in the House of Lords, 1833–6', *Lords of Parliament*, ed. R.W. Davis (Stanford, 1995), 124; T.K. Hoppen, 'Landownership and Power in Nineteenth-century Ireland: the Decline and Fall of an Elite', *Landownership and Power in Modern Europe*, eds R. Gibson and M. Blinkorn (1991), 168, and *Elections*, 167–8; Adonis, 'Political Role of the British Peerage', 31, 41–2; A. Jackson, *The Ulster Party: Irish Unionists in the House of Commons 1884–1911* (Oxford, 1989), 218, 220.

168. Proudfoot, *Urban Patronage*, 41, 229ff; Beales, 'The Electorate', 148; Hoppen, 'Politics, the Law, and the Nature of the Irish Electorate, 1832–1850', *EHR*, 92 (1977), 755, *Elections*, 332–3, 450–6, and 'Roads to Democracy', 566–7; Johnston, *Great Britain and Ireland*, 203.

169. Hoppen, 'Landlords', 68–9; White, 'Landlord Influence', 747–8.

170. Scotland 23.2 %, Wales 23.9%, England 19.7%.

171. The rise is somewhat illusory, however, since it included new non-Ascendancy parliamentary families such as the O'Connells.

172. See also the data in Appendix III, Table 3.5.

173. Proudfoot, *Urban Patronage*, 240, 258, 321; Somerville-Large, *Irish Country House*, 285–6; Hoppen, 'Landownership', 168, 174, and *Elections*, 165; Foster, *Modern Ireland*, 377; D. Large, 'The Wealth of the Greater Irish Landlords 1750–1815', *IHS*, 15 (1966), 21–47; Vaughan, *Landlord and Tenant*, 125.

174. Hoppen, 'Landlords', 67, 91–2, 'The Franchise and Electoral Politics in England and Ireland 1832–1885', *History* (1985), 208–10, and *Elections, Politics and Society*, 160–2.

175. For example, John George (MP 1859–66), son of a Dublin merchant, who made a fortune at the bar, purchased 2,000 acres, and built a castle: D. Walsh, *100 Wexford Country Houses* (Enniscorthy, 1996), 25.

176. Somerville-Large, *Irish Country Houses*, 275–84; R.F. Foster, *Paddy and Mr Punch: Connections in Irish and English History* (1993), 50–1; Hoppen, 'Roads to Democracy', 557, however, points to the exaggerated picture Hanham painted of patron control in the Irish counties in 1868.

177. Hoppen, 'Landownership', 172, 174–5, and *Elections*, 169, 337; Jordan, *Land and Popular Politics*, 170–1; Proudfoot, *Urban Patronage*, 320–2.

178. Batt, *The Moncks*, 232, 256; Somerville-Large, *Irish Country House*, 214; P. Buckland, *Irish Unionism: One – The Anglo-Irish and the New Ireland 1885–1922* (Dublin, 1922), i, 202 n.16, 204, 215.

179. E. Allyn, *Lords versus Commons: a Century of Conflict and Compromise 1830–1930* (New York, 1931), 25; Adonis, 'Political Role of the British Peerage', 10.

180. Jackson, *Ulster Party*, 57, 205, 232; Bardon, *History of Ulster*, 366; B.M. Walker, *Sentry Hill: an Ulster Farm and Family* (Belfast, 1991), 77–9, 141.

181. D. O'Sullivan, *The Irish Free State and Its Senate* (New York, 1972), 103–5; Buckland, *Irish Unionism*, i, 209–10, 279; Somerville-Large, *Irish Country House*, 353; Morrow, *Picnic in a Foreign Land*, 70, 284; V. Bary, *Houses of Kerry* (Whitegate, Clare, 1994), 41, 43; *The Spectator* (8 February 1997), 40; *Sunday Times* (14 April 1996) spec. sec. p. 29 and (6 April 1997), 'Rich List'.

182. Brett, *Buildings of County Antrim*, 71, and this does not include Shane's Castle, rebuilt on a more modest scale after being burned down in the 1920s but still the seat of the O'Neills.

183. J.G.A. Pocock, 'British History: a Plea for a New Subject', *JMH*, 47 (1975), 601–28, and 'The Limits and Divisions of British History', *AHR*, 87 (1982), 311–36.

184. See: R.G. Asch, ed., *Three Nations – a Common History? England, Scotland, Ireland and British History* c. *1600–1920* (Bochum, 1993); H. Kearney, *The British Isles: a History of Four Nations*

(Cambridge, 1989); G. Newman, 'Nationalism Revisited', *JBS*, 35 (1996), 118–27; A. Grant and K.J. Stringer, *Uniting the Kingdom? the Making of British History* (1995); S.G. Ellis and S. Barber, *Conquest and Union: Fashioning a British State, 1485–1725* (1995) and other works cited below.

185. Bradshaw and Morrill, *The British Problem*, 2; Colley, *Britons*, 155–93, and 'The Politics of Eighteenth-century British History', *JBS*, 25 (1986), 378; J. Black, *The Politics of Britain 1688–1800* (New York, 1993), 14; H.V. Bowen, *Elites, Enterprise, and the Making of the Overseas Empire 1688–1775* (1996), 52; J. Merriman, *A History of Modern Europe* (New York, 1996), 472; Lieven, *Aristocracy in Europe*, 10; Daunton, *Progress and Poverty*, 272–3; Cannadine, *Aspects of Aristocracy*, 2, 9–36, *DFBA*, 5–9, and 'The Fall of the British Nobility: 1789–1994', *The House of Lords*, ed. R. Smith (1994), 112.

186. Namier and Brooke, *HP*, i, 67; E.J. Cowan, 'Union of the Crowns and the Crisis of the Constitution in 17th Century Scotland', *The Satellite State in the 17th and 18th Centuries*, eds S. Dyrvik, K. Myland and J. Oldervoll (Oslo, 1979), 131–2; Bradshaw and Morrill, *The British Problem*, 11; J.S. Morrill, 'The Fashioning of Britain', *Conquest and Union: Fashioning a British State, 1485–1725*, eds S.G. Ellis and S. Barber (1995), 24–5, and *The Nature of the English Revolution* (New York, 1993), 96; Riley, 'Structure of Scottish Politics', 18.

187. Smyth, 'Like Amphibious Animals', 786–7; Hasler, *HP*, iii, 96–7; Heal and Holmes, *Gentry*, x.

188. K.M. Brown, 'The Origins of a British Aristocracy: Integration and Its Limitations before the Treaty of Union', 222–49, and S. Barber, 'A State of Britishness?', 310, *Conquest and Union: Fashioning a British State, 1485–1725*, eds S.G. Ellis and S. Barber (1995); L. Colley, 'Britishness and Otherness: an Argument', *JBS*, 31 (1992), 314–15; Jenkins, *History of Modern Wales*, 57–77; C. McKean, 'A Plethora of Palaces', 9, and A. Mackechnie, 'Design Approaches in Early Post-Reformation Scots Houses', 16, *Scottish Country Houses 1660–1914*, eds I. Gow and A. Rowan (Edinburgh, 1995); Canny, 'Irish, Scottish, and Welsh Responses', 147–8; Clark, *State and Status*, 336; L. Brockliss and D. Eastwood, *A Union of Multiple Identities: the British Isles, c. 1750–c. 1850* (Manchester, 1997), 1–8; F.M.L. Thompson, 'review', *PH*, 14 (1995), 389.

189. Halliday, 'Social Mobility', i–ii, 27–8, 30, 91, 104, 114, 117, 157, 176, 257, 281–97, 306–7, Appendix 23.

190. McCrone and Morris, 'Lords and Heritages', 176; Hutchinson, 'Nobility and Politics', 131–51.

191. A. Adonis, *Making Aristocracy Work: the Peerage and the Political System in Britain 1884–1914* (Oxford, 1993), 27, 31, 41–2; Hoppen, *Elections*, 167–8.

192. Families designated as 'English' in this study (with one or more MPs in 1660–1945) compiled only 2.5% of their years of service between 1660 and 1945 sitting for Welsh, Scottish or Irish seats and 0.4% of their years in the Lords as Scottish or Irish representative peers.

Chapter 5

1. N. Gash, *Aristocracy and People: Britain 1815–1865* (1979), 347.

2. 48% of families with an MP in 1765 had an MP in 1665 or earlier; 44% of those with an MP in 1665 had an MP in 1565 or earlier.

3. J.R.M. Butler, *The Passing of the Great Reform Bill* (1964), 255.

4. H. Nicolson, *The Desire to Please* (New York, 1943), 201–2; Bence-Jones, *Burke's Guide to Country Houses – Ireland*, 256.

5. G. Kitson Clark, *The Making of Victorian England* (1965), 51, 210, 212, 214.

6. E.A. Smith, *Lord Grey*, 327, and *House of Lords*, 4.

7. Rubinstein, *Capitalism, Culture, and Decline*, 140–1, 145, and 'New Men of Wealth and the Purchase of Land in Nineteenth-century Britain', *PP*, 92 (1981), 147; Searle, *Entrepreneurial Politics*, 202.

8. Cannadine, 'Fall of the British Nobility', 112, and *DFBA*, 18; Stones, *An Open Elite?*, 30, 402; A. Adonis, 'Survival of the Great Estates: Henry 4th Earl of Carnarvon and His Dispositions in the Eighteen-eighties', *HR*, 64 (1991), 54, and 'Political Role of the British Peerage', 2.

9. R.W. Davis, *Political Change and Continuity 1760–1885: a Buckinghamshire Study* (Newton Abbot, 1972), 108, 110; A. Ponsonby, *Decline of the Aristocracy* (1912), 102–3; Phillips, *Great Reform Bill*, 1, 10–11; Clark, *English Society*, 7, 94; Wasson, *Whig Renaissance*, 244–7; T.H.S. Escott, *England: Her People, Polity, and Pursuits* (New York, 1885), 317ff; G.W. Cox, *The Efficient Secret, the Cabinet and the Development of Political Parties in Victorian England* (Cambridge, 1987), 105.

10. *Parl. Deb.*, (4 October 1831), 1198, 1201–2; G. Kitson Clark, *Peel and the Conservative Party: a Study in Party Politics 1832–41*, 2nd edn (1964), 58, 180.

11. S.F. Woolley, 'Personnel of the Parliament of 1833', *EHR*, 53 (1938), 245; J.A. Phillips and C. Wetherell, 'The Great Reform Bill of 1832 and the Rise of Partisanship', *JMH*, 63 (1991), 623; Guttsman, *British Political Elite*, 18; Searle, *Entrepreneurial Politics*, viii.

12. Butler, *Passing of the Great Reform Bill*, viii; H.W. Carless Davis, *The Age of Grey and Peel* (Oxford, 1929), 231.

13. Phillips and Wetherell, 'Great Reform Act' (*AHR*), 411–16; M. Taylor, *The Decline of British Radicalism 1847–1860* (Oxford, 1995), 1, 7; J. Thompson, 'After the Fall: Class and Political Language in Britain, 1780–1900', *HJ*, 39 (1996), 800.

14. Clark, *English Society*, 7, 94, 409–12.

15. Baronets are often treated as if they were automatically part of the social and economic elite. (Guttsman, *British Political Elite*, 77 n.2 and 78–9.) This is a serious error. Stuart Halliday has demonstrated how diverse the backgrounds of men dubbed hereditary knights could be. (Halliday, 'Social Mobility', 155, 173–4, 301–2, and Appendix 23; a useful corrective to Stone's somewhat inaccurate portrayal, *An Open Elite?*, 241–2; Roebuck, *Yorkshire Baronets*, 22–4, 26, 309.) Comparatively few had estates large enough to weather improvident heirs or other economic setbacks, and hence many titles descended to humble successors. Table 2.3 in Appendix II shows how wide the gap was in wealth and parliamentary service between the nobility and baronets. See also Appendix III, Tables 3.7 and 3.9.

16. Beales, 'The Electorate', 143–9.

17. Woolley, 'Personnel of the Parliament of 1833', 246–7; V. Cromwell, 'The Victorian Commons 1832–1884', *The House of Commons*, eds R. Smith and J.S. Moore (1996), 119, 121.

18. M. Baer, 'The Politics of London, 1852–1868: Parties, Voters and Representation', (PhD thesis, University of Iowa, 1976), 451–2; Namier, *Structure of Politics*, 86–7; W. Bagehot, *The English Constitution*, rev. edn (New York, 1911), 235; W.C. Lubenow, *Parliamentary Politics and the Home Rule Crisis: the British House of Commons in 1886* (Oxford, 1988), 175; Whiteley, *SC*, 54; D.G. Wright, 'A Radical Borough: Parliamentary Politics in Bradford 1832–41', *NH*, 4 (1969), 148–9.

19. D. Spring, 'Some Reflections on Social History in the Nineteenth Century', *Victorian Studies*, 4 (1960), 55–64.

20. Thorne, *HP*, i, 43–4, 67; Harvey, *Britain*, 4; J. Cannon, *Parliamentary Reform 1640–1832* (Cambridge, 1973), 48, 220, and *Aristocratic Century*, 175; A.S. Turberville, *The House of Lords in the Age of Reform 1784–1837* (Westport, 1958), 244ff.; O'Gorman, *Voters*, 118–19, 262–82; Yorke, *Royal Tribes of Wales*, 155–6; Davies, 'Aristocratic Town-makers', 26, 34; J. Parry, *The Rise and Fall of Liberal Government in Victorian Britain* (New Haven, 1993), 48; Namier and Brooke, *HP*, i, 49; *VCH Cheshire* (1979), 137–8.

21. Sack, 'House of Lords', 919; E.A. Wasson, 'The Crisis of the Aristocracy: Parliamentary Reform, the Peerage, and the House of Commons 1750–1914', *PH*, 13 (1994), 297–311.

22. E. Richards, 'The Social and Electoral Influence of the Tentham Interest, 1800–1860', *Midland History*, 3 (1975), 116–48; Thorne, *HP*, i, 13, 37, 46–7, 54, 60; ii, 87–8.

23. Richards, *Leviathan of Wealth*, 27.

24. E. Richards, 'The Land Agent', *The Victorian Countryside*, ed. G.E. Mingay (2 vols, 1981), 454–5, and 'Social and Electoral Influence' 118–35; Maguire, *Downshire Estates*, 194.

25. Foster, *Politics of County Power*, 122–6, 130–44, 156; T.S. Nossiter, *Influence, Opinion, and Political Idioms of Reformed England: Case Studies from the North-east 1832–74* (New York, 1974), 35.

26. R.J. Olney, *Lincolnshire Politics 1832–1885* (Oxford, 1973), 232; Howe, *Cotton Masters*, 99; G. Nevill, *Exotic Groves* (Salisbury, 1984), 22.

27. Gash, *Reaction and Reconstruction*, 138; Nossiter, *Influence*, 52.

28. O. MacDonagh, *Early Victorian Government 1830–1870* (1977), 5–16; Cox, *Efficient Secret*, 29, 68, 134, 143; J.P. Cornford, 'The Parliamentary Foundations of the Hotel Cecil', *Ideas and Institutions of Victorian Britain*, ed. R. Robson (1967), 269; Hanham, *Nineteenth-Century Constitution*, 152–3.

29. Batt, *The Moncks*, 235; C. Russell, *TLS* (19–25 October 1990), 1124; Aspinall, 'Extracts from Lord Hatherton's Diary', 263.

30. D. Large, 'The House of Lords and Ireland in the Age of Peel, 1832–50', *Peers, Politics and Power in the House of Lords 1603–1911*, eds C. Jones and D.L. Jones (1986), 39; G. Kitson Clark, *An Expanding Society: Britain 1830–1900* (Cambridge, 1967), 17; Turberville, *House of Lords in the Age of Reform*, 252; Adonis, *Making Aristocracy Work*, 83.

31. J. Cannon, 'The British Nobility 1660–1800', *The European Nobilities in the Seventeenth and Eighteenth Centuries*, ed. H.M. Scott (New York, 1995), 75–6.

32. Guttsman's work (*British Political Elite*) has been widely influential and is much cited.

33. J.A. Jenkins, *Parliament, Party, and Politics in Victorian Britain* (Manchester, 1996), 103; Lubenow, *Parliamentary Politics*, 59. Some studies avoid these problems of definition by analysing 'interests' or educational backgrounds of MPs in multiple categories without combining totals – e.g. J.A. Thomas, *The House of Commons 1832–1901: a Study of Its Economic and Functional Character* (Cardiff, 1939), 2–22; Guttsman, *British Political Elite*, 41 – thus rendering the data, for the purposes of this chapter, unusable.

34. For further details, see: Wasson, 'Crisis of the Aristocracy', 297–311.

35. Jenkins (*Parliament, Party, and Politics*, 26 n. 10) argues that these figures may be distorted by the rapid expansion of the peerage in the early decades of the nineteenth century. In fact, while the proportion of peerage MPs rose by 51.6% between 1801 and 1830, the English peerage increased by only about 20–25% (depending on counts – 257– 267 in 1800 to 310–323 in 1830 – Beckett, *Aristocracy*, 486–7). The total peerage (including the Scottish and Irish) only rose by about 4 to 6% (492–508 to 511–524). So it is hard to see how the increase can account for the dramatic rise. Only forty-eight genuinely new United Kingdom peerages were created in 1800–1829 and thirty-three Irish ones. Extinctions would have reduced this inflow considerably. By contrast sixty new GB peerages were created in 1770–1799 and eighty-four Irish ones (excluding foreigners, women, reversed attainders, abeyances, royalty, promotions, eldest sons called to the Lords, brothers who were heirs presumptive, heirs made peers in their own right and eldest grandsons of peers.) Jenkins also noted that the figure for 1860 (25.2%) is only slightly lower than for 1801 (27.9) However, one needs to remember that by 1860, the House of Lords was much bigger (up at least 118 and possibly as much as 144, or over 50% among E, GB, and UK peers), while the percentage of peer-MPs went down. The proportion of peers represented in the Commons, had, therefore, been greatly reduced.

36. Christie, *BNE*.

37. Rubinstein, *Capitalism, Culture and Decline*, 141.

38. Guttsman, *British Political Elite*, 40.

39. R. Butt, *The Power of Parliament* (1967), 63.

40. Thompson, 'Britain', 24; Whiteley, *SC*, 56–8, 459.

41. J. Harris, *Private Lives, Public Spirit: Britain 1870–1914* (1994), 185; Cannadine, *DFBA*, 184.

42. T. Lloyd, 'Uncontested Seats in British General Elections 1852–1910', *HJ*, 8 (1965), 260–5; J. Davis and D. Tanner, 'The Borough Franchise after 1867', *HR*, 69 (1996), 306–27.

43. Whiteley, *SC*, 174, 200, 358, 504–5; Hanham, *Elections*, 26–7, 46, 48–9, 55; J.R. Vincent, *The Formation of the British Liberal Party 1857–1868* (Harmondsworth, 1972), 47.

44. Cannadine, 'Fall of the British Nobility', 111; H.J. Hanham, *The Reformed Electoral System in Great Britain 1832–1914* (1971), 12; Mingay, *The Gentry*, 74; Perkin, *Rise of Professional Society*, 41; Whiteley, *SC*, 476–80.

45. E.J. Evans, *The Forging of the Modern State: Early Industrial Britain 1783–1870* (1983), 353; W.L. Arnstein, 'The Survival of the Victorian Aristocracy', *The Rich, the Well-Born, and the Powerful*, ed. F.C.Jaher (Secaucus, NJ, 1975), 220; E.H.H. Green, 'An Age of Transition: an Introductory Essay', *PH*, 16 (1997), 2.

46. Beckett, *Aristocracy*, 433; M. Bentley, *Politics without Democracy 1815–1914* (1984), 250; Parry, *Rise and Fall of Liberal Government*, 12.

47. Hanham, *Nineteenth Century Constitution*, 23; A.B. Cooke and J. Vincent, *The Governing Passion: Cabinet Government and Party Politics in Britain 1885–86* (New York, 1974), 6.

48. H. Perkin, 'review', *AHR*, 97 (1992), 205.

49. P.H. Ditchfield, *The Old English Country Squire* (1912), 288.

50. It is true that as this study enters the twentieth century fewer years remain to accumulate MPs. None was counted after 1994. However, the tenure in the Commons for most families with fewer than six MPs was less than one hundred years from election of the first to the departure of the last MP. Thus, until 1894 the end date of the study a century later should not have had an appreciable statistical effect on the data. 'Six-plus' families were usually active electorally for centuries and *in theory* could have kept producing MPs well into the twentieth century.

51. Vincent, *Formation of the British Liberal Party*, 61–2.

52. Adonis, 'Political Role of the British Peerage', 1, 118–19, 121–2, 211, and 'Survival of the Great Estates', 54–62; J. Scott, *Who Rules Britain?* (1965), 130, 134; M.L. Bush, *The English Aristocracy: a Comparative Synthesis* (Manchester, 1984), 10–11; R. Quinalt, 'Warwickshire Landowners and Parliamentary Politics c. 1841–1923' (DPhil. thesis, University of Oxford, 1975), vii, 411, 422; Dewald, *European Nobility*, 9; A.J. Mayer, *The Persistence of the Old Regime: Europe to the Great War* (New York, 1981), 10–11, 15; A.J.P. Taylor, *English History 1914–45* (Oxford, 1965), 171; D. Cannadine, *Lords and Landlords: the Aristocracy and the Towns 1774–1967* (Leicester, 1980), 21–5; Thompson, *ELS*, 1; Habakkuk, *MDE*, 696–7; A. Marwick, *British Society since 1945* (Harmondsworth, 1982), 210.

53. Some sales were motivated by fear of a confiscatory state. Habakkuk, *MDE*, 681, 687; D. Spring, 'Land and Politics in Edwardian England', *Agricultural History*, 58 (1984), 26–9; Adonis, 'Survival of the Great Estates', 59; Cramb, *Who Owns Scotland Now?*, 172.

54. M. Beard, *Acres and Heirlooms, the Survival of Britain's Historical Estates* (New York, 1989), 139; Habakkuk, *MDE*, 624, 703–4; Perrott, *Aristocrats*, 149, 151–6; Clemenson, *English Country Houses*, 120–3, 151; P. Mandler, *The Fall and Rise of the Stately Home* (New Haven, 1997), 463 n.4. In 1998 about 1,400–1,500 country houses as complete entities in private hands still survive in the UK.

J. Cornford, *The Country House in England 1948–1998* (1998), 3. A 1990 list of the 200 richest families included fifty-four aristocrats. The list of the top 400, however, was inaccurate because a number of rich landowners such as Sir Watkin Williams Wynn, Lord Lambton and the Earls of Powis, Feversham and Yarborough were left out, while the fortunes of others were shown subsequently to have been grossly underestimated. Beresford, *Book of the British Rich*; J.V. Beckett, 'review', *PH*, 11 (1992), 176; Glover, 'Old Rich', 16; Yarborough left £67 million in 1991 – see T.R. Leach, *Lincolnshire Country Houses and Their Families, Part One* (Lincoln, 1990), 134; for corrective to Chomondeley see W.D. Rubinstein, 'review', *JMH*, 64 (1992), 396–7.

55. *CL*, 185 (5 September 1991), 94–9. These figures may be underestimates – the Duke of Portland, who had recently died and left his 64,000 acres to an heiress, is not counted and some other dukes noted at under 10,000 acres were listed with significantly larger holdings in a 1987 survey (Sutherland, *The Landowners*, 63). The heirs of the last Duke of Cleveland, the Lords Barnard, owned 53,000 acres in 1996 – *Sunday Times* (14 April 1996), special section 22, 29.

56. J.M. Robinson, 'Still in the Top Class', *Spectator* (16 November 1996), 9; D. Littlejohn, *The Fate of the English Country House* (Oxford, 1997), 111, 117; Wightman, *Who Owns Scotland*, 57. As the 1990s progressed, however, purely landed, non-urban fortunes failed to compete with the massive accumulations made by business and entertainment moguls. *Sunday Times* (6 April 1997), 'Rich List'.

57. *New York Herald Tribune* (8 September 1933).

Conclusion

1. A. Valentine, *The British Establishment 1760–1784* (Norman, 1970), i, x–xi.
2. Dewald, *European Nobility*, 62; P. Roosevelt, *Life on the Russian Country Estate* (New Haven, 1995), 29.
3. D. Cannadine, *Class in Britain* (New Haven, 1998), 18, and passim.
4. See, for example, M.W. McCahill, 'Open Elites: Recruitment to the French Noblesse and the English Aristocracy in the Eighteenth Century', *Albion*, 30 (1998), 599–629.

Index

* denotes a modern historian. Family is abbreviated 'f'.

217

Bulkeley f., 26, 97
burgesses, 10, 22–3, 27, 185, 191
Burgh (Bourke, Burke, DeBurgh, Clanricarde) f.,
130, 135, 136, 138, 208
Burke's publications, 29, 41, 187
businessmen, 27, 38, 79–87, 88–92, 98–9, 117–18,
140–1, 147, 153, 160–2, 195, 197, 199, 210
see bankers, brewers, builders, clothiers, coal
mining, distillers, financiers, industrialists,
ironmasters, merchants, nabobs, newspaper
proprietors, railway owners, shipowners,
textile manufacturing, West Indians
Butler (Ormonde) f., 131, 132, 136, 208
Byng (Torrington, Strafford) f., 65, 191

cabinet, 8, 45, 47–9, 97, 113, 131, 192, 205
cadets, 53, 104–6, 108, 113–14, 132, 137, 146
Cadogan f., 47, 73, 191
Cameron (Lochiel) f., 107, 110
Campbell (Argyll) f., 92, 105, 106, 108–10, 119–20,
202, 204, 205
Campbell (Cawdor) f., 95, 121, 205
Campbell-Bannerman, Sir Henry, 48
Cannadine, David*, 6, 146, 159
Cannon, John*, 49, 87
Capel f., 123, 191
Carew f., 191, 192
Carey, Robert 1st Earl of Monmouth, 10
Carnegie f., 205
Cartwright f., 16
Catholic Association, The, 133, 142
Caulfield f., 208
Cavendish (Devonshire, Hartington) f., 44–6, 76,
132, 142–5, 151, 158, 208
Cecil f., 5, 8, 47–8, 72, 98, 157, 158, 188, 191
Cecil, Robert Gascoyne 3rd Marquess of Salisbury,
8, 48, 151
Charles I, King, 61, 64, 70, 127, 146, 186
Charles II, King, 46, 115
Chaucer, Geoffrey, 20–1, 184
Chichester (Donegall) f., 122, 138, 142, 208
Chomondeley f., 47, 191, 195
Christie, Ian*, 62, 87, 195
Christmas f., 130, 140
Church of England, 70, 75, 162
Church of Ireland, 139, 210
Church of Scotland, 116
Church of Wales, 98–100
Churchill f., 13, 76, 151, 192
Churchill, Charles Spencer 9th Duke of
Marlborough, 8
Churchill, John 1st Duke of Marlborough, 73, 74

Churchill, Sir Winston Spencer, 3, 8, 48, 151
Civil War, the, 23–4, 51, 59, 60–1, 78, 103, 108,
113, 134
Clark, J.C.D.*, 86, 150
Clements (Leitrim) f., 144, 208
Cliffe, J.T.*, 35
Clifford f., 66, 195
Clive f., 28, 91, 191
clothiers, 80, 99
coal mining, 69, 99, 115
Cochrane f., 121, 202
Coke f., 116, 191
Coke, Robert, 28
Cole (Enniskillen) f., 143, 208
Colley, Linda*, 146
Commons, House of, 3–6, 15, 20, 21, 75, 80,
101–2, 104, 159, 178
attendance in, 23, 186
disappearance of families from, 49–56, 61, 63,
98, 100–2, 114, 133, 142–5, 155–8, 176, 192
Englishmen sitting for non-English seats, 15, 41,
95, 191, 212
Irish Commons, 122–3, 125, 129–30, 140, 191,
209
Irishmen sitting for non-Irish seats, 125, 132,
188, 191, 208
Irish MPs, 101–2, 125, 128, 132–3, 142–5,
172–3, 178, 209
lacunae in lists of MPs, 56, 128, 184
non-elite MPs, 37–8, 87, 162, 190
parity with House of Lords, 23, 24, 151
property qualifications, 4, 27
proportion composed of by elite, 25, 41–2, 62,
95, 100–1, 113, 118–20, 142–3, 149–57,
160–1, 165–73
Scotsmen sitting for non-Scottish seats, 95, 104,
108–10, 203
Scottish MPs, 101–4, 107–8, 110, 113, 118–20,
170–1, 178, 191, 202
size, 21, 24, 186
under age MPs, 32
under the Stuarts, 23, 61, 186
Welshmen sitting for non-Welsh seats, 94–5
Welsh MPs, 94–102, 119, 169, 178, 191
years of service in, 43, 45, 94–5, 108, 164, 191,
208, 212
see parliament
Compton f., 47, 66, 191, 195
Conolly f., 125, 132
Conolly, William, 123, 134, 139
Conservative Party, 101, 118–19, 121, 141
Convention of Estates (Scotland), 102, 112

Murray (Mansfield) f., 121, 205
Musgrave f., 192, 195
Myddelton f., 97, 99, 192

nabobs, 26, 62, 83, 91, 99, 117, 140, 210
Namier, Sir Lewis*, 6–7, 8, 15, 48, 92, 109, 117
Needham (Kilmorey) f., 125, 137, 143, 144, 158, 208
Neville f., 44, 66, 67, 185, 191, 192
'new men', 5, 29, 30, 35, 64, 65, 71, 87, 92, 98–9, 114, 117, 154, 160
'New Protestants' (Ireland), 134, 137, 140, 141
Newdigate f., 158, 192
newspaper proprietors, 83, 85
nobility see aristocracy, Lords, and peers
noble service, 71–2, 76, 115, 137
Noel f., 31, 192
nomination seats, 25, 30, 34, 44, 124, 126, 152–3
Normans, 47, 67, 98, 113, 122, 137
North f., 47, 192
Nugent f., 208

O'Brien f., 135, 208
O'Connell f., 136, 211
O'Conor (Don) f., 130, 136, 143
office-holding, 70–3, 75, 88–9, 98, 116, 118, 130, 137–8, 140, 147, 162, 199
Ogilvy (Airlie) f., 109, 205
'Old English' (Ireland), 122, 128, 134–6, 138, 141
O'Neill f., 135–6, 143, 145, 208, 211
Onslow f., 45
Osborne (Leeds) f., 65, 152, 192
Owen f., 97

Paget f., 185, 192
Pakenham (Longford) f., 145, 208
parliament, 3–4, 10–12, 20–5, 26–34, 40
  advantages of membership, 25–6, 29, 103
  frequency of sessions, 24, 56, 186, 192, 193
  importance of, 5, 23, 150–1
  Long, 27, 60, 61, 75
  Reformation, 22–3, 30
  size, 23–4
  and social rank, 4–5, 20–40, 94, 104–7, 123–7, 157, 159–61, 181, 192
  years of service, 43, 164, 191, 208
  see Commons and Lords
parliament, Irish, 3, 6, 15, 41, 122–31, 172, 183, 191, 207
  see Commons and Lords
parliament, Scottish, 3, 6, 15, 32, 41, 102–6, 113, 121, 170, 191, 202, 203, 208

parliamentary elite, 3, 5–6, 8, 10–11, 23–5, 34, 117, 147
  continuity, 5, 11–12, 21, 45, 49, 53–4, 69, 159–60, 162
  cross-referenced with other lists of elite, 34–7
  decline, 100–1, 133, 142–5, 147, 149–58, 160–1, 176
  defined, 1, 4, 15, 183
  Ireland, 96, 122–45, 146–7, 160, 172–3, 175–8, 207, 209
  merged elite?, 11, 93, 127, 145–8, 160
  new entrants, 46, 55–62, 87, 98–9, 101, 114–18, 133–4, 137–41, 163, 177
  'old' families, 46–7, 53–4, 59, 61, 63, 66–9, 92, 95–7, 98, 112–13, 115, 120, 135–7, 155, 163
  openness, 2, 11, 58–62, 64, 66, 87–92, 98–9, 118, 140–1, 147
  persistence of, 118, 150–2, 157–8
  Scotland, 1, 95, 96–7, 102–21, 146–7, 160, 170–1, 175–8, 204, 206
  size, 3, 11, 24, 41, 57–63, 94, 100–1, 107–8, 127–8, 159, 165–73, 175, 191
  Wales, 93–102, 117, 147, 160, 169, 175–8, 204
  wealth, 5–6, 11, 25, 27, 35, 42, 45, 46, 78, 94, 97, 107, 118, 120–1, 125, 131, 145, 157–8, 164, 174, 204, 206, 207, 216
Parsons (Rosse) f., 208
paymasters general, 73
Pecche f., 16
Peel f., 46, 85, 91, 192
Peel, Sir Robert 2nd Bt, 47
peers/peerages, 1, 4, 20, 29–30, 34, 107, 110, 151, 158, 164, 174, 183, 191
  abeyant, 33, 184
  creations, 23, 30–1, 34, 49, 60, 186, 214
  Irish, 30, 110, 124–5, 127–31, 136, 144, 146–8, 174, 188, 207, 209
  poor, 10, 131
  representative, 15, 103–4, 108, 109, 110, 112, 125, 131, 183, 204, 212
  Scottish, 102–14, 121, 125, 131, 146–8, 174, 202, 203
  sitting in the Commons, 30–4, 154–5, 188–9, 189, 192, 207, 214
  in Wales, 97, 99, 110, 147, 174
  see Lords
Pelham f., 45, 47–9, 192
Pelham-Anderson f., 46, 192, 216
Pennant f., 97, 99
Perceval f., 47, 127, 132, 192
Percy (Northumberland) f., 33, 67, 152, 158, 192
Perkin, Harold*, 86, 156